A POWER IN THE LAND

Richard Lomas

A POWER IN THE LAND: THE PERCYS

With a Foreword by
His Grace the Duke of Northumberland

TUCKWELL PRESS

First published in Great Britain in 1999 by
Tuckwell Press
The Mill House
Phantassie
East Linton
East Lothian EH40 3DG
Scotland

Copyright © Richard Lomas, 1999

ISBN 1 86232 067 5

British Library Cataloguing in Publication Data

A catalogue record for this book is available
on request from the British Library

The right of Richard Lomas to be identified as the author of
this work has been asserted by him in accordance with the
Copyright, Design and Patent Act 1988

Typeset by Hewer Text Ltd, Edinburgh
Printed and bound by
Cromwell Press, Trowbridge, Wiltshire

Contents

Contents

Contents

List of Illustrations

COLOUR PLATES

1. The 7th Earl of Northumberland
2. The 9th Earl
3. The 10th Earl
4. Syon House, by Griffier
5. The 11th Earl
6. Elizabeth Percy, Duchess of Somerset
7. The 1st Duke of Northumberland
8. The 1st Duchess
9. Alnwick Castle, by Canaletto
10. Alnwick Castle today

PLATES IN BLACK & WHITE

1. The 6th Duke of Somerset
2. The 1st Duke of Northumberland
3. The 2nd Duke
4. The 3rd Duke
5. The 3rd Duchess
6. The 4th Duke
7. The 5th Duke
8. The 5th Duchess
9. The 6th Duke
10. The 7th Duke
11. The 8th Duke
12. The 9th Duke
13. The 10th Duke
14. The 8th Duchess
15 The 10th Duchess
16. The three sons of the 10th Duke
17 The 12th Duke and Duchess

GENEALOGICAL TABLES

MAPS

Foreword

When I received the bulky manuscript of this book, I wondered how I could wade through another scholastic tome on my family history. Thankfully, and to Richard Lomas's great credit, this book is very readable as well as being extremely interesting. It fairly buzzes along with political intrigue, battles, executions, the great accumulations and disastrous losses of land and power over much of the last millennium. It is a story of heroism, duplicity, great judgement and equally great lack of it, of warriors, politicians, academics and the women who played vital roles in the fortunes of a dynasty.

The Percys were on the brink of disaster so many times, and yet managed to survive and thrive by determination, or by sheer good luck.

This book gives a 'warts and all' account of my predecessors, and is as interesting to the casual reader as it is to the historian. I wish it great success.

Northumberland

Introduction

In 1887, Edward Barrington de Fonblanque published *Annals of the House of Percy*. It is in two volumes with a combined length, including appendices, of 1,233 printed pages. This work, now long out of print, was the product of huge endeavour and is still valued by historians as a repository of a wealth of information about the Percy family.

But since Fonblanque's time, more facts have been brought to light; and styles, perceptions and interpretations have changed. It is these which prompted me to embark upon this book, the aim of which has been to bring together the results of research published during this century, not only about the Percys themselves, but also about the events in which they were involved. The result, which is far smaller than Fonblanque's double volume, seeks to trace the fortunes of the family in the context of national and regional events and to explain the parts its members played in them. Like Fonblanque, I believe this to be justified by the very longevity of the family, which has survived for almost 1,000 years, and by its impact on the development of England, Scotland and Great Britain, and on certain regions within them.

But unlike Fonblanque, I have divided my account into three rather than two parts. The first deals with the years up to the mid-fourteenth century, when the head of the family was of baronial rank with, from 1299, the title Lord Percy. In this phase, although possessed of a large estate in land, the Percys were in the second rank of the English nobility and were of regional more than of national importance. In the middle period, from the fourteenth to the seventeenth centuries, the head of the family bore the title Earl of Northumberland. This is the longest section of the book, because it was in these 300 years that the Percy family became hugely wealthy and achieved national status. There was hardly a moment when one member of the family was not of significance or importance, sometimes crucially so, in English politics. In the third phase (which except in terms of this book cannot be called final), the heads of the Percy family came to occupy the topmost niche in the scheme of nobility, a dukedom. But, while they were immensely wealthy aristocrats, their influence on national life diminished, although their regional importance continued.

Viewed generally and in the broadest perspective, the history of the Percys reveals three clear features. The first is that the family's progress was far from smooth and even. On numerous occasions, they met with political disaster, either through ill luck or poor judgement, and on two of these they appeared to be completely ruined. Moreover, on three other occasions, the family failed to produce a male heir, so that the Percy name would have disappeared but for deliberate decisions to retain or revive it. Lastly, although since the fourteenth century the family has been associated by title with Northumberland, and has owned a large estate there, its origins lay in Yorkshire. It was with this county that they had the longest association, which was not finally severed until the 1920s.

The constraints of space and the lack of information, particularly about the early centuries, mean that the book is mainly about the heads of the family. But not exclusively: where possible and desirable, wives and daughters and younger sons and brothers are given due attention. In no case, however, can it be claimed that the last word has been said: like other historians, I recognise that what has yet to be done is far greater than what has already been done. Indeed, writing this book has convinced me that almost every head of the family, and also many of its other members, deserve further study, with three being especially worthy of attention: the tenth earl (1602–1668), Elizabeth Percy, Duchess of Somerset (1667–1722) and the fourth duke (1787–1865); and in addition and in due time the tenth duke (1914–1988).

Those to whom I am indebted fall into two groups. In the first are the scholars upon whose researches I have drawn. All are listed at the end of the book. Here, I need say only that without their work, this book could not have been written. Then, there are those who have given me direct help. I most gladly thank for their generosity of time and interest: my wife, Joan, for her meticulous editing skills and for her detailed research into the castles and houses owned by the Percy family; my colleagues, Dr Donald Ratcliffe, Dr Philip Williamson and Mrs Jane Hogan, for advice about, respectively, nineteenth-century America, inter-war politics in

Introduction

Britain and the Sudan; Dr Colin Shrimpton, the Duke of Northumberland's archivist, and his colleagues, Ms Claire Baxter, Ms Louise Taylor and Mr Michael Johnson, for information about the estate and their help in selecting illustrations; Professor Norman McCord, Dr Ian Roberts and Mr Ernest Kirkby for information about various aspects of the nineteenth century; my elder daughter, Dr Kathryn Lomas, and Dr Martin Hatfield for help in obtaining information from the internet; Ms Nicky Ingram, the Collections Manager at Petworth House; Mrs Jozy Yeates and my younger daughter, Ms Clare Lomas, for their help and support on many occasions; to Mrs Wendy Shoulder, the Administrative Assistant of Durham University History Department, and her colleague, Ms Tracy Swaddle, for putting the first draft of the book on to the word processor and then frequently and cheerfully extricating me from electronic difficulties during the long revision process; and finally to His Grace the Duke of Northumberland for the information he freely supplied about his and the Duchess's ambitions and interests, for his encouragement, and for his generous Foreword to this book.

My debts are varied and immense, as are my thanks. Any errors, of course, are mine alone.

PART ONE

Barons and Lords

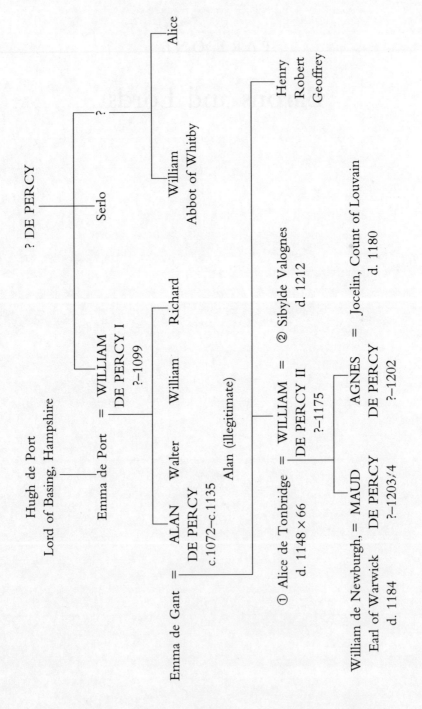

? DE PERCY

Serlo — ?

Alice

Hugh de Port
Lord of Basing, Hampshire

Emma de Port = **WILLIAM
DE PERCY I**
?–1099

William
Abbot of Whitby

Henry
Robert
Geoffrey

Emma de Gant = **ALAN
DE PERCY**
c.1072–c.1135

Walter   William   Richard

Alan (illegitimate)

① Alice de Tonbridge = **WILLIAM** = ② Sibylde Valognes
d. 1148 × 66   **DE PERCY II**   d. 1212
                    ?–1175

AGNES = Jocelin, Count of Louvain
DE PERCY   d. 1180
?–1202

William de Newburgh, = **MAUD
DE PERCY**
Earl of Warwick   ?–1203/4
d. 1184

2

ONE

Foundation

William de Percy I, ?–1099

The origins of William de Percy, the founder of the Percy family in Britain, are obscure and are almost sure to remain so. All that is certain is that he was a Norman, that his name was William and that he came from a place called Percy. The very fact that he was known as William dé Percy indicates that he was a member of the landowning class, although a not very prominent or important member. His place of origin also raises a problem in that there was more than one village in Normandy named Percy. The one favoured by earlier historians was Percy in the *département* of La Manche in western Normandy, close to the border with Brittany and situated about thirty kilometres west of Avranches in the direction of St Lô. More recently, however, it has emerged that towards the end of the eleventh century Percy in La Manche was owned by a family named Saint-Sauveur, the Vicomtes of Cotentin, who gave the church at Percy and the tithes owed to it in the township to the abbey they founded, Saint Sauveur-le Vicomte. Subsequently, the lordship of this Percy passed first to a family named Taissan and then to one named Paynel. In the early thirteenth century, the latter were still in direct control of Percy and had no tenants bearing that name. Therefore, there seems to be no evidence linking the English Percys with Percy in La Manche.

The alternative is Percy en Auge in the *département* of Calvados, located twenty-five kilometres south-east of Caen in the valley of the River Dives. In favour of this place are two pieces of evidence, although neither can be said to be substantial let alone conclusive. The first is that in 1180, Henry of le Puiset, the illegitimate son of Hugh of le Puiset, the Bishop of Durham, whose mother was Alice de Percy, granted to a Hugh Borel land in Percy and Mureres. The latter can be identified as Morières, a village only eight kilometres from Percy en Auge. A family called Morers, whose name is also believed to derive from Morières, were tenants of the Percys in Yorkshire in the time of Alice's father, William de Percy II, the grandson of William de Percy I.

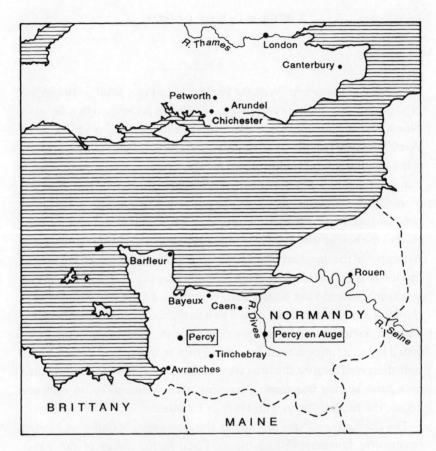

1. The Norman origins of the Percys

It is equally uncertain when William de Percy I left Normandy and came to England. It is possible, although generally thought unlikely, that he was a member of the invading army that landed on the Sussex coast late in September 1066 and defeated the English forces near Hastings on 14th October. The most likely alternative date is December 1067. In February of that year, Duke William, now King William I of England, returned to his duchy to deal with problems there and did not come back to England until December.

Nor can we be sure of William de Percy's age at the time of his arrival. The best guess is that he was born sometime between 1030 and 1040. Much earlier than this would have made him too old to uproot. Much later and he would have been too young to gain the experience necessary to do the work he did in England.

If he did come to England at the end of 1067, he arrived at the moment when William's position as king came under serious threat from the north of England. This was not simply the violent resistance of a native society to foreign conquerors, but a continuation of the north's struggle against a southern monarchy. Until the 1030s the north had been accustomed to the rule of earls, who may have been descendants of the old royal family of Northumbria and who strove to have the loosest possible relationship with the King of England. This autonomy had been gradually eroded during the reigns of Cnut (1017–1035) and Edward the Confessor (1042–1066), but the continuing desire for virtual independence was dramatically expressed in 1065 when the Northumbrians drove out their earl, Tostig, the brother of Earl Harold of Wessex, the man who became King Harold II of England in January the following year. Tostig had been forced on Northumbria, and he proved incapable of defending it from Scottish attacks, while at the same time seeking to impose unaccustomed taxation.

The Conqueror, therefore, inherited an unresolved problem, but initially he was far too occupied in trying to impose effective control over southern and midland England and to retain his grip on Normandy to do other than adopt a stopgap solution. This amounted to selling the earldom of Northumbria to whoever was willing to take on the role. The first volunteer was a certain Copsig, a Yorkshire thane. William's decision to accept Copsig's offer is strange in that Copsig was the right-hand man of the hated Tostig. William probably had no other option, and at this early stage in his reign he may well have been largely ignorant of the situation in Northumbria.

Not surprisingly, Copsig's reign was brief: a few weeks after taking up his appointment he was murdered at Newburn on Tyne by a rival, Osulf, who was himself killed shortly after. Consequently, when the Conqueror came back to England, Northumbria was without any form of Crown-appointed government. At this juncture, however, William found a much more suitable man, Gospatric. He was a very well connected Northumbrian aristocrat, for not only was he a leading member of the native family that had provided the earls of Northumbria until the 1030s, but he was also closely related to the royal families of Scotland and pre-Conquest England.

All this, however, was on the surface of a much more complex political situation involving three other men. The first of these was Edgar the Aetheling (Prince), the grandson of King Edmund (d. 1016). His mother was the daughter of a German bishop, whom his father, Edward, Edmund's son, had married during his enforced exile in Hungary following the conquest of England by the Danish king, Cnut. Edgar had returned to England only in 1057, and had fallen into the Conqueror's hands in 1066; but he managed to escape and took refuge in Scotland at the court of Malcolm III.

Malcolm had a very strong interest in northern England. In the early 1060s he had annexed Cumbria, and was almost certainly intending to make a similar gain east of the Pennines by annexing the land north of the Tees. This was not simply an indiscriminate land grab but was based upon an awareness that his late tenth-century predecessors had secured the land known as Lothian between the Tweed and the Forth, which had been part of the old kingdom of Northumbria. By acquiring the land between the Tweed and the Tees, he would be reuniting the two parts of the core of that ancient kingdom. Also, Earl Gospatric was his cousin and therefore he may have found the prospect of Malcolm's overlordship more attractive than that of William the Conqueror. Finally, in 1070 Malcolm married as his second wife, Margaret, Edgar the Aetheling's sister, through whom he could lay claim to England.

The third figure was Svein Estrithson, King of Denmark since 1047. As a nephew of Cnut he too could also lay claim to the English throne, a claim for which he had hopes of finding support in Yorkshire, where there had been a heavy settlement of Danes in the previous century.

As a united force these three men would have been formidable. In fact, long-term co-operation between them was unlikely since their aims and characters were basically incompatible. Nevertheless, in alliance with the native ruling class, they created a serious crisis which lasted until the end of 1069 and involved the Conqueror in three military expeditions into Northumbria.

The first followed an uprising in the spring of 1068, possibly caused by an attempt to impose the sort of taxation that had led to the revolt against Earl Tostig in 1065. William reacted rapidly before either the Scottish or the Danish king could intervene. Earl Gospatric and Edgar the Aetheling were involved, but fled to Scotland on William's approach. William's immediate solution was to build a castle at York and furnish it with a garrison of 500 men under a William Malet, and to appoint another man, Robert Fitz Richard, as Sheriff of Yorkshire.

The second uprising was sparked by William's attempt to extend his control to Durham, approximately seventy miles north of York. In February 1069, a force of 700 men under Robert de Comines arrived in Durham only to find the town deserted. They failed to heed the advice of the bishop, Aethelwine, that this was a trap. As a result, they were caught unprepared and totally wiped out. The revolt spread south into Yorkshire, and Earl Gospatric and Edgar the Aetheling returned from Scotland to assume leadership. Again, William was quicker to react than his enemies. He rushed north from the midlands, relieved William Malet besieged in York and defeated the native forces. He then commissioned a second castle at York and appointed a new sheriff, William Fitz Osbern, one of his most trusted men, in place of Robert Fitz Richard, who had been killed in the early days of the uprising.

But William's stay in York lasted only eight days, and it is therefore not surprising that no sooner had he returned south than the uprising was renewed and the Norman garrison was overwhelmed and massacred, except for Malet and Fitz Osbern. However, this time the native rebels were joined by a large Danish army which arrived in 240 ships under the command of King Svein's brother, Osbjorn. William again moved with his customary speed. After defeating the Danes and persuading their remnant to return home, he subjected parts of Yorkshire to what came to be known as the 'harrying of the North'. This was long considered to have been such a brutal and merciless killing of people and animals that many parts of the country were still totally desolate twenty years later. Recently, however, the evidence recorded in the Doomsday survey of 1086 has been re-examined and it is now thought that the devastation was nothing like so severe or the results as long lasting as first impressions suggest. Indeed, William probably had neither the time nor the man-power to inflict the deep devastation of which he was accused.

Nevertheless, 'the harrying of the North' put an end to native resistance, at least in Yorkshire. But the land north of the Tees remained beyond William's control, a fact publicly demonstrated in the last days of 1069 when he met Gospatric on the banks of the Tees and reinstated him as Earl of Northumbria north of that river (the far north of England was not finally brought under Crown control until the 1090s). Almost immediately after this, Malcolm III made his point by conducting a raid from Cumbria, across Stainmore and down Teesdale, one of his purposes being to underline, with as much brutality as William I of England, that the Tees was his southern boundary.

This situation continued for another three years until 1072, when William mounted an expedition into Scotland. Malcolm's inferior military capability meant that he did not dare risk battle. Instead, he retreated in order to bring William to negotiation. This took place at Abernethy in Perthshire with an outcome that was almost entirely to William's advantage: Malcolm did homage to William; gave his eldest son Duncan as a hostage; and agreed to expel his brother-in-law Edgar from his kingdom. Returning south, William was able to get rid of Gospatric, who promptly removed to Scotland, where his cousin, Malcolm III, pointedly gave him the earldom of Lothian. At Durham, William built a castle, installed a Frenchman, Walcher, as bishop in place of the doubtful Englishman, Aethelwine, and appointed Waltheof, the husband of his niece, Judith, as the new Earl of Northumbria. In effect, he had begun to shift Norman power northwards from York towards the Tyne.

It is known that William de Percy I played a major part in the events of these years, although unfortunately almost no detail has survived. That he was high in William's esteem is clearly indicated by his appointment in 1069 as the castellan at York and deputy to the sheriff, Hugh Fitz Baldric. William's confidence is further demonstrated by the numerous grants of land he made to Percy during the rest of his reign. Although acquired piecemeal, by 1086 when the Doomsday survey recorded the extent of Norman landholding, Percy's was one of the largest of the twenty-five estates granted to Normans in Yorkshire. In all, he held directly from the king land in 108 townships, amounting to almost 486 carucates. Carucates were not physical entities but notional units of land for the assessment and imposition of taxation and other burdens, and as they had no uniformity as regards acreage, they have an air of unreality. But if the commonest size, 120 acres, is applied, it means that Percy held over 58,000 acres.

He was also the tenant of a more important man than himself, Hugh de Avranches, Earl of Chester, from whom he held nearly eighty-four carucates of land in Whitby and Catton, amounting to perhaps 10,000 acres. Thus, his estate in Yorkshire comprised not far short of 70,000 acres. On top of this, the king also granted him almost eighty-six carucates in thirty-five places in the Lindsey district of northern Lincolnshire, which also must have amounted to about 10,000 acres. In round figures, Percy was in possession of 80,000 acres scattered over 160 townships. Finally, in distant Hampshire, Percy had acquired the manor of Hambledon as the result of his marriage to Emma, the daughter of Hugh de Port, Lord of Basing, who came from Port en Bessin on the Normandy coast, nine kilometres north of Caen. The fact that this was in the same region as Percy en Auge may be not without significance.

William de Percy I, therefore, was a major beneficiary of the second phase of William's conquest of England, earning the reward he no doubt deserved and certainly expected for his commitment to the king's enterprise. But grants of land on this scale were for future as well as past services. Like all other recipients of royal land grants, Percy was saddled with a quota of knights, that is, he was obligated to contribute a specified number of fully equipped and trained cavalrymen to the king's army. How the king's tenants-in-chief managed this obligation was up to them. Sooner or later, most solved it by granting parts of their estates to other men in return for the service of one or more knights. Percy adopted this solution more readily than most: by 1086 he had installed seventeen knights on his estate, and only three of his twenty-four fellow Yorkshire barons had exceeded this number. As most of the knights to whom he granted land were also tenants of other barons, a highly complex social network came into being in which connections and loyalties were far from being stable, certain and straightforward.

While wholeheartedly pursuing this policy, Percy was careful to retain the bulk of his land in his own hands: of the tenant farmers on his estate recorded in the Doomsday survey, 230 were on land he had retained and only 140 on land he had granted to his knightly tenants. The focal point of his estate was Topcliffe, twenty miles north of York and strategically located between the two main north-south roads, now the A1 and the A19. There he built a castle in the angle formed by the confluence of the River Swale and the Cod Beck. It was a typical motte and bailey castle of the period, comprising a high mound of earth surrounded by a ditch and topped by a wooden tower or palisade and fronted by an enclosed courtyard. It seems almost certain that he built another castle at Tadcaster, ten miles south-west of York, and perhaps one at Spofforth, four miles south-east of Harrogate, although there the later hall has obliterated earlier work. He also had a house in York in connection with his official duties. The closeness of these castles clearly indicates that the centre of Percy's interest and activity was in the heart of Yorkshire.

Percy's estate was not complete in 1086, but continued to grow between 1087, when his master, William the Conqueror, died and his own death twelve years later. That it did so was due to his continued loyalty to the Crown. William I was succeeded as King of England by his second son, William, nicknamed Rufus, and not by his eldest son, Robert, who was bequeathed his father's patrimony, the duchy of Normandy. This disposition, the result of the Conqueror's conscious decision, was a recipe for trouble. Robert's natural resentment at being denied the English crown made him an obvious focus for the discontents and ambitions of a restless baronage. The serious revolts against William II early in his reign were to a considerable extent the product of this situation. Rufus successfully dealt with these rebellions and punished many of his opponents by depriving them of their estates, among them Percy's earlier colleague in the subjugation of Yorkshire, Hugh Fitz Baldric. Conversely, those who gave Rufus their support were rewarded. These included Percy, although to what extent is not clear.

The Norman Conquest involved the widespread, although not total, dispossession of English landowners and their replacement by Normans. But it also coincided with a period of popular religious enthusiasm and reforming zeal within the ranks of the clergy, one important strand of which was a revival of the belief in the virtues and benefits of monastic life. In this respect northern England lagged far behind. Although in the pre-Viking period there had been a number of renowned monasteries such as Lindisfarne, Hexham and Jarrow, none had survived the turmoil and upheavals of the Viking era other than as abandoned and roofless ruins. For various reasons the monastic revival of the tenth century, inspired by continental examples which had made considerable headway in southern and midland England, did not spread north of the Trent.

By 1100, however, six monasteries had come into existence in Yorkshire at Selby, York (St Mary and Holy Trinity), Whitby, Allerton and Pontefract. In every case, the foundation stemmed from clerical initiative supported by landowners, who were willing and able to provide the necessary endowment. Their motives were mixed. Genuine belief played a part, particularly in the efficacy of prayer for the souls of the departed. But there were secular considerations as well. Monasteries were effective colonising agents, creating new settlements and stimulating economic activity. They were also very useful as places for the safe keeping of valuables, as comfortable retirement places and as the means of providing careers and livelihoods for relatives. And fashion came into it too: one did what one's social equals were doing.

William de Percy I was no exception, his contribution being to promote the restoration of the ruined monastery at Whitby. What happened, however, is not entirely clear and is likely to remain so, since there are two versions which cannot be fully or satisfactorily reconciled. One was produced in the abbey itself; the other was written by Stephen of Whitby, who was the first abbot of St Mary's Abbey, York. The weakness of the former version is that it was written two generations after the events it describes. The second, although composed close to the events, is suspect because it was almost certainly written to enhance its author's reputation.

However, the beginning of the story is clear enough. The central character was a certain Reinfrid, a knight who almost certainly was a member of the Conqueror's army that subdued Yorkshire in 1068 and 1069, during which time he saw the deserted ruins of the old monastery at Whitby. These seemed to have moved him to end his military career and to retrain as a monk, which he did at the west midland abbey of

Evesham. As it happened, the prior of that monastery, Aldwin, was not content to remain there. Instead, he became determined to go north in the hope of reviving monastic life at the famous centres about which he had read. In 1074, therefore, accompanied by Reinfrid and another monk, he left Evesham and travelled to Durham, where he obtained permission from the new bishop, Walcher, to occupy the monastic ruins at Jarrow.

But Reinfrid's true ambition was to settle at Whitby, not Jarrow, and after what was almost certainly a brief interval, he sought permission from William de Percy, who was the lord of Whitby. It is possible that Reinfrid may have served in one of the military units Percy had commanded a few years earlier, and that therefore the two men were already acquainted. The likelihood that this was so is increased by the fact that Reinfrid's son, Fulk, was or became Percy's steward, an important office in his estate administration, and one of his foremost military tenants.

Reinfrid's aims are not entirely clear to us, and may not have been to him. At Evesham he was described as 'unlettered' and so it is unlikely that at the time of his move to Yorkshire his intellectual development and academic training were more than rudimentary. In fact, there are slight indications that his real wish was to live a hermit's life. Like many other such men, his reputation attracted followers, with the result that within a short time a community of some size had come into being. One of this group was Stephen of Whitby, presumably a man of local origin. What happened next is now beyond certainty as a result of the two conflicting versions. What is clear, however, is that Stephen and Reinfrid were incompatible and almost certainly had sharply differing ideas about the community's future development. The outcome was that Stephen, with what he claimed was the backing of the King and of the Archbishops of Canterbury and York, migrated together with those who shared his ideas to another ancient monastic site at Lastingham, and then after a brief sojourn during which they must have built the present church, to York. There they founded St Mary's Abbey, with Stephen as its first abbot, a role he retained until his death in 1112. The remnant remaining with Reinfrid also left Whitby, not as the result of politics but of pirates, who made life on this coastal site impossible. They settled at Hackness, which is about twenty miles south of Whitby and not far from Scarborough, and it was during this period that Reinfrid was killed while on a business journey. It seems that he came across a group of workmen engaged in building a bridge over the River Derwent, and foolishly and impetuously he rushed to help them, only to be struck on the head by a falling timber. This tragedy appears to have occurred around the same time as William the Conqueror died in 1087.

These two deaths cleared the way for Percy to make a fresh start with his foundation. In place of Reinfrid he appointed his own brother, Serlo, as head of the community which now was able to return to Whitby. He also regained possession of the original endowment, which probably did not exceed 250 acres of land, which Stephen had continued to control after he removed to Lastingham and York. To this he added substantial amounts of property, sufficient to make Whitby financially viable as a fully-fledged monastery. His rapid and radical actions after 1087 suggest that, while the Conqueror lived, he had been restrained by the knowledge of royal support for Stephen of Whitby. But it is also possible that his sudden freedom of action was part of the reward for his support for William Rufus during the 1088 rebellion.

It is clear from these actions that Percy saw Whitby as his personal property and that he was annoyed and frustrated by the independent line Stephen of Whitby was able to adopt with royal backing. This proprietorial attitude is further revealed by the arrangements he imposed on Whitby. Both Reinfrid and Serlo were appointed to the office of prior, that is, second-in-command. The role of abbot, the head of the community, Percy assumed himself, even though he was a layman. By 1090, such an action and the assumptions that lay behind it were rapidly becoming politically incorrect as pressure rose from church reformers throughout Europe to liberate the church at all levels from lay control. Percy, however, seems to have been impervious to the new ideas, and as a result the situation at Whitby did not change until after Serlo's death. Even then the new abbot, although a monk of the Whitby community, was one of Percy's nephews. From all of this it is evident that Percy was a man of the old school who, having founded a monastery, expected to control it and have it work for the direct benefit of himself and his family.

Percy remained active in public life until the early 1090s at least, as is confirmed by the appearance of his name among the witnesses to documents issued by the King at courts held in places as far distant as Hastings and Lincoln. In 1096, however, he decided to join the military expedition promoted by Pope Urban II that became known as the First Crusade, the purpose of which was to regain Jerusalem from Moslem control. Given that he was almost certainly over fifty years of age, this was an extraordinary decision and one which indicates both a religious conviction, albeit of a conventional nature, and a continuing sense of adventure. And it seems likely that he reached his goal, since he is believed to have died on Mount Joy within sight of Jerusalem. If this is true, it must mean that his death occurred in June or July 1099, not, as is usually stated, in 1096. Sadly, the story that his heart was brought back to England and buried at Whitby is almost certainly without foundation, although it does suggest that contemporaries recognised that William de Percy's life had been extraordinary. To have started out as the son, possibly younger son, of a modest Norman landowner, to have become one of the leading figures of northern England and to have died at the end of one of the most extraordinary episodes in European history, indeed makes William de Percy I an exceptional man.

Evidence that his contemporaries also recognised him as an outstanding personality is the story written in the following century, probably in Bardney Abbey near Lincoln, about Percy and an entirely fictional but popular saint, St. Julian the Hospitaller, to whom travellers prayed for safety as they embarked upon a journey. The tale relates how Percy and his troops went on an expedition into Scotland, throughout which they assiduously prayed to St. Julian every day. Until, that is, the day before they got back to Topcliffe, when Percy told his chaplain not to bother. Inevitably, as in all such stories, disaster ensued. The castle at Topcliffe was found burnt to the ground, as was that at Tadcaster, while Percy's house in York had been wrecked by a storm. Worse still, when the party arrived at Nafferton, the house there was in flames and Percy's wife and infant heir, Alan, almost dead. It was now apparent, even to the most obtuse, that these catastrophes were not accidents. Final proof came when the party crossed the Humber to find shelter at Percy's manor at Immingham. There they were greeted by the reeve, who was very pleased to inform his master that he had been able to carry out the instruction in the letter Percy had sent to him five weeks earlier ordering him to have ready for that very day provision for 400 men and their horses. Percy denied having sent such a letter. Then, the miraculous explanation dawned on him, and he broke down and confessed his fault in slighting St Julian. All was now well, and the story ended with feasting and rejoicing.

Leaving aside the homiletic and didactic aspect of the tale, designed to reinforce the church's moral authority over even the mightiest of its flock, it serves to highlight Percy's standing and reputation: such stories were not usually told about people of no consequence. It may also be evidence of the size of military contingent that Percy led on the Conqueror's Scottish expedition in 1072 and a pointer to the date of birth of his heir, Alan. One final indication that Percy was a man who stood out is the descriptive nickname he acquired: *a la gernuns*, which translates as 'bearded' or 'whiskered'. The evidence of the Bayeux Tapestry is that Norman military men were short-haired and clean-shaven. It would seem that Percy ignored this fashion and in so doing gave rise to the name Algernon used by later generations of his family.

TWO

Consolidation

Alan de Percy, c.1072–c.1135
William de Percy II, ?–1174/5

William de Percy I was succeeded by his eldest son, Alan, who was probably born in or shortly before 1072. If so, he would have been in his late twenties at the time of his father's death. His control over the Percy inheritance coincided almost exactly with the reign of the younger of the Conqueror's sons, Henry I, who occupied the throne of England from 1100 until 1135. In the first years of his reign Henry, like his brother William, had problems with the disgruntled older brother, Robert. These were finally resolved in 1106, when Robert was defeated by Henry in a battle at Tinchebrai in Normandy and became a prisoner, a condition he was to endure for the rest of his life.

Success in defeating his rival meant that Henry, like William Rufus before him, had at his disposal the estates confiscated from men who had sided with Robert of Normandy. These enabled him to reward and promote men who had proved their loyalty or who had abilities he wished to employ in the future. In consequence, a clutch of new barons appeared in Yorkshire, notably Eustace Fitz John (Malton), Walter Espec (Helmsley) and Robert de Brus (Skelton). Their arrival made the Percys one of the older and more established Yorkshire families. But Alan de Percy also had been loyal, and as a result he too benefited from what has been aptly described as Henry I's 'tenurial engineering'. By 1135, Alan's Yorkshire estate was enhanced by acquisitions of land in fifty-eight townships, forty-five of which were new to the estate. Sixteen were from the Crown's own estate, the remainder came from the estates of the king's expropriated opponents. The most significant expansion was in Cravenshire, the most westerly district of the county. Overall, the Percy estate grew by 191 carucates, that is, nearly 23,000 acres at 120 acres to the carucate. At the time of his death, which occurred sometime between 1131 and 1135, Alan de Percy possessed over 760 carucates or getting on

17

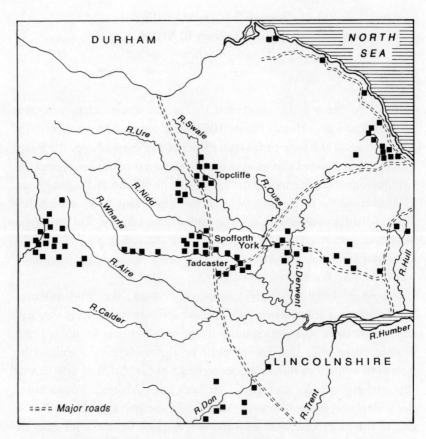

2. Percy property in Yorkshire, 1086

for 100,000 acres of land. Moreover, the substantial properties his father had held from the Earl of Chester were now held directly from the Crown, although when and why this change took place is not known. And the number of knights installed on the estate had increased to twenty-eight.

Another figure of considerable significance in Alan's career was Henry I's protégé, David I, King of Scotland, the youngest son of Malcolm III. David's mother, Margaret, was the sister of Edgar the Aetheling, and since he died without a male heir, David inherited his mother's family's claims to the English throne. This potential threat was recognised by Henry I, who neutralised it by marrying David's sister Edith (whose name was changed to Matilda, or Maud for short, when she came to England). David came south with his sister and was clearly recognised as an able man by his brother-in-law, so much so that Henry provided David with a highly advantageous marriage. His wife was Matilda, the widow of an English baron, Simon de Senlis, who brought with her the very substantial estate belonging to Simon's earldom of Huntingdon. At a stroke, David became a major figure in the English baronage. More important, however, was the fact that Matilda was the daughter and sole heir of Waltheof, the Earl of Northumbria whom William the Conqueror had appointed in 1072 but deposed and executed four years later. Waltheof's father was the Danish earl, Siward (d. 1055), who had been imposed on Northumbria by Cnut; but his mother, Ealdgyth, was the daughter of the last native earl. Through his wife, therefore, David was able to lay claim to the ancient earldom of Northumbria.

David became king of Scotland in 1124 as the result of the deaths of his two childless predecessors, his brothers Edgar (1097) and Alexander (1107), and he immediately began to institute revolutionary changes in his kingdom. One of these was the introduction of an Anglo-Norman baronage to whom he gave extensive estates. Possibly the most notable was Robert de Brus, who became Lord of Annandale; others included Hugh de Morville (Cunninghame and Lauderdale) and William de Somerville (Linton and Carnwath). The Percys also benefited from this policy, although in a very minor way. Alan's illegitimate son, also named Alan, became a valued member of David's court: he witnessed several of David's charters and together with his brother, Geoffrey, was granted a small estate in the Roxburghshire townships of Oxnam and Heiton.

Unlike Brus, Morville and other Anglo-Normans, Alan de Percy II did not found a Scottish dynasty. Both he and his brother gradually disposed of their properties to the family abbey of Whitby and to the newly founded Scottish monasteries at Kelso and Jedburgh. In the end, the lordship of both Oxnam and Heiton passed into the hands of the Colville family who, interestingly, were also Percy tenants in Yorkshire.

Alan de Percy was engaged in affairs of state, the witness lists attached to Henry I's acts showing him to have been at the English court in places as far distant from his Yorkshire base as Portsmouth, Winchester and Rockingham. Nearer home, he was one of those present in Durham in 1121 to arbitrate in the dispute between the cathedral priory and St. Albans Abbey over the ownership of Tynemouth Priory. The problem arose in the 1080s when monks from Jarrow crossed the Tyne at the invitation of Robert de Mowbray, the last Earl of Northumbria appointed by William the Conqueror, to reactivate monastic life at the ancient site at Tynemouth. Had this arrangement continued, it is all but certain that Tynemouth would have become, like Jarrow and Monkwearmouth, a dependent cell of Durham Cathedral Priory. But a quarrel between Robert de Mowbray and the bishop, William of St. Calais, led the former to expel the Jarrow monks and hand over the priory to the Hertfordshire abbey of St. Albans. The Durham monks were unwilling to relinquish their claim and in spite of the efforts made at the 1121 conference to find an acceptable solution, the issue remained unresolved until 1174, when Durham finally conceded defeat.

In spite of this involvement, Alan de Percy seems to have been less interested in church matters than either his father or his son. His years as head of the Percy family were notable as the period when the order of Augustianian canons reached the height of their popularity. This order, unlike the monasteries of the time which lived by the Rule of St. Benedict (d. 547), followed the more relaxed and less stringent Rule of St. Augustine (d. 430). Both monks and canons lived regulated, communal lives, but whereas monks were required to remain within their monastery, canons were permitted to work in the world outside its walls, in particular as parish priests. Their value in this role was fully appreciated by Thurstan, the man who became Archbishop of York in 1113. Thurstan was acutely aware of the serious inadequacies of the parochial system in his province, where many parishes were very large in area and had married priests who expected to pass them on to their sons. Such clergy horrified church reformers, whose ideal was a celibate, non-hereditary priesthood free of family ties and obligations. It seems likely that Thurstan's ideal was a parish system served by well-trained and celibate canons based in strategically located houses.

In this reformation policy he had the support, for political as well as religious reasons, of Henry I. Consequently, it is not surprising that in the following twenty years, eight Augustinian houses were founded in Yorkshire, or that many of them owed their origin to the generosity of the new members of the baronage introduced into the county by Henry I. For example, Helmsley was founded by Walter Espec in 1122, and Guisborough seven years later by Robert de Brus. From all of this activity the name of Alan de Percy was absent. Not only did he not found an Augustinian canonry, his only ventures into the business of monastic endowment were to confirm his father's grants and to make a small addition to the estate of St. Peter's Hospital in York, which was rededicated to St.Leonard around this time.

Alan's wife was Emma, a daughter of Gilbert de Gant (Ghent in modern Belgium), who owned some property in Yorkshire but was essentially a Lincolnshire landowner. Alan died sometime between 1131 and 1135 and Emma did not long outlive him. They had at least four sons, the oldest of whom was named William after his grandfather, and an unknown number of daughters. After his father's dynamic and far-ranging life, that of Alan seems undistinguished. Nevertheless, it should be recognised that he did not put a foot wrong politically, and he left an estate larger than the one he inherited from his father.

William de Percy II held this estate for at least forty years from the early 1130s until his death in 1174 or 1175. In the first half of this period, northern England was controlled by the kings of Scotland. This situation came about shortly after the death of Henry I in 1135. Almost immediately the throne was seized by Stephen, Count of Blois, who was a grandson of William the Conqueror and a major landowner in England as well as in France. By doing so, he thwarted Henry I's only surviving legitimate child, his daughter Matilda. Until his death in 1125, she had been the wife of the German emperor, Henry V, but she was now married to Geoffrey Plantagenet, Duke of Anjou. Henry had intended that Matilda should succeed him, and to overcome the disadvantage of her gender he had required his barons to swear to uphold her claim when he died.

First to do so was David of Scotland in his capacity as Earl of Huntingdon, and consequently when he invaded northern England in 1136 he could claim to be acting as Matilda's supporter. His true aim, however, was to realise his ambition of acquiring the earldom of Northumbria. David's invasion did not produce spectacular results. The two kings met at Durham, but their relative strength was such that Stephen was able to refuse David's demand. Two years later, the situation was more auspicious for the Scottish king. The war in England between Stephen and Matilda was going the latter's way, and this encouraged David to launch a two-pronged invasion of England. One thrust, led by his half-cousin, William Fitz Duncan, invaded Cumbria, while David himself advanced through Northumberland and Durham into northern Yorkshire. Fitz Duncan's expedition was successful in that he defeated a defending force at Clitheroe in Lancashire. David, however, met with military disaster. On 22 August, his army was totally defeated at Cowton Moor near Northallerton in what became known, because of the presence of banners from the minsters of York, Ripon and Beverley, as the Battle of the Standard.

David's invasion clearly caused a conflict of loyalties, especially for men like Robert de Brus with estates in both kingdoms. Some, like Eustace Fitz John, with estates centred on Malton in Yorkshire and Alnwick in Northumberland, plumped for David, while others such as Walter Espec, whose estates were around Helmsley in Yorkshire and Wark on Tweed in Northumberland, opted for the English side and fought under the command of Archbishop Thurstan. William de Percy II followed what appears to have been the family tradition by remaining loyal to the English king. He was comfortable in doing so, since his illegitimate uncle, Alan de Percy, was with David I in the Scottish army. Whatever the outcome, a Percy would be on the winning side.

David was able to snatch political victory out of military defeat. By 1139 Stephen's position was so precarious that he was forced to accept that he could not fight on two fronts. His solution was to make peace with Scotland in order to be free to concentrate on his difficulties in England. The two kings again met at Durham, and this time David got what he wanted, the earldom of Northumbria, except the Lands of St.

Cuthbert, that is, the estates of the bishop and cathedral priory of Durham. Despite this exemption, thereafter until his death in 1153 David I was the effective political authority between Tweed and Tees, although nominally power rested in the hands of his son, Henry, to whom he transferred the title of earl.

After this settlement, William de Percy's involvement was much more with William Fitz Duncan, Earl Henry's counterpart in Cumbria, who in the 1140s became the power in the west, not only because of his military victory at Clitheroe and David's diplomatic success at Durham, but also because of his marriage to Alice de Rumilly, heiress to the Cumbrian barony of Copeland and to a considerable estate in Cravenshire. This and Henry I's 'tenurial engineering' meant that Cravenshire was effectively divided between Percy and Fitz Duncan's lordship based upon Skipton. And it seems the two men developed a close relationship through their mutual interest.

This situation ended in 1157. Stephen died in 1154, without an heir as the result of the death of his son, Eustace, two years earlier. With this, he conceded defeat and acknowledged the twenty-one-year-old Henry Plantagenet, the son of Matilda and Count Geoffrey of Anjou, as his heir. On coming to the throne, Henry inherited a kingdom shorn of its most northerly districts. Young though he was, he was not prepared to accept this situation. Fortunately for him, the circumstances for recovery were propitious. The powerful and astute David of Scotland died in 1153. More significantly, his only son, Henry, had died the previous year. Consequently, David's heir was his twelve-year-old grandson, who became King of Scotland as Malcolm IV.

In 1157, Malcolm, now sixteen, was summoned to Chester by the twenty-four-year-old Henry II. There he capitulated to Henry's demand for the return of his lost territories. As a sop to his pride, he was granted the earldom of Huntingdon, and also the area of western Northumberland known as the Regality of Tynedale, which he and his successors were to possess until late in the thirteenth century. With the restoration of the earlier border, William de Percy's position as a border baron disappeared.

William de Percy II was far more active than his father in promoting the cause of monasticism. In addition to acceding to the request of the family monastery at Whitby for a confirmation of earlier grants (a sensible precaution for any monastery to take when the headship of the patronal family changed hands), William and both of his successive wives made positive and generous commitments to the new orders of monks that flourished in their lifetimes. The most important of these without doubt was the Cistercian or White monks, who enjoyed huge popularity and spectacular expansion in the 1130s and 1140s. Originating at Cîteaux in Burgundy, the order was promoted by the most charismatic figure of his age, Bernard of Clairvaux. The Cistercians were a puritanical order, practising harsh simplicity in all aspects of their lives. They refused to accept gifts of churches and settled land, preferring to found their houses in uncolonised wastes. They also adopted the concept of *conversi* (lay brothers), who did the physical and domestic work of the house, leaving the monks proper to concentrate on the liturgical services in church.

The first Cistercian house in England was founded at Waverley in Surrey in 1128. By mid-century, in little over twenty years the number grew to forty, of which eight were in Yorkshire. One of the earliest was Fountains, begun in 1132 in Skeldale near Ripon by a group of monks from St. Mary's Abbey, York, who had come to feel that the standards of their house as required by the Benedictine rule were not sufficiently strict or demanding. Six years after its foundation, Fountains was visited by a leading Northumberland baron, Ralph de Merlay, Lord of Morpeth. He was so impressed by what he saw that he immediately set about creating a Cistercian monastery, which was given the name Newminster, close to his town and castle. It was from Newminster that ten years later, in January 1148, twelve monks and ten *conversi* led by their abbot-designate, Benedict, set out to found yet another Cistercian monastery at Sallay (now Sawley) in the valley of the Ribble in Cravenshire.

This was done at the request of William de Percy II, who had the necessary buildings erected for them. Percy, however, was not alone in this enterprise, for several of his tenants helped by granting land to boost the endowment of the new house. His steward Robert, the grandson of the Reinfrid who had restarted monastic life at Whitby, gave land in Ilkley, while another of Percy's tenants, Norman Fitz Uhtred, whose name clearly indicates English ancestry, provided two carucates in Rimington. More important, however, was Swain Fitz Swain, who sold to the incoming community two carucates of land in Sawley and the moorland between Sawley and Clitheroe.

The foundations of Sallay neatly display three of the main characteristics of such acts: the major landowner taking the initiative, while being careful to keep his generosity within sensible limits; the association in the enterprise of several of his leading tenants, no doubt for reasons of prudence as well as piety; and the acquisition of endowment by means of commercial transaction as well as gift. As well as supporting his own foundation, Percy assisted two other Cistercian houses in Yorkshire. One was Byland, founded in 1138 at the southern end of the Hambledon Hills. The other was Fountains, to which he gave land in Malham and the Langstrother Forest, which was precisely the sort of empty upland country favoured by the Cistercians. In all, William de Percy II made eleven donations and confirmed fourteen others to nine Yorkshire monasteries.

Percy also supported monastic development in Lincolnshire. In or around 1154, he appears to have been instrumental in founding a nunnery at Stainfield, nine miles east of Lincoln. This was destined to be the only house of Benedictine nuns in the county and it remained small, poor and very obscure. More clearly authenticated is the assistance given by him and his daughter, Agnes, and her husband to a monastery at Sixhills, eighteen miles north-east of Lincoln and six miles east of Market Rasen. Sixhills was one of the fifteen houses of the monastic order founded by a Lincolnshire man, Gilbert of Sempringham. It was the only monastic order to originate in Britain and virtually all of its houses were in Lincolnshire and Yorkshire. Their distinctive characteristic was that they were houses of nuns supported by small canonries of male priests. Sixhills did not owe its foundation to the Percys but to a family named Gresley. Percy's daughter, Agnes, and her husband gave its endowment a considerable boost, however, by selling to it their nearby manor of Ludford. The price was £100, the money needed to finance Agnes' husband's pilgrimage to Jerusalem.

William de Percy II died in late 1174 or 1175. As he had directed, he was buried at Fountains Abbey, not at his own foundation at Sallay, or that of his grandfather at Whitby. In doing so, he was acknowledging that Fountains was the more prestigious house, as well as being closer to the centre of the Percy estate at Topcliffe. With his death, the Percy family entered a period of crisis which was to last well into the thirteenth century. Before looking into this, however, it is worth pausing to consider the Percy achievement in the first hundred years of their presence in England.

Three facts stand out. The first is biological: all three men lived a full span, at least by the standards of the age, and died leaving a male heir of full age. Secondly, by either accident or design, they had been politically adept in giving their loyalty to the Crown, which had rewarded them with sufficient land to place them amongst the leading landowners in Yorkshire. But, although big in Yorkshire, and with properties in north Lincolnshire, they were not yet great barons with a huge estate scattered across many counties. Therefore, their power and influence were only regional, not national. Finally, they had played a major part in the religious revival, particularly the expansion of monasticism. Here it is possible to see William I and especially Alan as being conventional, while William II appears to have had a more positive and active commitment.

THREE

Crisis and Recovery

Agnes de Percy. ?–c.1202 and Jocelin, Count of Louvain, ?–1180
Richard de Percy. ?–1244
Henry de Percy I, c. 1170–1198
William de Percy III, 1196–1245
Henry de Percy II, c. 1235–1272

If noble families can be said to have had a common overriding concern, it was to maintain, and wherever possible to enlarge, their estates in land. Essential to this aim was a son, since increasingly the English succession law favoured the principle of primogeniture, whereby the eldest son inherited the entire estate. Additional children might present problems, but these could be solved by effort and ingenuity. But failure to produce a son jeopardised the family's continued existence. No children would mean the reversion of the estate to the Crown, while having daughters only was likely to result in the division of the estate into equal portions which each girl would take with her into marriage. In this way, the estate would be fragmented and the fragments absorbed into the estates of other families. This problem faced the Percy family in the late twelfth century, but by good fortune they managed to overcome it, to survive and prosper.

William de Percy II married twice. His first wife, Alice de Tonbridge, whom he married sometime before 1154, died before 1166, the year in which he married his second wife, Sibyl de Valognes, the widow of another Yorkshire baron, Robert de Ros, Lord of Helmsley. Ironically, Ros was a beneficiary of the primogeniture rule in that he acquired part of the estate of Walter Espec who died in 1153 leaving daughters but no son. When Percy died sometime between October 1174 and the following Easter he had no surviving male heir, his only son, Alan, having died some years earlier. His heirs were his two daughters, Matilda and Agnes, the offspring of his first marriage.

Both girls married well. Sometime before 1154 Matilda became the wife of William, Earl of Warwick, the grandson of Henry de Beaumont, a close associate of William the Conqueror and a member of one of the leading families of Normandy. The marriage was childless, and when William died in 1184 while on a pilgrimage to the Holy Land, his widow successfully negotiated an agreement with the king, Henry II, whereby she paid the crown 700 marks (£466 13s 4d = £466 67p) for the right to remain in possession and control of the lands she had inherited from her father and to remain unmarried. This sort of arrangement was not uncommon. Kings were rightly concerned to maintain control over the marriages of the widows of their tenants-in-chief, since such women were entitled to a third of their deceased husband's estate for the remainder of their lives. This made the widows of the king's tenants economically very attractive, and kings expected to benefit by selling the marriage of widows to men they wished to favour, or whose loyalty they wished to ensure. Naturally, most women, having had their first marriage arranged for them by their father, preferred either to continue in widowhood, or to choose their own second husband. To secure this advantageous position, however, they had to be prepared to outbid potential husbands. Either way, the king stood to gain financially. Matilda evidently chose to buy her freedom, and she must have offered a sufficiently attractive price for it, for she remained a widow in possession of her land until her death, which occurred sometime between October 1203 and October 1204. Like her father, she was the benefactor of several Yorkshire monasteries, and like him chose to be buried at Fountains Abbey.

However, it was Agnes, the younger of the two sisters, whose life was to be of greater significance for the future of the Percy family. She, too, married, and to an apparently more prestigious person. Although he was a younger son, her husband, Jocelin, Count of Louvain (Leuven in modern Belgium), was the son of a European nobleman of the first rank, Godfrey, Duke of Lower Lorraine, who could trace his ancestry back to Charlemagne. Jocelin's arrival in England was directly connected with the marriage of his half-sister, Adeliza, to the English king, Henry I. Henry's first wife, Edith/Matilda, daughter of Malcolm III of Scotland, died in 1118. Henry appeared content not to remarry until 1120, when his only son and heir, William, was drowned in what became known as the White Ship disaster, when the vessel bringing him from Normandy to England was wrecked off the port of Barfleur. The need to produce another son and heir now made a second marriage imperative.

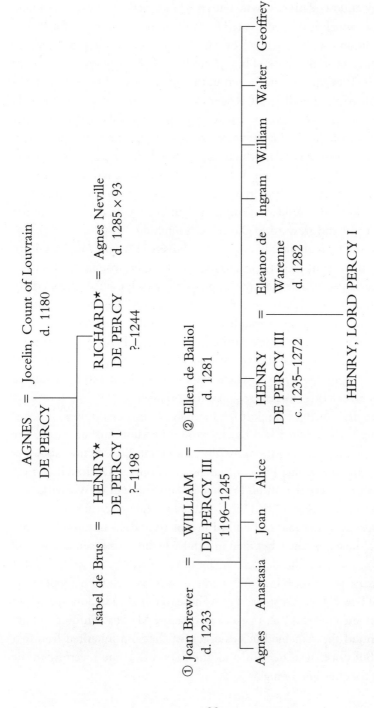

* There is a possibility that Richard was older than Henry.

Henry endowed his new wife with the huge estate centred on Arundel in Sussex, which had been created by William the Conqueror for Roger de Montgomery, a member of another of the leading families of Normandy, who had backed him in his bid for the English throne. This barony had reverted to the crown in the first decade of Henry's reign as the result of the rebellion of Roger de Montgomery's son, Robert de Bellême. As we have seen, Henry's second marriage failed to produce the hoped-for male heir. This drove the king to try to secure the succession for his daughter, Matilda, which led to Stephen's usurpation and the turmoil of his reign. Having failed to bear a royal child, after Henry's death in 1135, Adeliza was free to marry again, which she did in 1138. Her new husband, William d'Aubigny, had been a close associate of her first husband and steward of the royal household.

It was they who granted, sometime between 1138 and Adeliza's death in 1151, the barony of Petworth to her half-brother, Jocelin, the husband of Agnes de Percy. The barony comprised Petworth itself and property in thirty-three other townships, mostly in western Sussex and eastern Hampshire, amounting to roughly a quarter of the Arundel estate. This event is of major significance in the history of the Percy family, since it brought to them one of their most valued and favoured possessions, and arguably began the process which would turn them into a family of national rather than merely regional importance.

In the light of their support for monasteries in Lincolnshire, it is not surprising to find Agnes and Jocelin doing the same further south. The objects of their generosity were the important Benedictine abbey at Reading and the smaller Premonstratensian canonry at Durford in Surrey. Jocelin's piety, like that of his brother-in-law, the Earl of Warwick, also included a pilgrimage to the Holy Land, which he undertook in 1174 on the proceeds of the sale of Ludford manor to Sixhills nunnery. He too survived the experience, but died in 1180. He did so as Jocelin, Count of Louvain, not as Jocelin de Percy. There is no truth in the tradition that upon marriage he took his wife's name: it was his sons who adopted the name of Percy. Like her sister, Agnes chose to remain a widow and not to remarry. She died in 1202, a year or two before Matilda. Throughout her widowhood she remained in possession of the land inherited from her father, but not that of her husband, the Petworth estate reverting to the Crown for the time being.

In contrast to her sister, Agnes had eight children, two of whom, Henry and Richard, were male, and it is with them that a serious problem emerges. Traditionally, Henry is thought to have been the elder. He was almost certainly born around 1170, since in 1190 he paid 500 marks (£333 6s 8d = £333 34p) 'relief' (the sum of money paid to the Crown by the heir of a tenant-in-chief for permission to succeed to his inheritance) for his father's barony of Petworth. Shortly after this, he married Isabel, daughter of another Yorkshire baron, Adam de Brus of Skelton in Cleveland. Although the marriage was of short duration – Henry died in 1198 – it was long enough for the couple to produce a son, William. As a minor and heir to a tenancy-in-chief, William became a ward of the Crown. Two years later, the new king, John, in line with common practice, sold the wardship and marriage of the boy to one of his most trusted but much disliked administrators, William Brewer, who thereby gained control over William's great aunt Matilda's portion of the Percy estate when she died in 1204.

William came of age in 1214, when he married Brewer's daughter Joan, and laid claim to the other half of the Percy estate which, since the death of Agnes de Percy in 1202, had been in the hands of his uncle, Richard. In doing so, he began a dispute that lasted thirty years and was aired in public on no fewer than six occasions. Although these resulted in some minor adjustments, basically William continued in possession of Matilda de Percy's portion while Richard retained those properties that had been allocated to Agnes de Percy. The conflict was eventually resolved and the unity of the estate restored by the failure of Richard de Percy and his wife, Agnes, daughter of Geoffrey de Neville, Lord of Brancepeth and Raby in Durham, to have any surviving children, whereas William and his second wife, Ellen, daughter of Ingram de Balliol, Lord of Barnard Castle in Durham and Prudhoe and Redesdale in Northumberland, had a son, Henry. He succeeded to both halves of the estate following the death of his great-uncle, Richard, in 1244 and of his own father, William, in the following year.

This long-running quarrel raises a particular question: why was Richard de Percy, the younger son, allowed to deprive his nephew of what should have been regarded as his rightful inheritance? A recent suggestion is that Richard was in fact older than Henry, and that it was intended that Richard should inherit the Percy estate, while Henry

31

would be provided for by his father's barony of Petworth. According to this argument, it was Richard who was the injured party as the result of being denied half of his inheritance by King John and his close associate, William Brewer, and by the stubbornness of his nephew. Although there is some evidence that Richard was older than Henry by about ten years, this must be regarded as hypothesis rather than fact. Indeed, the only certainty is that neither version is fully capable of proof. What is certain, however, is that the Percy estate became divided as the unfortunate consequence of the failure of two earlier marriages to produce a male heir. It was reunited seventy years later by the fortunate chance of two later marriages producing between them only one surviving son.

If Richard were the rightful but thwarted heir to the Percy estate, it would help to explain his role in the events that led to King John's enforced acceptance of the Magna Carta and the civil war that ensued. The core of the opposition to John comprised seven northern barons, five of whom had the bulk of their property in Yorkshire : Eustace Fitz John, William de Mowbray, Peter de Brus, Robert de Ros and Richard de Percy. All these men can be shown to have had personal grievances against the king, Richard's being – assuming he was the older brother – John's part in depriving him of half of his inheritance for the benefit of one of his henchmen.

In the end, virtually all the English baronage came to oppose the way John exercised his rights as monarch and as feudal overlord. It was not that they denied or wished to deprive him of his rights: what in the end proved to be beyond their endurance was John's excessive partiality, capriciousness and viciousness. By one means or another, John managed to ensnare virtually half the baronage in debt through the high charges he imposed for reliefs, wardships, the marriages of minors and widows, and scutage (the cash levied in lieu of military service). They were also heavily penalised for offences against the Crown, especially trespass against the extensive royal forests. To pay what they owed to the Crown, many barons borrowed from Jewish usurers, but this did not afford an escape, since the Crown had absolute control over the Jewish community, and John was always ready to buy up the debts owed to its members by his barons. But most of the barons were the authors of their own misfortunes, and in turn were prepared to behave in a harsh and unscrupulous manner towards inferiors in their power. When all allowances are made, however, it was John's actions which drove a wedge between Crown and baronage, when co-operation between them was the natural order and was necessary for social harmony and sound government.

But why were the northern barons in particular so hostile? Probably because under John northern England felt the full weight of royal government for the first time. He was the first king of England to visit the north regularly, to know it and the leading members of its society at first hand, and to be determined to impose upon it the same degree of control to which England south of the Trent had long been accustomed. Almost inevitably, the barons of northern England, used to a free hand, would resent and resist.

This sense of grievance led to action as early as 1212, when a group of northern barons, which included Richard de Percy, plotted to assassinate John while he campaigned in north Wales. They then intended to invite Simon de Montfort, who had gained an international reputation through his successful leadership of the crusade against the Albigensian heretics of southern France, to come to England as king. This plot was thwarted by John's early knowledge and quick reaction, but his position was now so weakened that he was unable to exact retribution. The crisis was merely postponed. It was finally precipitated by the collapse of John's foreign policy.

On the death of his brother, Richard I, in 1199, John had inherited the huge French empire of their father, Henry II, which stretched from the Channel coast to the Pyrenees. Between 1202 and 1204, the northern part of this empire, comprising the provinces of Normandy, Brittany, Maine and Anjou, was conquered by the King of France, Philippe II. John was not prepared to accept these losses, and in the years that followed he devised a recovery strategy involving a two-pronged attack by a group of allied states along France's northern border combined with an English invasion launched from the province of Poitou, to the south of Anjou. Paying armies and allies required a great deal of money, hence John's incessant and ruthless pursuit of his barons' wealth and his demand that they serve in a military capacity overseas, a commitment they were reluctant to undertake. By late summer 1214, John's strategy was in ruins. The English baronage was distinctly lukewarm and that of Poitou even more so. Then, at the end of July, Philippe II won a resounding victory over John's northern allies at the Battle of Bouvines, between Tournai and Valenciennes.

John was now vulnerable to his baronial opponents and in the end could not avoid accepting the conditions laid down in the Magna Carta, since the more radical barons from the north were joined by men of more moderate opinion from the midlands and the south and by the most eminent figure in English public life, Simon Langton, Archbishop of Canterbury. What John agreed to in June 1215 was essentially an attempt to define the king's rights more precisely so as to set limits on his scope for exercising them, most particularly in his dealings with the church and the baronage. The most radical and therefore contentious aspect, which reveals the depth of baronial mistrust, was the committee of twenty-five barons set up by clause sixty-one of the Magna Carta to act as a watchdog over the king's behaviour. It is an indication of the extent of his involvement in the rebellion that Richard de Percy was chosen as a member of this committee.

The Magna Carta produced war not peace. To the northern barons, its terms were too generous and lenient to the Crown, forced on them by their more moderate southern colleagues. On the other hand, for John they were an intolerable infringement of his God-given freedom of action to rule as he saw fit. The outcome was civil war, which John, showing his usual dynamic energy, would probably have won had it not been for the invasion of a French army under Philippe II's son, Louis, to whom the rebels promised the English crown. But what really took the heat out of the situation was John's death at Newark on 18 October 1216. Fighting continued into the following year, when the rebels suffered a severe defeat at Lincoln. But with John gone, there was little reason not to make peace with the regency government set up for his nine-year-old son, Henry III, especially as it agreed to confirm the Magna Carta and guaranteed that there would be no reprisals. With these assurances, one by one the rebel barons submitted, Richard de Percy being one of the last to do so.

Richard's subsequent career suggests that his animosity had been against John, rather than the Crown as such, since throughout the remainder of his life there is clear evidence of his active involvement in public life, attending court, acting as a royal justice and serving in a military capacity, most notably on the abortive expedition in 1230, when the young Henry III made a futile attempt to recover Poitou, which had been conquered by the French in the late 1220s. With the loss of Poitou, the English empire in France was reduced to the duchy of Gascony, the area between the sea, the Pyrennes and the River Dordogne. More privately, he made gifts of land to the family foundation, the monastery at Sallay, to St Leonard's Hospital at York and to Fountains Abbey, where, like his grandfather, he chose to be buried.

In contrast, and not surprisingly, the career of his nephew, William, took a different course. He chose to side with John. He was among those barons who agreed to take part in the Poitou expedition of 1214 and he fought for the king in the civil war of 1215–17. Although there is no evidence of collusion, this meant that whichever side came out on top, the Percy interest would be safeguarded. In the end, however, the two men remained divided, even in death, since William chose to be buried at Sallay.

With the deaths of Richard and William, the Percy estate was reunited in the hands of Henry de Percy II. In the strictest sense this is an inaccurate statement in that, at the time of his father's death, Henry was a minor, and as such he and his lands passed into the wardship of the king. In fact, Henry secured possession of them only four years later, when he was probably no more than fourteen years of age. This was the result of a bargain made with the Crown whereby, in return for a payment of £900, he was granted the right to have his land and to marry at will.

The years of Henry de Percy II's adult life (he appears to have come of age in 1257) were those of the second half of the reign of Henry III (1216–1272), when again England experienced tension and conflict between Crown and baronage. As under John, the underlying cause was the personality and actions of the king. Discontent with Henry III's performance as monarch developed in the years after 1227, when his minority ended and he assumed direct control of the processes of government. The root cause of this discontent was financial. Henry was unable, or disinclined, to live within his means, largely as the result of commissioning expensive building projects, notably Westminster Abbey, undertaking hopeless attempts to recover his lost inheritance in France, and lavishing land and money on his favourites and his wife's French relations (Henry's wife, whom he married in 1236, was Eleanor, daughter of Raymond-Berengar IV, Count of Provence, and Beatrice of Savoy).

The crisis was precipitated by a totally unrealistic foreign policy decision. Between 1252 and 1254, Henry entered into an agreement with the papacy whereby the English church would finance the conquest of the Kingdom of Sicily, which comprised the island of Sicily and the southern third of the Italian peninsula. Its rulers were a dynasty of German origin, to which the popes were implacably opposed. The agreement was to the effect that, once the current German ruler, Manfred, had been defeated and removed, the kingdom would be ruled by Henry's younger son, Edmund, as a vassal of the pope. By 1258, as a result of this contract, Henry was in deep trouble. The English church, which he had not taken the trouble to consult, was naturally recalcitrant and refused financial help. Meanwhile, the pope was getting increasingly angry and frustrated by Henry's lack of action, even to the extent of threatening him with excommunication and England with an interdict.

In desperation, Henry was driven to appeal to the baronage for money. But they too were entirely unsympathetic, pointing out that Henry had undertaken this commitment without seeking their advice or support. Instead, they used the power the king's predicament gave them to embark upon what, had it been permanent, would have been a constitutional revolution. By what were called the Provisions of Oxford, a council of fifteen was set up to institute a programme of reform of the royal household and the organs of central government, the effect of which was to place the Crown under baronial supervision. They also insisted upon the banishment of the most influential royal favourites. At first, these drastic actions had the support of almost all the wealthiest and most powerful nobles in England, and consequently, by contrast with the 1214 rebellion, it was dominated by men whose centres of power lay south of the Trent. Paradoxically, the most charismatic of these men, who became the leader of the radical wing of the reform party, was a foreigner. Simon de Montfort was the son of the man who had suppressed the heretical movements in southern France and had been considered as a possible replacement for John. Simon the younger, who was without doubt a man of energy and ambition, came to England in the 1230s, married the king's sister, Eleanor, and successfully laid claim to the earldom of Leicester.

Like his father, Henry was not prepared to accept any constitutional change which would place structural limits upon his freedom to rule. Almost inevitably, divisions developed within the ranks of the baronial opposition, and as a result there followed several years of political conflict and turmoil, culminating in civil war between the early months of 1264 and the spring of 1266. Initially, the opposition forces were successful, defeating the king at a battle on the outskirts of Lewes in Sussex in May 1264. But the Crown's supporters were able to regroup, and in August of the following year they won what proved to be decisive victories at Kenilworth and then at Evesham, where de Montfort was killed. Fighting continued into 1266, but with the defeat of the last baronial army at Chesterfield in Derbyshire in May, the rebellion was at an end and royal authority restored.

It is clear that Henry de Percy II was actively engaged in these events, although unlike his uncle he did not play a leading part, and in particular he was not chosen to be a member of the committee of fifteen. There were two reasons for this. One was that he was not in social and economic terms in the front rank of the baronage, and as has been noted, it was such men who dominated and led the resistance to Henry III. The other is that, having been born around 1235, he had only just attained his majority when the crisis began to develop. Had he been older, he might have been more prominent.

The surviving fragments of information suggest that initially he may have been among the king's opponents, and that because of this his lands were declared forfeit. But by 1260, as the baronage became split into royalist and rebel groups, Henry de Percy veered towards the king's side. He did so as a follower of one of the leading members of the royalist party, John de Warenne, Earl of Surrey (1231–1304), who was the most powerful figure in Surrey and Sussex, that is, where Percy had his Petworth estate. Certainly he was with Warenne at Northampton in April 1264, when the baronial army ambushed the king's troops, capturing a number of them, and again a fortnight later, when Warenne successfully defended Rochester Castle in Kent against a rebel attack. Both men were also together in the royal army at Lewes, but there Percy was captured, or, as one contemporary chronicler alleged, surrendered in panic. Not so Warenne, who escaped and was one of the organisers of the royal army that won the decisive victories in the west midlands. Percy, however, remained a captive until after de Montfort's defeat and death at Evesham.

All this suggests that Percy was in southern England throughout, but other evidence indicates otherwise. He was clearly recognised as a northern baron, since he was commissioned together with several others, including John de Balliol, Robert de Neville and Adam de Jesmond, to keep the peace north of the Trent, that is, to ensure that the north remained loyal to the Crown. And he was also summoned to serve in forces mustered to oppose the rising power of Llewellyn, the ruler of the province of Powys in North Wales. It would seem that he was considered able and competent enough to serve the state, especially in military matters.

Henry de Percy II did not marry until 1268, when he was thirty-three years of age or thereabouts. This was rather late for a first marriage, but there is no known reason for the delay. When it finally took place, it was a clear demonstration of his close association with John de Warenne: his wife was the Earl of Surrey's daughter, Eleanor. It was a prestigious match, for not only was John de Warenne a man of national importance to whom Henry III owed a great deal, but his wife, Alice, was related to the royal family. She was the daughter of Isabelle of Augoulême, King John's widow, who returned to her native France after John's death and married a leading member of the French nobility, Hugh de Lusignan, Count of La Marche.

Their marriage was short-lived, since Henry de Percy II died on 29 August 1272 at the early age of thirty-seven. The cause of his death is not known. However, in the four years of their marriage, he and his wife produced two sons. The elder, John (presumably named after his mother's father), was born in 1270, but died prematurely sometime between 1285 and 1293. The second, Henry, was born on 25th March 1273. In manhood, this man was to begin the thrust which was to raise the House of Percy to the uppermost ranks of the English nobility.

FOUR

The Scottish War and the Northward Shift

Henry, Lord Percy I, 1273–1314

It is all too easy for historians to talk of turning points. This said, it would be hard, if not impossible, not to regard the career of the third Henry Percy as one of the most significant and formative in the family's history. For it was he who began the process which was to transform the Percys from a middle-rank baronial family based in Yorkshire, but with important assets in Sussex, into one of the wealthiest and most influential members of the English nobility. His success came, as it so often does, through a combination of personal ambition and ability and the circumstances of the time.

The background to his story starts with another turning point, in this case in the history of Britain. On the night of 19th March 1286, Alexander III of Scotland, while returning to St. Andrews from Dunfermline, was killed when in the dark he rode over a cliff near Kinghorn on the Fife coast. This was, of course, a personal tragedy. But it was also the cause of a constitutional crisis which came to involve England as well as Scotland. Alexander and his first wife, Margaret, had three children, two sons and a daughter. Both sons, Alexander and David, had died at an early age without leaving heirs, in 1284 and 1281 respectively. The daughter, Margaret, had also died early (in 1283), but she had produced a daughter, also named Margaret. The father, however, was Eric II, King of Norway, and so the fate and future of the dynasty that had ruled Scotland for over four centuries rested with a little girl living in a distant country.

Responsibility for governing a Scotland bereft of its natural ruler was assumed by a committee of six leading figures - two bishops, two earls and two lords - known as the Guardians. These men entered into discussions with the King of England, Edward I (1270–1307), who claimed, and to a degree was acknowledged, to be the overlord of the Scottish kings. The outcome, known as the Treaty of Birgham, envisaged the return of Margaret to Scotland to be placed in Edward's guardianship until she was of marriageable age and might marry Edward's eldest son, the future Edward II, who was a year younger than his prospective bride. Before his untimely death, Alexander III had discussed the possibility of this marriage with Edward I. This was not simply because of the circumstance that Alexander's first-wife, Margaret, the grandmother of the little Maid of Norway, as she was known, was Edward's sister. Had the contemplated marriage taken place, the subsequent development of Britain almost certainly would have been very different.

The marriage did not take place. Although Eric of Norway agreed, albeit with some reluctance, to return his daughter, she died shortly after arriving at Orkney in the autumn of 1290. The worst Scottish fears were now realised: the country had no king and no one with an undeniable claim to be king. There were over a dozen men who were able to put forward some sort of case, but only two could be considered serious contenders. They were John Balliol and Robert Bruce, both descended from Alexander III's great-uncle, David, Earl of Huntingdon, who died in 1219. His son, John, predeceased him, but he was survived by his two daughters, Margaret and Isabel, who married respectively Alan, Lord of Galloway, and Robert Bruce, Lord of Annandale. John Balliol, who was Margaret's grandson, appeared to have the stronger claim in that his grandmother was the elder of Earl David's daughters. However, although the rules of royal and feudal succession favoured the eldest child, they were not yet so firmly fixed as to preclude argument. This enabled Bruce to point out that he was Isabel's son, whereas Balliol was only Margaret's grandson. Furthermore, Bruce argued that Balliol's claim came through the female, namely his mother, Dervoguilla, Alan and Margaret's daughter who married John Balliol's father.

The issue was sufficiently fraught and entangled to earn and merit the descriptive title of the Great Cause. Inevitably, Edward I was involved, not only in his role as overlord but, as he pointed out, as someone with a claim of his own through his descent from the daughter of the Scottish king, Malcolm III, who had married his ancestor, Henry I of England. Edward, however, did not press this claim and indeed behaved with what seemed to be commendable impartiality. In the end, after an exhaustive debate and investigation lasting two years, the decision was in favour of Balliol, a verdict to which there could be no serious objection since, although both competitors, as they were known, had a just claim, the

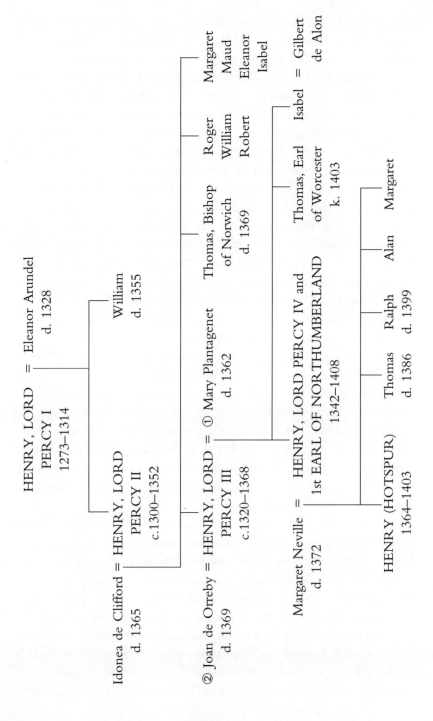

HENRY, LORD = Eleanor Arundel
PERCY I   d. 1328
1273–1314

William
d. 1355

Idonea de Clifford = HENRY, LORD
d. 1365   PERCY II
                              c.1300–1352

Thomas, Bishop
of Norwich
d. 1369

Margaret
Maud
Eleanor
Isabel

Roger
William
Robert

② Joan de Orreby = HENRY, LORD = ① Mary Plantagenet
d. 1369   PERCY III   d. 1362
                            c.1320–1368

Thomas, Earl
of Worcester
k. 1403

Isabel = Gilbert
            de Alon

Margaret Neville = HENRY, LORD PERCY IV and
d. 1372   1st EARL OF NORTHUMBERLAND
                           1342–1408

HENRY (HOTSPUR)
1364–1403

Thomas   Ralph   Alan   Margaret
d. 1386   d. 1399

41

weight of Balliol's seniority was decisive. Consequently, on 30th November (St. Andrew's Day) 1292 Balliol was enthroned at Scone as King John of Scotland. The following month, like his predecessors, he did homage to the English king during the Christmas festivities at Newcastle.

King John's reign lasted less than four years and ended in his humiliation. The heart of the problem was differing views of his role and status. King Edward of England now expected to treat King John of Scotland rather like one of his barons, requiring conformity to his wishes and obedience to his orders. On his part, John expected to be, and to be treated as, an independent monarch like his predecessors. The crisis came with Edward's demand for Scottish troops to form part of the army to serve in Gascony, the last remnant of the English empire in France. John resisted as, it must be said, did many English barons. But he compounded his 'offence' by an appeal for support to Philippe IV of France, Edward's enemy, who was seeking to reassert his authority over Gascony. To Edward, what had begun as defiance now became treason.

Edward's reaction was drastic and dramatic. On 26th March 1296, he invaded Scotland with a large army. Four days later his troops stormed Berwick and massacred several thousand of its male inhabitants. Thereafter, Edward encountered only slight resistance as he swept through eastern Scotland as far north as Elgin. John was captured, and in a humiliating ceremony at Montrose, had the insignia of royalty stripped from his garments. The removal of the Stone of Destiny from Scone to Westminster symbolically signalled that, for Edward, the kingdom of Scotland was at an end. Confident that the Scottish question was solved, Edward returned south, leaving John de Warenne, Earl of Surrey, to govern this newly conquered province.

But this was the beginning, not the end, of a war which was to wax and wane for over three hundred years until James VI of Scotland became James I of England. Scottish resistance to Edward's enforced union was activated by William Wallace, a Lanarkshire man of knightly family, and Andrew Moray, a man of baronial status whose lands lay in the northeast. Against expectation, they had great success: on 1st September 1297, they completely routed the English army at Stirling Bridge, a victory to which English military incompetence significantly contributed. At a stroke, Edward's conquest was undone. But over the remaining ten years of his reign, he assiduously applied himself and his huge resources to re-establishing his control over Scotland. His effort began spectacularly in July 1298 with his defeat of the Scottish army at Falkirk, a defeat which destroyed Wallace's reputation as a commander. Thereafter, Edward's almost constant military pressure, combined with his diplomacy designed to eliminate French and papal support for the Scots, gradually had its effect. By 1305, virtually all the leading nobles of Scotland had submitted and had accepted Edward's overlordship, so that the English king felt able to issue an ordinance setting out the arrangements for the future government of Scotland, which were very similar to those of 1284 for Wales.

The peace was a peace of exhaustion not of reconciliation, and consequently it did not last long. It was ended by a rash and unplanned act, which was at the same time criminal and sacrilegious. On 10th February 1306, in the church of the Franciscan friary at Dumfries, Robert Bruce, the grandson of the 'competitor' of 1292, murdered John Comyn, Lord of Badenoch, the head of the senior branch of Scotland's most powerful family with extensive estates throughout the country, which had played a leading and at times dominant role in the nation's affairs for nearly a hundred years. Comyn was struck down in anger and almost certainly because he was refusing to back Bruce's claim to the throne, which was not surprising given the close relationship between the Comyn and Balliol families.

Although he had himself enthroned at Scone, support for Bruce as king was initially very limited, and he soon found himself a fugitive from his enemies, Scots as well as English. But he did have his backers, and over the following twelve years he gradually made himself master of Scotland, first by winning the civil war against the Balliol–Comyn faction, and then by eliminating one by one the English garrisons in the strategically located castles. His greatest military triumph, for which he will always be remembered, was his defeat of the English army at Bannockburn near Stirling in June 1314. Memorable it may be, but Bannockburn was in reality one event, albeit a major one, in a much longer and more arduous struggle. After Bannockburn another four years of fighting were required to rid Scotland of the English, and a further ten years were to elapse before Bruce finally achieved recognition of himself as King of Scots.

His eventual success was primarily due to his military and political abilities and unswerving determination, but he also owed much to the change of king in England. On 7th July 1307, as he was preparing to invade Scotland yet again, Edward I died. His successor, his son, Edward II, was a man of very different calibre and character. Inclined to idleness and lacking a military disposition, he allowed the initiative in Scotland to slip into Bruce's hands. He was also hampered by the serious financial problems he inherited from his father and distracted by the emergence of an opposition group among the baronage. Their concern was twofold: the maladministration in many sectors of Edward's government and his addiction to a Gascon knight, Piers Gaveston, an addiction which may well have had a homosexual basis. By 1310, the opposition was strong enough to force Edward to accept a committee of twenty-one known as the Ordainers, who produced in the following year a reform programme. Allied to this was the demand that Gaveston be exiled. Edward's resistance to all of this provoked violence, which resulted in the judicial murder of Gaveston in 1312 by the earls of Lancaster, Arundel and Hereford. In the light of these distractions, it is perhaps not surprising that two years later Edward suffered such a humiliating defeat at Bannock-burn.

The year 1314 was also an important one in the history of the House of Percy, for it saw the death of the first Lord Percy at the early age of forty-one. He was born on or about 25th March 1273, some seven months after his father had died. He was not his father's immediate successor, since he had a brother, John, who had been born two years earlier. Nothing is known about John Percy, not even the precise date of his death, which occurred sometime between 1285 and 1293. Because of this, however, it was Henry who succeeded to the estates upon attaining his majority in 1294. Little is known about his early years, although there are hints that he distinguished himself in the jousting lists. This was not simply an exciting sport but also an important element in training for a military career. Upon attaining his majority, he was immediately summoned to serve in the army in Gascony, although in the event the campaign was diverted to Wales. The following year he took part in a diplomatic mission to Scotland headed by his grandfather, John de Warenne, Earl of Surrey. Thus, even before the outbreak of the Scottish war, he had had a taste of the activities that were to dominate the rest of his life.

The war began on 26th March 1296, which may have been Percy's twenty-third birthday. He must have taken part in the horrendous storming of Berwick and the massacre of its townsfolk on 30th March, since he was knighted by the king on the following day. He subsequently fought in the battle near Dunbar which for the time being ended Scottish resistance, and presumably in the rest of that year's campaign. Clearly he had found his vocation, for in the remaining years of Edward I's reign he was on campaign in Scotland or engaged in preparations for campaigning there. And his promotion was rapid. The records of the army assembled in 1298 that was to defeat William Wallace at Falkirk reveal Percy as one of the 110 bannerets, the men commanding squadrons of between ten and twenty men-at-arms (heavy cavalry). In that battle, he was a prominent member of the fourth or reserve division commanded by his grandfather, the Earl of Surrey.

The 1298 campaign is notable for the production of one of the earliest 'rolls of arms', lists of commanders and the knights who fought with them illustrated by paintings of their heraldic arms. This document, known as the Falkirk Roll, was produced by Percy's private herald, a man named Walter le Rey Marchis, whose abilities were shortly to lead to his transfer into the king's service. At this date, heralds were a new phenomenon, who were just beginning to emerge as a group distinct from minstrels, who recorded great military events. Clearly, not only was Percy successful, but he was also not inhibited by false modesty. This confidence was fully justified, for in the following year, 1299, he was awarded the title of Lord Percy by royal writ. In the years that followed, he served in all the invasions of Scotland. He was part of the expedition to Caerlaverock in Dumfriesshire in 1300 and was present at the siege and capture of Stirling Castle in 1304. By 1306 he was in command of all the men-at-arms serving on the western border as well as having administrative responsibilities in Cumbria and the south-western districts of Scotland.

As he expected, Percy benefited materially, at least in theory, from his services; and the size of his reward is a good measure of the worth of those services. In 1299, he was granted the Scottish estates of Ingram de Balliol centred on Urr in Kirkcudbright and Red Castle on the Angus coast between Arbroath and Montrose. This was not a random acquisition since, although in English eyes Balliol was a traitor, he and Percy were closely related, both being grandsons, albeit via different wives, of William de Percy III who died in 1245. As was Edward I's intention, Percy now had a direct and personal incentive to support the royal aim of subjugating Scotland. And further gains followed. In 1304, Percy was granted the earldom of Buchan with its wide estates in northern Scotland, which had been forfeited by John Comyn. His tenure was brief, however, since the estate had to be restored to the Comyns when they renewed their allegiance to Edward I after the murder of John Comyn by Robert Bruce. In compensation, Percy was granted the earldom of Carrick, which had been confiscated from Robert Bruce in 1306. Had Percy been able to retain any of these Scottish estates, he would have been one of the wealthiest and most powerful men north of the Border.

It was not to be. Following Edward I's death in 1307 and the failure of his son Edward II to press on with the policy of conquest, English control was gradually eroded and with it the ability of Percy and others like him to hang on to and profit from their Scottish gains. In the light of his losses and his faltering military career, it is not surprising to find Percy as one of the Ordainers, the magnates who sought through the Ordinances of 1311 to control Edward II's actions. He was among those barons who secured Gaveston's surrender at Scarborough in 1312, but not, as far as is known, was he party to the judicial murder at Warwick that followed.

Percy did not long outlive this incident. He died early in October 1314 some fourteen weeks after the Battle of Bannockburn. He was only forty-one years of age. The cause of his death is uncertain. He is known to have been summoned to the army which invaded Scotland, but there is no evidence that he served or was present at Bannockburn on 23rd–24th June. Unlike Robert de Clifford, another of Edward I's able young northern captains with whom he was closely associated, he was not killed in this action. It is possible that he was wounded and that he died of his wounds a few weeks later. But the silence of the records argues that he was not there and that consequently his death was due to non-military causes. He was buried at Fountains Abbey, where his defaced tomb can still be seen.

His place of burial is a reminder that the Percys were still a Yorkshire family. But it was the first Lord Percy who acquired Alnwick in Northumberland, the place with which the family has so long been associated. The story of the acquisition is complicated and around it hangs a slight suspicion of unfair play. The barony of Alnwick, the largest in Northumberland, was created by Henry I some time before 1130. Throughout the twelfth and thirteenth centuries it belonged to the de

Vesci family. In 1297, however, the then owner, William de Vesci, died without leaving any legitimate children. The previous year he had created a complex legal settlement by which he granted his entire estate to Antony Bek, Bishop of Durham, who immediately regranted it back to him, with two remainders contingent upon de Vesci dying without a legitimate male heir. By the first, his properties in Yorkshire and Lincolnshire were to pass to his illegitimate son, also William, who was known as William de Vesci of Kildare (he was so called because his father was, in addition to being a landowner in England, the lord of Kildare, and his mother was Devorgilla, daughter of Donal Roe Mac-Carthy, Prince of Desmond). By the second remainder, however, the barony of Alnwick was to return to Antony Bek.

This is what happened. But in 1309, twelve years after de Vesci's death, Bishop Bek sold Alnwick and its estate to Henry Percy for an unrecorded sum, but one large enough to have made it necessary for Percy to borrow from Italian bankers. So far the story is straightforward, but not long after the transaction was completed rumours began to circulate to the effect that Bek had no right to sell, since he was not the owner but was holding the estate in trust for future generations of the de Vescis. Against this, however, there is no evidence in the surviving documents relating to the sale to suggest that it was not *bona fide* or that Bek's possession was in any way restricted. Nevertheless, there may have been just enough doubt to cause Henry, Lord Percy II, who had recently come of age, to pay 700 marks (£466 13s 4d = £466.67p) to Gilbert de Aton on 2nd September 1323 in return for de Aton's confirmation of Percy's father's purchase of Alnwick. By this date, William de Vesci of Kildare was dead (killed at Bannockburn) and de Aton was the undisputed heir general of William de Vesci who died in 1297. Consequently, it has been argued that was Percy prepared to pay a large sum of money to avoid what might have been a long and costly legal action. Why Percy was so keen to acquire Alnwick? The answer is that, not only was it a very valuable property, but it was located conveniently halfway between the old Percy estates in Yorkshire and the acquisitions in Scotland. And the castle would also be a convenient base for military operations in Scotland and a ready refuge in the event of defeat.

Percy's military career and property acquisitions in Scotland and Northumberland would seem to suggest that his eyes were turned northwards. While this was certainly true, there are indications that

3. Main centres of the Percy estate in the North

he also enhanced his links with Sussex, particularly with the Fitz Alan family. Originally lords of Clun and Oswestry on the Welsh border, the Fitz Alans inherited the earldom of Arundel in 1243, although they appear not to have used the title until around 1290. The family from whom they acquired this earldom were descended from Adeliza, the second wife of Henry I and half-sister of Percy's ancestor, Jocelin, Count of Louvain, and her second husband, William d'Aubigny. As the Percy estates centred on Petworth were part of the great honour of Arundel, it was natural that Percy should seek to establish a fruitful relationship with the new power in Sussex. And the relationship may have involved marriage. It is traditionally believed that Percy's wife, whom he probably married in the late 1290s, was Eleanor Fitz Alan and that she was very closely related (daughter or sister) to Richard Fitz Alan, Earl of Arundel. However, there is no conclusive proof of this. The known facts are that Percy's wife's maiden name was Eleanor Arundel, that she was the sister of a Sir Richard Arundel, one of Edward I's household knights, who had very little property, and that neither he nor she feature, in any of the accounts or genealogies of the Fitz Alan family. At the same time, the Fitz Alans were using their title as a surname, and it seems unlikely that a man as ambitious as Henry Percy would have married beneath him.

Further support for the idea that Eleanor was a member of the Fitz Alan family is the adoption by Percy in the late 1290s of a new armorial device. The arms that he and all previous Percys had used were five gold lozenges on a blue ground. Instead, he now displayed a blue lion rampant on a gold ground. It is possible that these were the arms of his Louvain ancestor, but perhaps it is more significant that the Fitz Alan arms were different only in colour, namely, a gold lion rampant on a red ground. His new arms may therefore have been intended to emphasise a newly forged link with the Fitz Alans, and also to underline their common descent from the family of the dukes of Lower Lorraine. The change was made very public, the new device appearing in the Falkirk Roll produced by Percy's own herald in 1298, as well as on his seal. Whatever the truth of Eleanor's origin, it is almost certain that she rests on the north side of the sanctuary of Beverley Minster under what is arguably the finest fourteenth-century tomb in Britain which, unlike her husband's, is undamaged.

FIVE

Towards an Earldom

Henry, Lord Percy II, 1301–1352
Henry, Lord Percy III, c.1320–1368

The northward thrust of Percy ambition and interest was maintained by Henry, Lord Percy II, but not immediately. The second Lord Percy was born at Leconfield in the East Riding of Yorkshire on 6th February 1301 and was therefore only thirteen years old when his father died. His minority lasted until 26th December 1321, when he was declared to be of age and invested with his father's estates. His emergence into public life was completed in the following year when he was knighted at York by Edward II.

Being a minor meant that Percy was not really involved in the problems and crises that beset England in the early years of Edward II's reign. For the northern counties the most urgent and pressing problem was their persecution at the hands of Robert Bruce, from 1306 Robert I of Scotland. This began as early as 1311 and continued almost incessantly until May 1323, when a thirteen-year truce (which was to last a mere four years) was agreed. The persecution took the form of fast-moving raids by small armies of light cavalry, which were able to penetrate as far south as mid-Yorkshire. The Scots profited from these raids in two ways. Some English communities were able to organise themselves sufficiently to raise enough money to buy off the invaders. For Bruce, who systematically encouraged them to do so, this was an excellent means of replenishing his treasury. In effect, it was he and not the English king who was taxing the far north of England. Where the money was not forthcoming, however, property was destroyed and valuables and livestock were stolen. It was the lure and appeal of such plunder that was the great attraction for Bruce's subjects who manned his armies. Both king and subjects were therefore satisfied. But for Bruce, all this activity was a means to a political end. His real purpose was to force the English government to the negotiating table where, as the price of peace, Edward II would have to acknowledge him as King of Scots.

Edward II was totally unwilling to abandon his father's claim to the overlordship of Scotland while at the same time being powerless to make his claim a reality or even to find ways of defending his own kingdom. In addition to his military inadequacy, he was distracted from the task by a long-running dispute with a baronial opposition led by his cousin, Thomas, Earl of Lancaster. The chief cause of this was a new royal favourite, Hugh Despenser, son of the Earl of March, who aroused hatred and envy by his arrogance and greed to acquire land. In 1321, Edward was forced to agree to the exile of the Despensers, father and son. He went along with this, but only until he could gather together his own forces. The issue was decided in a short civil war in 1322, which ended with the defeat of the baronial opposition at Boroughbridge in Yorkshire, ironically at the hands of an army from the very Border region that the king was unable to defend. Lancaster and at least thirty of his associates were executed, while others fled abroad leaving Edward free to abolish the Ordinances at a parliament held at York.

It was on this occasion that Henry, Lord Percy II entered public and political life. The very fact that he was knighted at this time suggests that he was active on the side of the Crown; indeed there is some evidence that he fought with the royal army at Boroughbridge and captured two rebel knights and their esquires. Thereafter, and perhaps in part because of what he had witnessed, his commitment to royal service seems to have been unswerving. His career was to last for thirty years, during which time he was all but constantly engaged in matters relating to Scotland and the Border, where he took an active part in the revival of English fortunes. Throughout the rest of Edward II's reign, the Scots remained in the ascendant and northern England continued to suffer, although not to the same degree as in the previous decade. In 1327, Edward II was deposed by his wife, Isabella, and her lover, Roger Mortimer, Earl of March, and later murdered. The new king was Edward III, son of Edward II and Isabella, but as he was only fourteen years old, he was monarch in name only. It was during Isabella and Mortimer's brief period in power that peace was concluded with Scotland. By the Treaty of Edinburgh agreed in 1328, Robert Bruce secured what he had striven so hard to achieve for twenty-two years, English recognition that he was King of Scotland.

Two years later, in October 1330, Edward III, now eighteen years old, overthrew the illicit regime of his mother (who was required to retire completely from public life) and Roger Mortimer (who was executed). The previous June, Robert I of Scotland had died, probably of leprosy, leaving his hard-won kingdom to his six-year-old son, David II. Suddenly the political balance had shifted: England now had a young and dynamic king, who was not prepared to accept what he called the 'shameful peace', while the government of Scotland was in the hands of the guardians of a child monarch, who in 1334 was sent to France for safety.

The English counter-attack against Scotland began surreptitiously. In 1332, a group of English nobles, known as the 'Disinherited' because they had been deprived of their Scottish estates, launched an invasion of Scotland. They were accompanied by Edward Balliol, the son of King John (who died in 1315), who hoped to regain his father's lost throne. This small force landed in Fife, won a surprise victory at Dupplin Moor, and enthroned Balliol at Scone. The Scots had been caught unprepared, but they soon rallied and expelled Balliol. Edward III now came into the open. In 1333, he invaded Scotland with a large army, laid siege to Berwick and defeated a Scottish army at Halidon Hill just north of the town. Significantly, both of these victories were won by what was to prove the most effective military tactic of the fourteenth century, the use of dismounted men-at-arms in conjunction with archers wielding the longbow.

Edward III continued his efforts to subdue Scotland by means of annual invasions and permanent garrisons in strategically located castles such as Roxburgh, Jedburgh and Stirling. In 1337, however, he decided to reduce his commitment to what was proving to be an unpopular, expensive and unproductive policy in favour of aggression towards France. There had been tension between the kings of England and France for nearly a hundred years arising from the English king's possession of Gascony and his right to the title Duke of Aquitaine. Added to this was Edward's claim to the throne of France as the nephew of Charles IV, who died in 1328 without a direct male heir. At that time, Edward was too young to press his claim, and Philippe of Valois, Charles IV's cousin, became King of France as Philippe VI. But in the late 1330s, Edward prepared to challenge Philippe VI's right to the French throne, if only as a diplomatic weapon. This change of foreign policy, which began what came to be called the Hundred Years War, made it possible for the Scots gradually to regain control of the southern parts of their country. By 1341, the situation there was sufficiently secure for David II, now nearing his eighteenth birthday, to return from France. He immediately showed that he had inherited his father's hostility towards England, and as a result England found herself faced with an enemy on two fronts. In the course of 1346, however, Edward succeeded in neutralising both threats. In August, he personally commanded the army which crushingly defeated a French army at Crécy in Ponthieu. Two months later in October, an army raised in the northern counties of England won a decisive victory over a Scottish army at Neville's Cross on the outskirts of Durham. David II, who had willingly responded to the French appeal for help by invading England, was captured and remained a prisoner of the English king until 1357. This defeat, together with the loss of their king, seriously reduced the ability of the Scots to threaten England in the foreseeable future. Worse still, the English took control of the Scottish border counties, thereby creating an effective buffer zone against further attacks.

What part did Henry, Lord Percy II, play in these events? Although not many details have survived, enough are available to make it clear that his involvement was virtually continuous, that it took three different but related forms, and that he was one of the most important men on England's northern border. He held many of the public offices noblemen were expected and required to hold. At various times he was the keeper of the royal castles at Scarborough, Skipton and Bamburgh, all of which were close to his estates, and all with an important role in the defence of northern England. He also served as Warden of the Marches, an office with which his family was to have a long and close association. The concepts of a march as a defined frontier district, and of a warden as an officer with special powers and responsibilities within its boundaries, were responses to war. They developed rapidly in the first half of the four-teenth century, although the apparatus did not achieve its full and final form until the 1380s. Two marches, comprising Northumberland and Cumberland-Westmorland, emerged, and from 1345 were known re-spectively as the East March and the West March. In 1381, the East March was divided into the East March and the Middle March, although in practice until the sixteenth century they were normally united under the same warden.

Until the late 1380s, the wardens held office under special commissions, but thereafter the more permanent arrangement of a contract specifying terms and length of service became the norm. Initially, the warden's duties were military: basically, he took over the military aspects of the sheriff's role, calling out and commanding the military forces of his march, and in times of war controlling all the castles within its boundaries. Gradually, however, civil duties were added: holding Warden Courts which enforced the March Laws, the body of Border law which had been codified in 1249 but was in origin much older; and holding Truce Days, when he met his opposite Scottish number at one of the designated places on the Border to receive complaints and hand over malefactors. He also acquired the power to agree truces of up to two months and issue safe conducts. Although his powers appeared to be great and extensive, he was constrained, as was the sheriff, by having to respect the many 'liberties' (districts of private jurisdiction) and to work with and through their officers.

Primarily, however, Percy was engaged in the business of raising and commanding contingents of troops and in this he played a leading part in the radical transformation of English military organisation and tactics prompted by the disastrous defeat at Bannockburn. By the late 1330s, English armies were ceasing to be composed of men-at-arms who fought on horseback, accompanied by a large body of under-trained, poorly equipped and badly disciplined infantry. Increasingly, armies were made up of units of men-at-arms and archers in roughly equal numbers, both mounted for speed of movement (a lesson taught by the Scots), but in battle fighting on foot in a co-ordinated fashion according to a clearly formulated tactic. Moreover, recruitment no longer relied on the traditional methods based upon the feudal obligation of the landowning class and the general liability to military service of all men between the ages of sixteen and sixty. Rather, both men-at-arms and archers were volunteers, paid at agreed rates and with the guarantee of such things as recompense for lost horses and safeguard from lawsuits while on active service. In effect, they were becoming essentially professional troops, and as such they were to prove almost invincible during the hundred years after 1330.

Percy was one of the most active men in northern England in these developments and he took part in almost all the campaigns in Scotland and in the defence of northern England in the 1330s and 1340s. He appears not to have been involved in the invasion of Fife in 1332, essentially because he was not one of the 'Disinherited'. Once Edward III had made the war official, however, he became fully engaged. He was a member of the army which took Berwick and won the Battle of Halidon Hill in 1333. Two years later, together with another prominent northern landowner, Ralph Neville, Lord of Raby in County Durham, he repelled a major raid into Redesdale, and he was heavily involved in the campaigns of 1336, 1337 and 1338. Some indication of Percy's prominence is afforded by the details of the force raised to invade Scotland in 1337, which was ordered to assemble at Newcastle-upon-Tyne on 7th May. Of the twenty-five men who agreed to raise between them 501 men-at-arms, the largest contingent comprised the 120 furnished by the commander, the Earl of Warwick; the second largest retinue, however, was Percy's eighty which was twice the size of the next largest contingent. In the following decade, he took part in Edward III's short campaign in Scotland in the winter of 1341/42 and commanded the force sent to relieve the garrison at Stirling in 1344.

His most notable military engagement, however, was at Neville's Cross in 1346, when he commanded the third division of the English army. When Edward III invaded France, he was fully aware of the likelihood of a Scottish invasion, and consequently his army was raised in the south, leaving northern resources to deal with any Scottish incursion. The nominal commander of this northern army was the Archbishop of York, William de la Zouch, whose office gave him precedence. Under him, however, the main military commanders were Percy, Lord Neville, and the Sheriff of Yorkshire, Thomas de Rokeby. The following year, the success of Neville's Cross was reinforced by an invasion of Scotland, in which Percy was prominently involved, which resulted in the re-establishment of the English-controlled buffer zone in the Scottish Border counties.

War is rarely continuous, and is almost always accompanied by complementary diplomatic activity. Here too Percy played a notable role. In 1328, he was one of the four English commissioners sent to negotiate the peace treaty with Bruce, and he also took part in the negotiations which led to the marriage between the young David II of Scotland and Edward III's sister, Joan. Five years later, he was the chief English representative at the meeting at Perth of Edward Balliol's one and only Scottish parliament. His diplomatic experience was again called upon in 1350, when talks took place with the Scots with a view to securing a lasting peace.

In the middle ages, men did not fight merely for king and country, but also, and perhaps in many cases primarily, for personal gain and advancement. Percy was no exception; indeed, he was very much a man of his age and class who used his services and his opportunities to increase his wealth and enhance his status. From Edward III who, in contrast to his father, knew how to match service and reward, Percy gained considerably. His first acquisition was the estate of a fellow Northumberland baron, Sir John Clavering. Clavering's lands were entailed on his male descendants, but since he was old and childless, it was known that his estate would revert to the Crown. This happened in 1332. The Clavering estate was immediately given to Percy, who in return relinquished an annual fee of 500 marks (£333 6s 8d = £333 34p) he had been granted in 1327 for his services on the Border. The gain was substantial, for the Clavering estate comprised considerable properties centred on Warkworth, Rothbury, Newburn and Corbridge. Two years later, he added the manor of Thirston in mid-Northumberland, but of much greater significance were the Northumberland estates of the Earl of Dunbar, most notably the barony of Beanley. Dunbar was descended from Gospatric, the Earl of Northumbria deposed by William I in 1072, whose grandson had been granted Beanley by Henry I. He was one of the many nobles with estates in both England and Scotland who were forced to choose which nation to join. Dunbar's decision to be a Scot meant the expropriation of his Northumbrian lands, which were granted to Percy in 1335. Through these acquisitions, within a period of twenty-six years the Percy family had become the largest landowners in Northumberland.

Percy also gained extensively in Scotland. The estates granted to his father by Edward I in Galloway and Angus had been confiscated by Robert Bruce, but Percy used the opportunity presented to him by his role as one of the English peace negotiators in 1328 to secure their restoration. This matter was satisfactorily completed in 1331, hence his disinclination to join the 'Disinherited' when they invaded Scotland the following year, although the fact that these lands had once belonged to the Balliol family may have been an additional consideration. In fact, he acknowledged the validity of the Balliol claim by paying 200 marks

(£133 6s 8d = £133 34p) to a member of that family to head off any possible legal challenge. With Edward Balliol's Scottish gamble appearing, perhaps against all the odds, to succeed, Percy became a willing participant in the venture. He entered into a contract with Balliol whereby he agreed to serve Balliol in Scotland (saving his prior duty to Edward III) in return for a substantial grant of land. The consequence of this agreement was the award of Annandale and Moffatdale in 1333. He did not secure possession, however, as Edward III insisted that the estates in question be granted to his cousin, Edward de Bohun, whose father, Humphrey de Bohun, Earl of Hereford, had been given them by Edward I in 1306. In 1334, therefore, Percy relinquished his claim to Annandale and Moffatdale, in reward for which Edward III granted him Jedburgh and Jed Forest, the keepership of Berwick Castle and an annual pension payable out of the customs duties collected at Berwick. In fact, the income from the recompense was greater than that from the original grant. Here it is possible that the English king's generosity was deliberate and was linked to the fact that Percy did not press his claim to the Scottish earldom of Carrick, which had been granted to his father in 1306. The restoration of the earlier acquisitions, together with Edward III's grants, made Percy for the time being one of the wealthiest nobles in Scotland.

Henry, Lord Percy II, died after a short illness of unknown nature at Warkworth in February 1352. He was fifty-one years of age. He was buried at Alnwick, although in his will he directed that he should be interred at Sallay Abbey, an indication perhaps of a continuing attachment to his family's Yorkshire roots. His widow, Idonea, was a daughter of Robert, Lord Clifford, who had been ennobled by Edward I in 1299 at the same time as Percy's father and been killed at Bannockburn. It was a most appropriate alliance between two of the young men who had come to the fore through their military abilities in the early years of the Anglo-Scottish war. Henry and Idonea had a large family. In addition to the heir, Henry, who became Lord Percy III, their second son, Thomas, became Bishop of Norwich in 1356, while two of their daughters married leading members of the Border baronage: Margaret became the wife of Robert Umfraville, Lord of Prudhoe and Redesdale, and Maud married Ralph Neville, Lord of Raby.

Although almost everything known about Henry, Lord Percy II, points to his total involvement in military and closely related matters connected with the Border, his will exposed another side to his nature. He revealed that he had set aside 1000 marks (£666 13s 4d = £666 67p) to pay for a pilgrimage to the Holy Land, a sum which his heir was to have, provided he fulfilled his father's commitment. How serious this intention was, we cannot tell. It may have been genuine piety, or merely a show of it; or it may have been an expression of a wish to travel and to see parts of the world other than the war-torn lands of northern England and southern Scotland.

Unlike his father, Henry, Lord Percy III, was of full age when he succeeded to the title, having been born, probably in 1320, and probably at Seamer near Scarborough. Like his father, however, he pursued a successful military career. When the French war got under way in the late 1330s, Percy was fast approaching military age. It is not surprising therefore to find that he was a member of the Earl of Arundel's retinue in 1339. This connection may indicate that Percy had grown up and received his education and training in the earl's household. If so, it would add support to the idea that his paternal grandmother was in fact a member of the Fitz Alan family. His presence in the Arundel household would also have had the advantage of placing him close to the Percy lands around Petworth, an important consideration in the light of his father's almost total involvement in northern matters.

The Arundel link meant that Percy's early military career took place in and against France, and it included war at sea as well as on land. Almost certainly he took part in the naval battle of Sluys in 1340, by which England gained command of the Channel and so prevented a projected French invasion. This control, which lasted for several years, also enabled English armies and equipment to cross to France in safety. Ten years later, he is known to have been involved in another sea battle, this time off Winchelsea against a Castilian fleet operating as an ally of France.

On land he may have been a member of the expeditionary force which invaded Brittany in 1342 and won an important victory at Morlaix. Four years later, in 1346, he was certainly in the larger army Edward III took across to Normandy, with which he won the great victory at Crécy and which in the following year secured the surrender of Calais. Shortly thereafter, he was in Gascony in the force commanded by one of Edward's III most able captains, his cousin, Henry of Grosmont, Earl of Lancaster. These fragments of evidence suggest that Henry Lord Percy

III was involved at various times in all the strands of Edward III's strategic plan to defeat France, which was a three-pronged attack from Normandy in the north, Brittany in the west and Gascony in the south. By the time he succeeded his father, Henry Percy III was in his early thirties and had gained wide and varied military experience through involvement in most of the important military and naval engagements in the first phase of the Anglo-French war.

His father's death and his succession to the title required him to shift northwards to undertake what was fast becoming the traditional Percy role, the defence of northern England and control of southern Scotland. Like his father, he was Keeper of Berwick and Warden of the Marches. He was also Keeper of Roxburgh, one of the main Scottish border castles, and Sheriff of Roxburghshire, duties which would have enabled him to maintain control of the family's recently acquired estate around Jedburgh. This may have been the extent of his involvement in defence, since his life after 1352 coincided with a period when the Border was largely peaceful, thanks to Neville's Cross. In fact, in the 1350s there was only one serious outbreak of fighting, in 1355–56, when the Scots briefly occupied the town of Berwick but were punished by Edward III, whose retaliation in the winter of 1356 was severe enough to be remembered as 'Burnt Candlemas'.

It is unclear whether Percy was involved in this episode, although the fact that he had recently been appointed to the keepership of Roxburgh hints that he may have been. But it is known that he was also with Edward III about this time, for he crossed to France with the king as marshal of the royal army, a clear indication of his status and importance. Because of this he is unlikely to have been present at the Battle of Poitiers in 1356, when Edward III's son and heir, Edward, known as the Black Prince, inflicted another crushing defeat on the French and captured their king, John II. The battle was an attempt by the French to block the Black Prince's northward advance from Gascony, the strategic aim of which was to link up with Henry, Earl of Lancaster, whose operational base was Normandy. If Percy was involved, which is likely, it would have been with this northern force. If there is doubt here, there is none about his presence in the huge army which Edward III assembled at Calais in 1359. Edward's aim was to capture Rheims, where French kings were crowned, and to bring the war to a triumphant conclusion by his own coronation as

King of France. This campaign, however, failed to achieve its aim as Rheims refused to open its gates, and exhaustion drove the two countries to enter negotiations which ended with the Treaty of Brétigny. With the war in France ended for the time being, Percy probably returned to northern England where in the early 1360s he was employed in an ambassadorial role in Scotland.

Henry, Lord Percy III, married twice. His first wife, whom he married in 1334, was Mary, sister of Henry of Grosmont, Earl of Lancaster. The match was entirely appropriate since both were prominent members of Edward III's military establishment. Mary, however, died in 1362, and three years later Percy married an heiress, Joan, daughter of John, Lord Orreby. Percy himself died in 1368 at the age of forty-eight. Both he and his first wife elected to be buried at Alnwick, probably in the Premonstratensian canonry, a clear indication, it would seem, that the Percy family was, and felt itself to be, firmly rooted in the far north of England. With hindsight, it may be argued that the death of Henry, Lord Percy III, brings to an end the first phase of the family's history. The stage was set for their rise in social status and an almost permanent leading role in the political life of the nation.

PART TWO

Earls

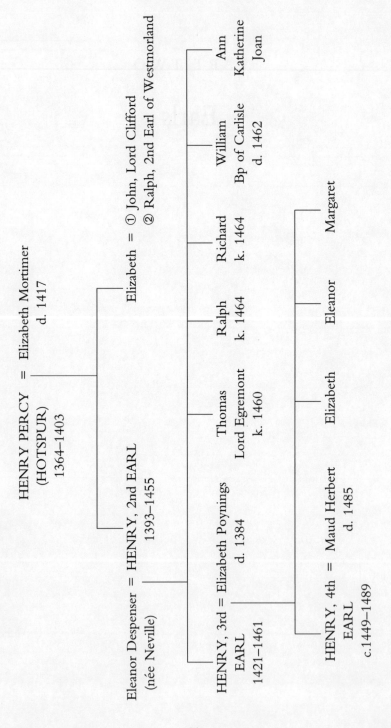

SIX

The Earldom Gained and Lost

Henry, Lord Percy IV, and
First Earl of Northumberland, 1342–1408

Henry, Lord Percy IV, the man destined to acquire an earldom for himself and his descendants, was born on 10th November 1342, and was therefore twenty-six years old when his father died in 1368. Little is known about his upbringing, but it is likely that his formative years were spent in the household of his uncle, Henry of Grosmont, Earl (Duke from 1351) of Lancaster, who was not only an outstanding military commander, but also a civilised man of letters. Percy's first known public appearance was as a member of Lancaster's entourage during the invasion of France in 1359, when he would have been seventeen years of age. He must have been a young man of some promise since he was knighted in 1361, and by 1366 had become one of the twenty-six knights of the Garter, the chivalric order founded by Edward III in 1348. In these years he is known to have been involved in Border matters with his father, and also independently. Consequently, when his father died, he was well prepared to undertake the many and varied roles to which he had been born.

During the next ten years much of his public life was spent in, or concerned with, France. The expedition of 1359, of which he had been a member, resulted the following year in the Treaty of Brétigny, whereby Edward III agreed to abandon his claim to the French throne in return for French recognition of his full sovereignty over the Duchy of Aquitaine, including Gascony. This treaty was never implemented, probably because neither the French nor the English were sincere in their acceptance of its terms. Consequently, what was apparently a permanent peace turned out to be no more than a brief interlude.

The war broke out again in 1369, the driving force in England being Edward III's third son, John of Gaunt, Duke of Lancaster (the title he acquired in 1362 by his marriage to Blanche, daughter and heir of Henry of Grosmont, who had died the previous year). By this time the king's health and his interest in war were failing. His eldest son, the warlike Edward, known as the Black Prince, was already suffering from the disease (probably dysentery) which caused his death in 1376, and his second son, Lionel, Duke of Clarence, was already dead. The war had two aspects. One was the long-range expeditions, known as *chevauchées,* in which English armies swept through France plundering and destroying property. Although these forays caused much misery and hardship, they were strategically futile in that they did not result in decisive battles. In fact, English control was reduced to a coastal strip south of Bordeaux. The other was the naval conflict for control of the Channel, which England also lost as the result of a defeat off La Rochelle in 1372. This phase of the Hundred Years War ended with Edward III's death in 1377 and the accession of his ten-year-old grandson, Richard II, the Black Prince's son and heir.

The war failed to produce the great victories and great profits of Edward III's earlier years, and consequently it aroused little enthusiasm, especially amongst members of parliament, who were required to vote the taxation to pay for fleets and armies. During these years, Henry Percy was actively involved in warfare, usually in association with John of Gaunt, who was a contemporary, a relation by marriage and, at this stage, a friend. It is a testimony to Percy's ability and the quality of his service that in 1376 he was made Marshal of England.

Percy's real interest, however, lay not in France but in northern England and the Scottish borders, and it was here that most of his time was spent from the late 1370s. This phase of his career had two distinct but closely related aspects, military and political. In 1369, a fourteen-year truce between England and Scotland was agreed. It should have lasted until 1383, but the death of Edward III and the accession of the minor, Richard II, was the signal for a renewal of Scottish aggression. The annual instalments of the ransom of David II, which continued to be paid even after his death in 1371, ceased; and Durham Cathedral Priory's cell at Coldingham in Berwickshire was seized and handed over to Dunfermline Abbey. Moreover, the Scottish border lords, the Earl of Douglas and the Earl of March, began an aggressive drive to recover control of most parts of the Scottish lowlands which had fallen into English hands as the result of the Battle of Neville's Cross.

By the end of 1383, this activity had reduced English control to little more than the strategic castles of Berwick, Roxburgh, Jedburgh and Lochmaben. The capture of the last-named, in February 1384, provoked an English retaliation in the form of two large-scale raids (in effect *chevauchées*), the first in 1384, led by John of Gaunt, the second in the following year, led by Richard II, now eighteen years old and emerging from tutelage. Although they caused widespread destruction of property, they were fruitless since the Scots, like the French, shrewdly declined to engage a superior enemy in a set-piece battle, but removed themselves and their portable goods from the path of the invaders.

This phase of the war culminated in 1388 in the Battle of Otterburn. This event became the subject of one of the best known of the Border Ballads, and as a result is commonly seen as an incident of local importance arising from a long-standing feud between the Border families of Percy and Douglas. This view is valid, but only up to a point. Between these two families there was a serious and long-standing dispute about the ownership of Jedburgh and Jed Forest, the extensive district stretching southwards from the Teviot to the Border at Carter Bar. Shortly before he died, Robert I of Scotland granted this huge estate to one of his closest associates, Sir James Douglas, but, as we have seen, in 1334 following his victory at Halidon Hill, Edward III of England bestowed it up on Henry, Lord Percy II. Since that date the English control of the Border region had ensured Percy possession, but it is also clear that the Douglas family had in no way abandoned its claim.

To concentrate on this aspect, however, would be to ignore the much wider significance of the battle as a major incident in the long Anglo-Scottish conflict, and indeed in the Hundred Years War. The battle was the result of a carefully planned attack upon England by the government of Robert II (1371–1390), which was intended to take advantage of Richard II's political embroilment with the Appellants, a formidable opposition group within the English nobility. The Scots hoped to force the English government to negotiate from a position of weakness, as it had been obliged to do in 1328, and thereby to secure a permanent peace and an English-free Scotland. The plan was for a three-pronged campaign, which included an attack on English lands in Ireland, as well as a double invasion of England. Here the main thrust was in the west under Robert II's second son, Robert Stewart, Earl of Fife (later Duke of

Albany). The incursion into the East March led by James Douglas, second Earl of Douglas, was essentially a diversionary raid, but it was this that involved the Percys and led to Otterburn.

Regrettably, it is impossible to recount exactly what happened, since there are no fewer than eight medieval versions (three Scottish, four English and one French, by the famous Jean Froissart, who was able to talk to French knights who had taken part). None, however, was written by an eye witness. Even the precise date is not known, although it was after the 4th and before the 18th August. What appears to have happened is that Douglas's force advanced southwards through Northumberland on what again must be seen as a *chevauchée*. Its progress was halted at Newcastle, which was protected by its twenty-foot-high wall and defended by a garrison commanded by Percy's twenty-four-year-old son and heir, Sir Henry Percy, better known by his nickname, Hotspur. There may or may not be truth in the story that, in a skirmish outside the northern wall of the town, Douglas captured Percy's pennon and taunted Percy that he would display it at Dalkeith, unless Percy was able to recover it.

Douglas's force was not equipped to besiege Newcastle, and therefore it began its return journey to Scotland, via Redesdale. Its progress was almost certainly slowed by booty taken in the course of its southward sweep. Consequently, when Hotspur's scouts reported that the Scots were camped just north of Otterburn, he decided upon a forced march and a surprise attack. That he covered the thirty-two miles in a day suggests that his force was mounted. Even so, it was late in the day when he sighted the Scottish camp. Some accounts have the battle fought in the gloaming; others say it was by moonlight. Which is correct depends upon the time in the month: the moon was new in early August, but full towards the middle of the month. Whatever, the outcome was a comprehensive Scottish victory, which included the capture of Hotspur and his brother, Sir Ralph Percy, and it was marred only by the death of the Earl of Douglas. Hotspur was soon ransomed for a very large sum, to which Richard II contributed £3,000, a testimony to his recognised importance to Border defence.

How many men took part is, as always with medieval battles, a matter for speculation. Jean Froissart claimed that the English dead numbered 1,840, a figure made credible by the discovery in 1877 of the remains of

1,200 skeletons under the foundations of the part of the local parish church of Elsdon known to have been built around 1400. This would in turn support the claims that Percy's force was between 7,000 and 9,000 strong. The size of the Scottish force would seem to have been smaller, possibly as few as 3,000 men. If so, it was outnumbered by at least two to one, which perhaps explains Hotspur's rush to battle. It has been pointed out that Otterburn has the distinction of being the only occasion when a Scottish invasion resulted in a major military victory on English soil. Yet Scotland made no strategic gains: there was no peace treaty, but only another renewal of truce in 1389, which left Berwick, Roxburgh and Jedburgh in English hands.

Another matter was of the utmost importance to the Percys. It too concerned the Border, but it was also of political significance nationally. This was the award, on the occasion of Richard II's coronation in 1377, of the title Earl of Northumberland to Henry, Lord Percy IV. This elevation appeared to be a formal recognition of the power and status of the Percys on the Border. Yet, the following twenty years saw an almost constant attempt to undermine or reduce their influence. It was begun by John of Gaunt and led to a marked cooling of the hitherto friendly relationship between him and Percy. In 1379, Gaunt, then the dominant political figure in London, was appointed Lieutenant in the Marches. His commission gave him full power in matters of Border defence and the supervision of truces, and it clearly indicated that the wardens of the Marches were subordinate to him and under his direction. In addition, Gaunt took steps to ensure that men loyal to him were appointed as wardens, the most notable being John, Lord Neville of Raby, an able soldier who had served under him in France and Spain. Gaunt's base for his intrusion into Border affairs was the barony of Embleton in North-umberland, which he had acquired as part of the great estate of the duchy of Lancaster. The barony was small and did not yield a large income, but in Dunstanburgh, which was built in the 1310s, it possessed one of the largest and certainly the most up-to-date castles in Northumberland.

In the end, however, this proved to be an inadequate power base, and after the 1384 expedition into Scotland, Gaunt accepted that local men, especially the Percys, were the linchpins of Border defence. In fact, in 1386 he left England to pursue a greater ambition, the Crown of Castile, to which he had a claim as the husband of Constance, the heir of her father

King Pedro I. In the 1390s, however, Richard II too adopted an anti-Percy policy, firstly by appointing his own relatives to the wardenship, and then by promoting the Nevilles. John Neville died in 1388, but by 1397 his son, Ralph, was considered fit to assume the role of rival to the Percys. In that year, he was made Earl of Westmorland, a title supported by the grant to him of two large Cumbrian estates based upon Penrith and Sowerby. At the same time, independently of the Crown, although with its approval, he inherited the Northumbrian baronies of Bywell and Bolbec. Suddenly, the Nevilles had achieved parity with the Percys.

Before looking at the political crisis that developed at the end of the 1390s, it is important to look at another aspect of Percy's career, the one which perhaps was closest to his heart, namely, the enlargement of his estate. His efforts in this respect were immensely successful: in just over twenty years between 1373 and 1395 he acquired several important properties which greatly increased the size of his estate and significantly altered the pattern of landownership in Northumberland and Cumberland.

His first major success was in 1373 when, for £760, he bought from the Crown the wardship of Elizabeth and Philippa, the daughters and heirs of David of Stathbogie, Earl of Atholl, who had died four years previously. Atholl was one of the nobles who had possessed estates in both England and Scotland but had forfeited their lands north of the Border earlier in the century when they or their predecessors had opted to give their allegiance to the King of England. Percy set about attaching Atholl's estate to his own by marrying Elizabeth to his second son, Thomas, and Philippa to his youngest son, Ralph. In part he was successful, in that the land assigned to Elizabeth and Thomas (who died in Spain c.1389) eventually reverted to the main estate, although not until the middle of the next century. The marriage of Philippa and Ralph (who died c.1399), however, was annulled, and she married again, taking her share of the estate out of the Percy orbit. The lands involved were well scattered and included properties in Kent, Wiltshire, Norfolk and Lincolnshire. These were probably of secondary interest to Percy compared with the land in Northumberland, which included the manor of Mitford with its castle, and substantial properties in the Regality of Tynedale, which were inherited by Atholl from another Anglo-Scottish family, the Comyns.

Percy gained far more from his dealings with another ex-Anglo-Scottish magnate, Gilbert de Umfraville. He, too, had lost his Scottish lands, while retaining the empty but nonetheless status-enhancing title of Earl of Angus, acquired in 1243 by one of his ancestors as the result of marriage to a Scottish heiress. In 1375, Umfraville, who was sixty-five years old and childless, granted or sold to Percy half of his Northumberland estate, comprising the barony of Prudhoe with its large castle and nine villages. (The other half, the Regality of Redesdale, was to pass to his half-brother, Thomas de Umfraville.) Gilbert died in 1381, and three years later Percy, who had been a widower since the death in 1372 of his first wife, Margaret, daughter of Ralph Neville, Lord of Raby, married his widow, Maud. The marriage to Maud gave Percy a firmer grip on the Umfraville property in Northumberland. But this was not his only gain, for Maud was not merely Gilbert de Umfraville's widow, but also the sister and heir of another major Border landowner, Anthony, Lord Lucy of Egremont. Lucy, who was childless, was persuaded to settle his considerable estate upon Maud and her new husband. Consequently, when Lucy died, Percy acquired another Northumbrian property, the small barony of Langley, and also a much greater prize, the huge Cumberland barony of Cockermouth, which included no fewer than thirty-five villages.

The last major acquisition was made in 1395, when Percy persuaded the Hylton family to make over to him eight manors in Northumberland in exchange for land of equivalent value in Yorkshire. These manors were original members of the barony of Alnwick which, as the result of their recovery, was fully reconstituted. Percy's willingness to trade property in Yorkshire for land in Northumberland is a clear indication of where the family's centre of interest now lay. This impression is reinforced by several smaller acquisitions he made, most by purchase, but one as the result of the failure of heirs, all of which, significantly, were in Northumberland. And as well as these gains made by the earl, a number of Northumbrian estates were also acquired by his heir, Hotspur, notably four manors secured as the result of an unredeemed mortgage, and in 1399, as a gift from the Crown, the remaining Comyn properties in the Regality of Tynedale.

By the end of the fourteenth century the Percy family were far the largest landowners in Northumberland. Their success had been achieved through service to the Crown, shrewd dealing in the marriage market and a willingness to use their growing power in pursuit of their aims. As a result they had replaced, and to a large extent had taken over, the estates of the earlier nobility, most of whom had had dual nationality, which the conflict between England and Scotland turned into a handicap.

Towards the end of the 1390s, the Percys became deeply involved in national politics and played a central role in bringing about a change of dynasty. Richard II had succeeded to the throne as a minor, and therefore it was not until 1385 that he began to play an active part in government. Very quickly, he aroused opposition through his predilection for favourites, extravagant expenditure on personal interests and an unwillingness to be guided and advised. His opponents were among the most powerful members of the English nobility: Thomas of Woodstock, his uncle and Edward III's youngest son; Richard Fitz Alan, Earl of Arundel; his brother, Thomas Arundel, Bishop of Ely; Thomas Beauchamp, Earl of Warwick; Thomas Mowbray, Earl of Nottingham; and John of Gaunt's son and heir, Henry of Bolingbroke, Earl of Derby. Known collectively as the Appellants (a word deriving from a legal term meaning accusation), these men used their control of parliament in 1388 to humiliate the young king by securing convictions for treason against several members of his government and men close to him personally. The most notable was Richard de Vere, Earl of Oxford, on whom Richard had unwisely and provocatively bestowed the title Duke of Ireland. In the end, only two of those convicted were caught and executed, Sir Nicholas Brembre, and the Chief Justice, Sir Robert Tresilian. The Appellants' control of the government did not last long. In May 1389, Richard declared himself to be of full age, which undoubtedly he was, and that he would now rule as an adult monarch. The Appellants did not have enough popular support to stand in his way.

Richard's vengeful nature did not allow him to forget the slights done to him, and in 1397 he set about exacting revenge. He had the Earl of Arundel arrested, tried and executed, and his brother, Thomas, now Archbishop of Canterbury, exiled; and he also procured the murder of his uncle, Thomas of Woodstock. The Earls of Nottingham and Derby, however, were spared. They had made their peace with Richard, who rewarded their return to loyalty by granting to them, respectively, the titles Duke of Norfolk and Duke of Hereford. Percy was not seriously involved in this, yet his position was also weakened. In 1396, he was removed as Warden of the East March and replaced by his son, Hotspur, while Hotspur's previous office, Warden of the West March, was given to one of the king's favourites, John Holland, Earl of Huntingdon. In the following year, Richard significantly enhanced both the status and wealth of Ralph Neville. Inevitably, the Percys construed these as hostile acts, which lessened their loyalty to Richard.

This was to prove a major factor in the political crisis that developed in 1398 and 1399. It began, seemingly harmlessly enough, in a quarrel between the two former allies, Thomas Mowbray, now Duke of Norfolk, and Henry of Bolingbroke, now Duke of Hereford. The quarrel became sufficiently bitter to raise the prospect of trial by battle. In September 1398, Richard intervened and imposed a harsh and far from even-handed settlement. Both men were exiled, Norfolk for life, but Bolingbroke for only ten years, and with a promise that should his father, John of Gaunt, die he would inherit his title and estates. But when Gaunt died in the following year, Richard reneged, increased Bolingbroke's sentence to exile for life and confiscated his estates, which he then distributed among his supporters. Belatedly, deviously and capriciously, he had completely avenged the humiliation of 1388.

Bolingbroke's response to this double-cross was rapid. Late in June, while Richard was in Ireland, he returned to England, landing at Ravenspur on the Humber. Three months later, at the end of September, he forced Richard II to abdicate and took the throne as Henry IV. In the train of events leading to this conclusion, Henry Percy, Earl of Northumberland, played a major, and at times crucial, role. The events themselves are fairly well established, but what is not, because of the propagandist nature of much of the contemporary evidence, is the motives and intentions of the leading participants.

The basic facts are that Bolingbroke was met by several members of the northern nobility, including the earl and Hotspur, at Doncaster on or about 8th July 1399. That they came – and came armed – was in itself an act of treason and an indication of their basic inclination. It was at Doncaster, however, that Bolingbroke swore on relics brought from Bridlington Priory that his purpose was to claim his rightful inheritance and secure the reform of royal government, but not to depose Richard, or seek the throne for himself. As he advanced westwards, his army grew in size, and by the time he reached Chester in mid–August it was clear that support for Richard, who had returned from Ireland at the end of July and taken refuge in Conwy Castle, had ebbed away. At Chester, Bolingbroke again swore that his aims were to regain his title and estates and to reform the government, but not to depose Richard. It was at this point that Percy played a crucial role, as the leader of the deputation that went to Richard to persuade him to meet with Bolingbroke at Flint. In fear and with great reluctance, Richard agreed, but only after the earl swore that Bolingbroke had solemnly sworn that he did not seek the throne. Once at Flint, however, Richard was seized and shortly after-wards removed as a prisoner to the Tower of London. There he was persuaded or forced to abdicate, and a few weeks later, in October, Henry Bolingbroke was crowned King Henry IV. Henry Percy's support for this act was clearly and publicly revealed by his role as the new king's sword bearer at his coronation. The details of Richard's fate are uncertain, but to let him live would have been too risky. In all probability, he was murdered early in 1400.

The obvious questions are more easily asked than answered. Did Bolingbroke return to England resolved from the start to remove Richard and become king; if not, when did he take the fateful decision? And to what extent did he deceive the Percys, or were they throughout willing accomplices and parties to the plot? There are no certain answers to these and many subsidiary questions. But all those involved were highly ambitious men with very few scruples, who were engaged, and with open eyes, in a deeply dangerous and risky business where failure meant death. This said, with their knowledge of Richard's capacity for ruthless revenge and his total untrustworthiness, they must have known that they had no realistic alternative to deposition, although it is possible, for reasons that will shortly become apparent, that Hotspur may have had greater reservations than his father about Bolingbroke's right to the throne.

Whether the Percys were innocent dupes or cynical perjurers may be open to debate. What is not is the rewards they received from Henry IV. The earl was reinstated as Warden of the West March, appointed Constable of England and Lord of the Isle of Man, and given custody of two-thirds of the lands of Edmund, Earl of March, during his minority. Hotspur did equally well. He was made Warden of the East March, appointed Admiral of England, Captain of Roxburgh Castle, Justice of Chester, Lord of Anglesey and Constable of Chester, Flint, Conwy, Caernarfon and Beaumaris Castles.

In the summer of 1399, Henry Bolingbroke and the Percys were allies and almost certainly to some degree conspirators. By the summer of 1403, they were at war, a war which was to end in disaster for the Percy family. Although a great deal of uncertainty surrounds this reversal of commitment, it is absolutely clear that, in the latter half of 1402, relations between the new king and his leading supporters turned sour. The most obvious evidence of this is the bitter complaint by the Percys that Henry had not paid them what was due to them for defending the Border. The government's financial records, however, contain very little to support their claim. In fact, they had been paid substantial sums, which, even if they did not fully reimburse them, should have been sufficient to prevent the degree of anger revealed in the complaints. The true causes of Percy discontent must be sought elsewhere.

It is at this point that the younger Percy comes to the fore. He was born in 1364, and from a very early age he was actively engaged in military matters. It was the vigour with which he pursued these that earned him the nickname given to him by the Scots, 'Hotspur'. In fact, the original spelling, 'Haartspore', might be more accurately rendered as 'Hardspur'. The difference is immaterial, however, since both words convey the idea of a dynamic, dashing soldier. It is not surprising, therefore, that in 1383 he was lured, as were many adventurous young knights, including in fact Henry Bolingbroke and in fiction Chaucer's 'gentil parfit knyght', to Prussia to fight alongside the Teutonic Knights against the heathen Baltic tribes. However, he was immediately recalled to take part in the less glamorous and less worthy campaign in Flanders led by the bishop of Norwich. Apart from this and brief tours of duty in Calais in 1386–87 and Aquitaine in 1393–94, his military activity took place on the Border.

Hotspur's greatest hour of glory was his victory at Humbleton Hill, just north of Wooler, on 14th September 1402. This battle was the outcome of a course of events virtually identical to that which ended at Otterburn in 1388, but with the opposite result. In 1400, the newly crowned Henry IV led an expedition into Scotland, in which Hotspur had taken part, and earlier in 1402 the Scots had suffered a defeat at Nesbit Muir. It was in retaliation for these blows, therefore, that the Scots launched a raid into

Northumberland which penetrated as far south as Newcastle. As they were returning home through the valley of the River Till, they were ambushed by Hotspur a few miles north of Wooler. The result was a total defeat for the Scots, thanks to the effectiveness of English archery. Seven Scottish nobles were killed, and twenty-eight were taken prisoner, including their leaders, the fourth Earl of Douglas, known as Archibald the Tyneman (the Loser), and Murdoch Stewart, Earl of Fife, a nephew of the Scottish king. English losses are said to have been no more than five. But it might have been different. Hotspur, with characteristic impetuosity, apparently wanted to charge the enemy, rather than let the archers fight the battle at a distance. Had he not been dissuaded, the result could have been another Otterburn.

It was now that the quarrel with the king began. Henry IV demanded that Douglas be handed over to him. In this he was in the right, since the rule was that the king had the right to have and to ransom the enemy leaders captured in battle, upon payment, of course, of suitable compensation to the captor. Hotspur, however, refused to hand over Douglas, unless the king agreed to ransom Hotspur's brother-in-law, Sir Edmund Mortimer, who was a prisoner in Wales. Mortimer's captor was Owain Glyn Dŵr, who, in 1400, had begun a rebellion with the aim of making himself Prince of Wales, in effect the ruler of an independent principality. It is reported that the meeting between Hotspur and the king became so heated that the king struck Hotspur in the face and drew his sword against him, insults to honour that could not be lightly dismissed. Curiously, Shakespeare, to whom Hotspur owes much of his fame, missed using this obviously dramatic scene in Act I of *Henry IV* (Part I), and instead has him rather tamely declaring 'By Heaven, he shall not have a Scot of them; No, if a Scot should save his soul, he shall not: I'll keep them, by this hand'.

But this alone may not explain why the situation became so serious. Beneath what ought to have been little more than a storm in a teacup, albeit a serious one, was the far deeper question of Henry IV's right to the throne, a matter of more direct concern to Hotspur than to his father. Henry IV was undoubtedly of royal blood, being the son of John of Gaunt, Duke of Lancaster, the third son of Edward III. And as Richard II did not have any children, the only thing that stood between Henry and a fully legitimate claim to the crown was the offspring of Edward III's second son, Lionel, Duke of Clarence, who died in 1368. Clarence had no son, but he did have a daughter, Philippa, who married Edmund Mortimer, third Earl of March. From this union there were two significant offspring. One was Roger Mortimer, fourth Earl of March, who, until his death in Ireland in 1398, was Richard II's officially designated heir. Mortimer and his wife had a son, Edmund, born in 1391, who became fifth Earl of March upon his father's death. The third Earl of March's other child was a daughter, Elizabeth, who became Hotspur's wife in 1379. They too had a son, Henry, born in 1393. By the law of succession, the young Edmund Mortimer, and after him Henry Percy, Hotspur's son, could claim greater right to the throne than Henry of Bolingbroke. When the crisis arose in 1399, both boys were too young to be considered as Richard II's successors. This did not mean that their claims were forgotten or abandoned, but rather that they were held in abeyance for possible future use. As Henry IV was now proving not to be the hoped-for puppet king, doubts about the legitimacy of his crown were available for exploitation. Consequently, either from genuine conviction, or for tactical reasons, early in July 1403 the Percys issued a manifesto in which they claimed that the king had played false and had broken his oath by seizing the throne, and in so doing had deprived young Mortimer of his rightful inheritance.

The quarrel, or rather the first phase of it, was resolved by battle near Shrewsbury on 21st July 1403. Hotspur began to raise troops in Cheshire, which was likely to be a good recruiting ground in that Richard II had been popular there, and rumours were circulating, possibly encouraged by Hotspur, that he was still alive. Almost certainly he was doing so preparatory to linking up with Glyn Dŵr, who was now in alliance with his erstwhile captive, Hotspur's brother-in-law, Sir Edmund Mortimer, an alliance cemented by the marriage of Mortimer and Glyn Dŵr's daughter, Catherine. However, Henry IV with his army moved quickly north to Shrewsbury, thereby interposing himself between Hotspur and Glyn Dŵr. Clearly, Hotspur had been outmanoeuvred, and he was therefore forced to fight on ground of his opponent's choosing, and with a smaller army. In the battle that ensued, Hotspur was killed. He was buried at Whitchurch, but he was not allowed to rest in peace. His body was exhumed, and in the grizzly custom of the time, his head was cut off and displayed at York, while his body was quartered and the parts displayed at London, Newcastle, Bristol and Chester. Only after a year of this indignity were his remains returned to his widow for burial in York Minster. Also killed, but by execution after the battle, was Hotspur's uncle, Thomas Percy, Earl of Worcester.

The defeat at Shrewsbury and the death of Hotspur did not end the rebellion. Although the Earl of Northumberland was arrested, he was not seriously punished, partly because he had been in Yorkshire and so could argue that he was not involved. But, in addition, the king may not have felt strong enough to attempt the total destruction of the Percys. The revolt was resumed in 1405, and with several new recruits, the most notable being Richard Scrope, Archbishop of York. Its aim was made clear enough in the agreement drawn up between the Earl of North-umberland, Glyn Dŵr and the young Earl of March, who was now fourteen years old. It envisaged no less than the tripartite division of the kingdom: Glyn Dŵr was to get Wales and the counties bordering it; the Percys were to have the North and certain eastern counties; and Mortimer was to have the remainder of England. To our minds, this may look like fantasy politics, but it represented not merely the combined wishes, but also the legitimate claims, of the three parties, at least as they saw them. Again Henry IV was too quick for the rebels. The uprising was soon put down, and several of its leaders, including the Archbishop of York, were executed. This was unprecedented, and the fact that Henry executed the second most senior figure in the English church may tell us something of his anxiety.

Among those not caught was the old Earl of Northumberland, now over sixty years of age. He escaped to Scotland, where he had already taken his grandson for safety. This time there could be no way back. Nor was there much hope of help from Wales, where Glyn Dŵr's power was waning. Consequently, the earl's invasion from Scotland early in 1408 was a forlorn hope. The venture got as far as Bramham Moor, near Wetherby in Yorkshire, where, on 19th February, it was easily defeated by local forces led by the sheriff, Sir Thomas Rokeby. The earl was amongst those who were killed. Fourteen months earlier, he and his brother had been attainted in their absence and their lands and titles declared forfeit. Thus, in less than a decade, the Percys had fallen from kingmaker to oblivion.

As a postscript, it needs to be said that an alternative view of Percy aims has been advanced. This sees their real ambition lying to the north, in

1. CHARLES SEYMOUR, 6TH DUKE OF SOMERSET 1662–1748 (JOHN CLOSTERMAN).
He married in 1682, as her third husband, Elizabeth Percy, daughter and heir of
the 11th Earl of Northumberland. Known for his pomposity as the 'Proud Duke,'
he was largely responsible for the present form of Petworth House, Sussex.
Petworth House, Courtauld Institute of Art Photographic Survey.

2. HUGH SMITHSON (PERCY 1750), 1ST DUKE OF NORTHUMBERLAND 1714 OR
15–1786 (SIR THOMAS GAINSBOROUGH). He began life as a baronet, but through
his marriage became Earl and then Duke of Northumberland. He played an
active part in the political life of Britain during the 1750s and 1760s.
*The Duke of Northumberland. Photograph: Photographic Survey, Courtauld Institute of Art.
Also Plates 3–8.*

3. HUGH SMITHSON (PERCY 1750), 2ND DUKE OF NORTHUMBERLAND 1742–1817 (GILBERT STUART). Eldest legitimate son of the 1st Duke, he had an early career in the army, serving in the Seven Years War and in the early stages of the War of American Independence. He had an illegitimate half-brother, James Smithson, who was an eminent scientist and left his estate to found the Smithsonian Institution in Washington, D C.

4. HUGH PERCY, 3RD DUKE OF NORTHUMBERLAND 1785–1847 (JOHN DOWNMAN 1815). The eldest son of the 2nd Duke. He did not enjoy a favourable reputation either in London political circles or in Northumberland. However, he made a considerable contribution to the development of the gardens at Syon House, Middlesex.

5. CHARLOTTE FLORENTIA, 3RD DUCHESS OF NORTHUMBERLAND 1787–1866 (SIR THOMAS LAWRENCE). A granddaughter of Robert Clive, the conqueror of India, she was the official governess of the future Queen Victoria during the reign of William IV.

6. ALGERNON PERCY, 4TH DUKE OF NORTHUMBERLAND 1792–1865 (GUSTAV POPE). Youngster brother of the 3rd Duke. Arguably the most distinguished Duke of Northumberland. He served in the Royal Navy during the Napoleonic War and became an Admiral in 1862. He was a patron of scholarship and a most able and caring estate administrator; and he was briefly in the Cabinet in the 1850s.

7. GEORGE PERCY, 2ND EARL OF BEVERLEY AND 5TH DUKE OF NORTHUMBERLAND 1778–1867 (GUSTAV POPE). His father was the younger son of the 1st Duke who was created Earl of Beverley in 1790. He succeeded his cousin, the childless 4th Duke, in 1865 when he was eighty-seven. Not surprisingly, he held the title for only two years, dying in 1867 in his ninetieth year.

8. LOUISA, WIFE OF THE 5TH DUKE OF NORTHUMBERLAND 1781–1848 (WILLIAM OWEN). She was a granddaughter of John Stuart, 3rd Earl of Bute, a close political associate of the 1st Duke. She was never Duchess of Northumberland since she died before her husband succeeded to the title.

Scotland, where, it is argued, they hoped to expand their possessions and power. But, as their resources were inadequate to the task, they needed the help of the English Crown. This Henry IV was unwilling to give, hence their wish to replace him with a boy to whom they were related and whom they hoped to control. Whether true or not, this helps to reinforce the impression that the first Earl of Northumberland and his son were men of almost boundless ambition. Like Icarus, however, they flew too close to the sun, their wings melted, and they crashed to earth.

SEVEN

Political Minefield: the Wars of the Roses

Henry Percy, Second Earl of Northumberland, 1393–1455
Henry Percy, Third Earl of Northumberland, 1421–1461
Henry Percy, Fourth Earl of Northumberland, c. 1449–1489

The careers of the second, third and fourth earls of Northumberland, covering the years 1408 to 1489, need to be considered together. Although different in character and personality, there were certain common features to their lives. The most obvious is their commitment to the House of Lancaster. This may have been due to family tradition or to the lessons of 1403, 1405 and 1408, but this loyalty was costly and at times threatened total disaster. Also very evident is their commitment to their estates, both to preserve what they had and to expand them whenever possible. This, however, applied only to their property in England. They had to accept the permanent loss of their Scottish possessions. Because of this, and also because they were drawn deeply into the maelstrom of national politics, their centre of gravity shifted southwards. Whereas in the late fourteenth century Percy interest seemed to lie primarily in the Border region, both in England and in Scotland, in the fifteenth century their activity was much more obviously focused on Yorkshire. This did not mean a total loss of interest in the Border. Indeed, for much of the fifteeth century, a Percy was normally Warden of the East March, but the Border was no longer the urgent and demanding matter it had been for much of the fourteenth century. Although a permanent peace settlement was out of the question while parts of southern Scotland were still under English control, there were few major incidents or invasions, and the Border regions enjoyed an uneasy and only occasionally violent existence.

A proper understanding of the course of Percy fortunes during these seventy-five years requires an awareness of the two power structures with which they were involved. One is the Neville family, which in these years came to be the great rival and enemy of the Percys. The rise of the

81

Nevilles was phenomenal, and primarily due to the virility and political skill of Ralph Neville, first Earl of Westmorland, who had no fewer than twenty-three children. With his first wife, Margaret, a daughter of the Earl of Stafford, he had nine. The eldest of them, his heir, John, died in 1423, leaving a young heir, Ralph. Consequently, when the earl died two years later in 1425, it was this boy who inherited his title as second Earl of Westmorland. But he did not inherit the estate, except for the patrimonial property of Raby, in County Durham. The remainder of the vast array of Neville properties in Durham, Yorkshire and elsewhere was settled on Richard, the eldest son of his second marriage, to Joan Beaufort, daughter of John of Gaunt by his third wife, Katherine Swynford. She and Neville had fourteen children, all of whom were used to the advantage of the family. Apart from one son, Robert, who became Bishop of Durham, all were married to good effect. Of greatest importance for the family's fortune was Richard's marriage to Alice Montagu, daughter and heir of Thomas, Earl of Salisbury. In 1429, Richard inherited his wife's land and her father's title. In his turn he too pulled off a major coup in the marriage market by securing for his son, also Richard, Anne Beauchamp, sister and heir of the childless Earl of Warwick. The younger Richard inherited lands and title from his wife and then from his father. As well as being 'Warwick the Kingmaker', he was the greatest non-royal landowner in England. The first earl also arranged good marriages for his younger sons, so that at one stage five Nevilles were simultaneously members of the House of Lords. He was equally successful for his daughters, three of whom married dukes, one an earl and a fifth a viscount. In national terms, the Nevilles had outstripped the Percys, but in Yorkshire the two families were still evenly matched, both having extensive estates which interlocked with each other: a virtual recipe for bitter rivalry.

The other important power structure was the Crown and its apparatus of government. Henry IV died in 1413, and was succeeded by his son, Henry V, who so spectacularly and successfully restarted the war against France. Henry died prematurely in 1422, however, leaving a six-month-old son, Henry VI. This meant a long minority during which England and its newly acquired empire in France were governed, respectively, by the king's uncles, Humphrey, Duke of Gloucester (d.1447), and John, Duke of Bedford (d.1435). Henry was deemed to have come of age and fit to exercise the royal role in 1437. But fit he was not, and never became so. In fact, he probably qualifies as the weakest and most inadequate of England's medieval kings. He was totally unfitted by temperament and character to impose his will and drive the organs of government. He was easily dominated, and consequently he was unable to deal firmly but even-handedly with the various factions and family interest groups that were the political nation. Nor was he at all interested in that perennial preoccupation of the medieval world, war. The empire in France, which his father had won, was gradually lost, and he had neither the ability nor inclination to stem the tide of defeat and retreat. It is ironic, therefore, that while the dynamic father is always portrayed as a national hero, renowned for his victory at Agincourt in 1415, the effects of which lasted less than fifty years, the despised son is remembered for Eton and King's College, Cambridge, two institutions which still flourish. Such backbone as he had resided in his French wife, Margaret, daughter of the impecunious but well-connected René, Duke of Anjou. The marriage, which took place in 1444 when groom and bride were twenty-three and fifteen respectively, was prompted by the French king, Charles VII, as part of his campaign to rid France of English presence.

Inevitably, the ground the king should have occupied was taken by others. The first dominant figure was William de la Pole, Duke of Suffolk, but he was ousted and murdered in 1450. His place was taken by Edmund Beaufort, second Duke of Somerset, a grandson of John of Gaunt and Katherine Swynford, and therefore a great-grandson of Edward III. The domination of government by what was a clique of Beauforts meant the exclusion of the most powerful member of the royal family, Richard Plantagenet, Duke of York, who could trace his descent back to both the second and fourth sons of Edward III, respectively, Lionel, Duke of Clarence and Edmund, Duke of York. Indeed, until 1453 when Queen Margaret gave birth to a son, Edward, York was the heir to the throne. His exclusion from the inner core of government was an insult to his rank and status, an act of political folly and a guarantee of trouble.

These days were far in the future, however, when Henry Percy, the second Earl of Northumberland, emerged on to the stage. He was born on 3rd February 1393, to Hotspur and his wife, Elizabeth, daughter of Edmund Mortimer, third Earl of March. He was therefore eleven years of age when, following Hotspur's death at Shrewsbury, his grandfather, the first earl, took him to Scotland for safety. Consequently, his upbringing was at the Scottish court. Here it should be explained that in 1406, the ailing Robert III, who had been King of Scotland since 1390, decided to send his heir, James, to France. The reasons were his own health, his heir's youth (James was only eleven years old) and the dangerous political situation in Scotland. But by ill luck the ship carrying him was ambushed off Flamborough Head and James became a prisoner in England. Tragically, news of this helped to hasten Robert III's death a few weeks later. James I of Scotland was to spend the first eighteen years of his reign, until 1424, as a 'guest' of the English king. During his enforced absence, the government of Scotland was in the hands of his uncle, Robert, Duke of Albany, until 1420, and then of Albany's son and successor, Murdoch, who, as Earl of Fife, had been captured at Humbleton Hill.

The possibility that Henry Percy might be rehabilitated was opened in 1413 by the death of Henry IV which brought a new and more forgiving regime to power in England. The process began in October 1414 when, at Berwick, Percy married Eleanor, the widow of Richard Despenser. Her father was Ralph Neville, first Earl of Westmorland, and her mother his second wife, Joan Beaufort. Percy's mother-in-law was therefore the new king's aunt, and it is she who is believed to have smoothed the path for Percy's return. The year 1414 was also significant in that Percy came of age. As he had not been directly involved in his father's treason, and as his father's and grandfather's lands were legally entailed upon him, he was granted permission to seek restitution of his inheritance. There was, however, a diplomatic factor, and negotiations relating to this delayed his return to England until February 1416. It concerned Murdoch, Earl of Fife, whose father, Robert, Duke of Albany, was more anxious to secure the release of his son from English captivity than to negotiate the return of his nephew, the young King James. In the end, it was agreed that he and Percy should be exchanged, but with Murdoch paying a ransom of £70,000. In fact, it was Percy who had to pay the money, and then try to recoup his outlay from the Scots.

Although Hotspur's son is always regarded as the second Earl of Northumberland, the award of 1414 was strictly a new creation. That aside, regaining the title was a straightforward matter. Not so the recovery of the estates. In 1414, these had not been granted to Percy; all he secured was the right to sue in the Court of Chancery for the entailed estates of his father and grandfather. Happily, Percy was able to show good and incontrovertible title to these lands. But there was a very serious obstacle to his actually regaining possession of them, namely, the king's brother, John, Duke of Bedford, to whom a large portion of them had been granted. There was no way such a powerful individual could be dislodged, and Bedford remained in possession until his death in 1435; and even then it required an act of parliament (passed in 1439) to secure their return. The same act, however, gave Percy the additional right to claim the entailed estates of his great uncle, Thomas Percy, Earl of Worcester. From the Percy point of view, the most important of these was the castle and manor of Wressle, six miles east of Selby, in the East Riding of Yorkshire. This, however, together with a manor in Lincoln-shire, had been acquired by an influential member of the government, Ralph, Lord Cromwell of Tattersall. The question of the ownership of Wressle was to become a serious issue and the cause of bitter conflict in the 1450s.

The 1440s, however, did see the earl regain possession of the lands granted in the late fourteenth century to Hotspur's younger brother, Thomas. His son, known as Henry Percy of Atholl, died in 1432 leaving no male heirs, and under the terms of the original grant his lands reverted to the main Percy estate in 1440 upon the death of his widow. By this date, but by unknown means, the properties acquired by Hotspur had also been regained, and two important additional properties had been acquired, a house in Hull and the large Essex manor of Dagenham. The result was that by the time of his death in 1455, the second earl had recovered, with a few exceptions, the entailed properties of his father, grandfather and great uncle, and had made new acquisitions.

In the summers of 1416 and 1417, he was on campaign with the king in France. Presumably, Henry V wanted to keep an eye on him and get his measure. Percy must have passed muster, for the remainder of his public life was largely spent on Border matters. Most significantly, from 1417 until 1434, and from 1440 until his death, he was sole Warden of the East March, for which he was paid (or at least entitled to) a substantial annual stipend. In addition, he was a member of various diplomatic commissions sent north to hold discussions with the Scottish government, and in 1424 he was among those who ceremonially escorted James I to the Border on his return to Scotland from captivity in England.

These activities had long been standard work for the Percys, but they also became closely involved in the extraordinary political events of the 1450s. By 1453, when the crisis developed, Percy was sixty years of age and consequently the military aspects were handled by his sons, Henry, Lord Poynings, and Thomas, Lord Egremont, the latter being a man of particularly violent temperament. By this time, the situation in England was deteriorating. Lawlessness was on a greater scale than normal, due largely to the government's unwillingness to tackle the problem. Politically, the reputation of the government as regards honesty and competence was at a low ebb, with the Duke of Somerset seen as the chief culprit. On the sidelines was the Duke of York, frustrated by his exclusion from the king's council and animated by a range of personal differences with Somerset. Early in 1452, he tried and failed to force his way into government, a rebuff which made his position even more precarious. Then, in August 1453, the situation worsened as Henry VI became insane.

The Percys, however, were at this stage more concerned with a personal and local problem, which involved them in a bitter quarrel with the Nevilles. The matter at issue was the castle and manor of Wressle, which had belonged to the first earl's brother, but was now, as we saw, in the possession of Ralph, Lord Cromwell. The matter came to a head in August 1453 when the marriage took place at Tattersall Castle of Cromwell's heir, Maud Stanhope, and Sir Thomas Neville, a younger son of the head of the Neville clan, Richard, Earl of Salisbury. By this marriage, Wressle would pass upon Cromwell's death into Neville hands and be permanently lost to the Percys. To them this was an intolerable prospect, and it led them to an intemperate act. On 24th August, as the bridal party was returning from Tattersall to the Neville stronghold at Sandhutton, it was attacked on Heworth Moor, east of York, by Lord Egremont and 700 Percy retainers. Seemingly, there were no fatalities, and the Nevilles were able to make good their escape, but the 'Battle of Heworth' exposed the extent to which powerful men could and would seek to settle their differences by the use of force.

The government did nothing. Indeed, it had been rendered even more incapable of action by Henry VI's insanity. In October, Neville and Percy looked poised to clash again. Both mustered their forces, Neville at Sandhutton, Percy at Topcliffe, but neither side risked advancing the four miles between the two castles. In fact, the more serious development in the autumn of 1453 was the widening of the conflict as the two parties looked for allies. The Nevilles found theirs in the Duke of York, whose wife, Cecily (known as the Rose of Raby), was the Earl of Salisbury's sister. Their mutual requirements were clear: the Nevilles wanted help in dealing with the Percys; York needed support in his drive to become Protector, in effect head of government during the king's incapacity, the duration of which could not be known. For their part, the Percys joined forces with Henry Holland, the young Duke of Exeter. He was descended from John of Gaunt and his first wife, Blanche of Lancaster, and consequently considered that he had more right than York to be Protector.

During the course of 1454 the York–Neville alliance triumphed. In March, York's undoubted right to be Protector was acknowledged, and both Somerset and Exeter were imprisoned. And on 1st November, the Nevilles and Percys finally clashed in a battle at Stamford Bridge, near York. The Neville army, commanded by the Earl of Salisbury's sons, Sir Thomas and Sir John Neville, defeated the Percy force under Lord Egremont and his younger brother, Richard, largely due to the desertion of Peter Howard, the bailiff of their manor of Pocklington, and the men he was leading. Egremont and Richard Percy became captives and were sent to Newgate Prison in London.

But York's triumph was short-lived. At the end of December 1454 the king recovered his wits and consequently York's role as Protector came to an end. Early in 1455, Somerset was released from prison and resumed his place at the centre of royal counsels. In this situation, the Earl of Northumberland had no real option but to ally himself with the king and his supporters. The crisis came in May. Under Somerset's influence, an enlarged royal council was summoned to meet on 21st May at Leicester. It was obvious to York and Salisbury that the purpose of this meeting, away from London where Somerset was highly unpopular, was to act against them. Consequently, they decided to make the first move.

With an army of around 5,000 men they intercepted the king and his entourage, which included Somerset and the Earl of Northumberland, at St. Albans. York demanded the removal and imprisonment of Somerset. The king refused, and the Duke of Buckingham tried but failed to negotiate a compromise settlement whereupon York and Salisbury took to force. In a short battle in the streets and vennels of the town the royal forces were defeated, thanks to the initiative shown by Salisbury's son, the Earl of Warwick, and the toughness of 600 troops from the Border, led by Sir Robert Ogle. The king was slightly wounded and made captive, and forty-three of his entourage were killed. The dead included the Duke of Somerset and the Earl of Northumberland. In fact, there seems little doubt that for York and Salisbury, the main aim of the battle was to ensure the deaths of their respective enemies. As a contemporary perceptively remarked, when Somerset and Percy had been killed, the battle was over.

The second Earl of Northumberland had been head of the house of Percy for forty-one years. His son, the third earl, was to enjoy the role for less than six. Like his father, however, he too was to die fighting in the Lancastrian cause. Born on 25th July 1421, he was therefore almost thirty-four years of age when he succeeded his father.

During the four years following the events at St Albans, political tension remained high, for the deaths of Somerset and Northumberland had solved nothing. There was no general wish to see Henry VI removed, and still less to have the Duke of York as his replacement. Henry was therefore fully restored to liberty, but the Crown's authority increasingly was wielded by Queen Margaret, a woman of far greater resolution. With the succession of her young son, Edward, to ensure, she set about the task of securing control over the machinery of government. One by one, York's appointees were removed from office and replaced by Lancastrian loyalists. These included the new Earl of Northumberland, who in February 1457 was appointed to the traditional Percy posts of Warden of the East March and Keeper of Berwick. He was joined by his brothers, Thomas, Lord Egremont, and Richard, who the previous November had effected a daring escape from Newgate Prison by bribing their guards to supply them with weapons and then fighting their way out over the roof in true Hollywood fashion.

It would have required an unlikely and uncharacteristic change of many hearts for the two sides to settle their differences amicably. That said, an attempt was made in March 1458 to promote a general reconciliation. That this was a pious but unfounded hope, however, was clearly revealed when all parties turned up to the meeting at St. Paul's Cathedral in London with armed retainers. The signal for the outbreak of violence was, as it had been in 1455, the summoning of an enlarged royal council to meet outside London, this time at Coventry. The omission of the Duke of York and his Neville allies and their followers from the invitation was an ominous and obvious pointer to the fact that the queen's intention was to use the occasion to proceed against them. Their response was to organise a counter-meeting of their supporters at Ludlow. The queen's attempt to prevent this resulted in a small battle at Blore Heath, in Shropshire, on 23rd September 1459.

The next eighteen months were the crux of the Wars of the Roses. In that time eight more battles of increasing scale and ferocity were fought, until a resolution was achieved in the spring of 1461. Broadly, the pattern was of Yorkist success from Blore Heath in September 1459 until Northampton in the following July, when their victory gave them control of the person of Henry VI and of London and Westminster, the seats of government. The Earl of Northumberland appears not to have been present at Northampton, but his eldest brother, Lord Egremont, was killed in the fighting.

In late 1460 and early 1461, the Lancastrians staged a recovery. On 30th December 1460, a Yorkist army was severely defeated at Wakefield by a large Lancastrian army, which included the Earl of Northumberland. The Duke of York was killed, and the head of the Neville clan, the Earl of Salisbury, was captured and executed. Leadership of the Yorkist cause now passed to the next generation, York's son, Edward, Earl of March, and Salisbury's son, Richard, Earl of Warwick. The consequence of Wakefield was to hand the initiative to the Lancastrians, and they immediately headed south with the aim of securing London. On 17th February 1461, they defeated Warwick at a second battle at St. Albans and in doing so recovered the person of the king. But London shut its gates, so depriving them of the greater prize. This proved to be the turning point. A few days before the St. Albans engagement, the young Earl of March had proved his military ability by winning a battle at Mortimer's Cross, in Herefordshire. He then rejoined the defeated Warwick, and together they pursued the retreating Lancastrian army. On 28th and 29th March, the two forces met in what was one of the largest battles ever fought on British soil, at Towton, between Tadcaster and Ferrybridge. The result was a total victory for the Yorkists. The list of Lancastrian dead, both during and after the battle, was long. It included Henry Percy, third Earl of Northumberland, and his brother, Sir Richard Percy.

Towton made the Earl of March king, as Edward IV. But it did not mark the end of the war. Lancastrian resistance continued in Northumberland, orchestrated by the queen, who was able to call upon the help of England's traditional enemies, Scotland and France, and the help of Henry Beauford, third Duke of Somerset, a man of considerable military ability. The potential Lancastrian recovery was thwarted by the skilful diplomacy of the new king and the military action of the Nevilles, notably the Earl of Warwick's brother, John Neville, Lord Montagu. It was he who, in the spring of 1464, won two small battles, at Hedgeley Moor south of Wooler, where the dead earl's second brother, Sir Ralph Percy, was killed, and near Hexham. The ex-king, Henry VI, deserted by his wife and son, became a fugitive and was eventually captured in 1465, hiding in Lancashire. With his imprisonment in the Tower of London, the war was over. For the Percys it had been a time of disaster: the earl and his three brothers were killed in successive battles, and in 1461 the earl was posthumously attainted, so that his title and estates were forfeit to the Crown.

Ironically, prior to this the earl had brought about a considerable enlargement of the Percy estate. He did so by his marriage in 1434 to Eleanor Poynings. Her father, Richard, predeceased her, and consequently she became the sole heir of her grandfather, Robert, Lord Poynings. When he died in 1446, Henry Percy, the future third Earl of Northumberland, acquired the title and the lands in the right of his wife. But there was a slight complication, in that Lord Poynings had willed part of his estate to Eleanor's uncle, her father's brother, Robert. He was killed at St Albans in 1461, fighting in the Yorkist army, and because of this it was Eleanor, now Countess of Northumberland, who gained control of his lands, even though he left a young son. The Poynings inheritance was substantial. The bulk of it was in Sussex, where the Percys had long possessed considerable property around Petworth, but there were also manors in Dorset, Surrey, Kent, Norfolk and Suffolk. When Eleanor's husband was killed at Towton a few weeks later, the whole of the Poynings estate reverted to her.

The death and attainder of the third earl and his brothers appeared yet again to mark the end of the House of Percy. And in most respects it did so for almost ten years. The third earl, however, died leaving a son, Henry, who had been born in 1449 and was therefore only twelve years old. With the death of his uncle, Sir Ralph Percy, in 1464, he became a captive and spent the next five years in prison in London, first in the Fleet and then, from September 1465, in the Tower. His release and restoration were to stem from the political crisis which blew up in 1469 and dominated English public life until 1471.

In many respects this crisis was a replay of the one ten years earlier, only this time with the opposite result. At its heart was Richard Neville, Earl of Warwick, whose ambition it was to dominate and control the king and direct royal policy. But in Edward IV he was dealing with a very different man to Henry VI. In foreign affairs the two men had sharply opposed views. Warwick favoured an alliance with France, whereas Edward inclined towards France's enemy, Burgundy, then a powerful duchy covering much of eastern France and the Low Countries. One reason for Edward's preference was that his sister, Margaret, was married to the ruler of Burgundy, Duke Charles; but in addition, he had to consider England's important economic links with Flanders, then Burgundian territory. Equally important was the domestic problem caused entirely and un- necessarily by the king's rashness. On 1st May 1464, Edward secretly married Elizabeth Woodville, the daughter of a man of mere knightly status and the widow of another, Sir John Grey, who had been killed in 1461 at St Albans fighting for the *Lancastrian* cause. Her only connection with the upper levels of society was through her mother, Jacquetta, daughter of Pierre de Luxembourg, Count of St Pol, and widow of Henry V's brother, John, Duke of Bedford. Edward's marriage was an act of political stupidity: kings were expected, and indeed needed, to marry for political advantage, not personal gratification. To compound the folly, Edward then advanced his wife's family, which included five brothers and seven sisters, by means of marriages to available members of the nobility. By his action, he thwarted Warwick's hopes of getting him married to a French princess, and also removed from the marriage market all the potential husbands for Warwick's daughters (he had no sons), Isabel and Anne. The upshot was that Warwick came to a secret understanding with the king's brother, George, Duke of Clarence, an unstable and ambitious man who, until the queen bore a son in 1470, was heir to the throne. What these two men, individually and collectively, hoped to achieve is not certain, but it is very likely that they intended to depose Edward IV and place Clarence on the throne.

The crisis began in the summer of 1469 with a rebellion in northern England led by Robin of Redesdale, a mysterious figure who, despite his name, was probably a Yorkshire knight. If Warwick and Clarence were not actually behind his rebellion, they were certainly willing to make use of it. They took the opportunity of cementing their alliance by the marriage of Clarence and Warwick's elder daughter, Isabel, a match which Edward IV had specifically forbidden. They also defeated, at Edgecote in Oxfordshire, a royal army led by William Herbert, Earl of Pembroke, and Henry Stafford, Earl of Devon, both of whom were captured and then murdered. Shortly there after, Edward himself fell into the hands of Warwick's brother, George Neville, Archbishop of York. Despite these successes, it was clear that they had no significant support, either among the nobility or the general populace. Consequently, in September Edward was set free and life seemingly returned to normal.

If the events of the summer of 1469 were an anxious time for the king, they were a godsend to the House of Percy. On 27th October, Henry Percy, now twenty years old, was released from the Tower and performed fealty to Edward. In March of the following year, he was restored to his title and his estates. This may have been part of a general round of reconciliation, or the pretence of such. But it may also be seen as a move by Edward IV to increase his support among the nobility. The time gap between release and restoration was made necessary by the need to negotiate a deal with Warwick's brother, John Neville, Lord Montagu. In 1464, as the young Henry Percy was entering the Fleet Prison, John Neville was being invested with his estates and title as Earl of Northumberland, his reward for stamping out the last vestiges of Lancastrian resistance in the north. If Percy was to be restored, Neville would have to be compensated. The solution was to grant to Neville the lands of the murdered Earl of Devon and to elevate him in the peerage to the rank of Marquis of Montagu.

As in 1460, however, any attempt at reconciliation was almost bound to be phoney and futile. Warwick and Clarence surreptitiously renewed their rebellion by helping to foment an outbreak of violence in Lincolnshire. But again this did not succeed, and in July 1470 Warwick left the country. His purpose was to change political tack. On 22nd July, he cynically reconciled himself to Henry VI's queen, Margaret of Anjou, and entered an alliance with her, which was sealed by the betrothal of

Warwick's second daughter, Anne, to Margaret's son, Edward, the Lancastrian heir to the throne. Put simply, Warwick ditched Clarence for what he thought would be a better option. Now for the third time he fomented rebellion in northern England, and this time he was successful. Not surprisingly, he was joined by his brother, the newly minted marquis, and together they outmanoeuvred Edward IV. In the early days of October, the king, together with his brother, Richard, and his father-in-law, sought safety by fleeing the country and taking refuge in Holland, a territory belonging to his brother-in-law, the Duke of Burgundy.

Five months later, in March 1471, financed by Duke Charles of Burgundy, Edward set sail from Flushing with around 1,200 troops in thirty-six ships. Some days later, this invasion force landed at the mouth of the Humber. In the days that followed, the newly restored Earl of Northumberland played a crucial role, although there is some uncertainty about his actions and motives. There are contemporary claims, which cannot be lightly dismissed, that it was Percy who wrote to Edward encouraging him to return. When Edward did so, however, Percy was far away in Northumberland, and the king got a sullen and unsupportive reception in the East Riding, an area of Percy dominance. The reason may have been the strength of local resentment caused by the heavy loss of life at Towton. Another deterrent may have been the presence at Pontefract of John Neville with a small but potentially threatening body of troops. On the other hand, Percy may well have been playing the waiting game and was not prepared to move until it was clear who was gaining the upper hand.

In fact it was Edward IV who rapidly secured victory. As he headed south from the hostile territory of York, he steadily gained recruits, and after securing control of London, won a decisive victory at Barnet on 14th April over the combined forces of Warwick and Montagu, both of whom were killed. On the same day Margaret of Anjou and her son, Edward, landed in Devon. Their plan was to move north up the Welsh border to recruit in Cheshire and Lancashire, but on 4th May they were intercepted by the king at Tewkesbury in Gloucestershire. Again Edward IV was victorious, and again his victory was enhanced by the death of a dangerous enemy, in this case Edward, Henry VI's heir. Meanwhile, the Earl of Northumberland had made his move by securing control over the northern counties for Edward IV. In the weeks that followed, the final

Neville effort, by an illegitimate nephew of the Earl of Warwick, was defeated on the outskirts of London. Shortly after this, it is likely that the former king, Henry VI, was quietly murdered.

Edward IV reigned for another twelve years and during that time Henry Percy, fourth Earl of Northumberland, remained unequivocally loyal and was rewarded for that loyalty. In June 1470, he was appointed Warden of the East and Middle Marches, and in August 1475 he was made Sheriff of Northumberland for life. In 1483 he acquired the last of the frontier posts traditionally held by the Percys: Keeper of Berwick. The reason for the longer delay was that Berwick had not been in English hands until the previous year. In 1461, as the price of the help she needed from Scotland to retrieve her fortunes in England, Margaret of Anjou returned Berwick (and promised to hand over Carlisle) to the Scottish government. It remained in Scottish hands until 1482, when it was recaptured by an army commanded by the king's youngest brother, Richard, Duke of Gloucester. Inevitably, the Earl of Northumberland played a notable part in this event, which saw Berwick change nation for the last time.

That Richard of Gloucester was in command was no accident, for in the 1470s he had become Edward IV's viceroy in northern England. His power base was the estates of the junior branch of the Neville family, and after 1478, those of the Duke of Clarence, who was executed for treason. These, together with the wardenship of the West March, gave Richard a commanding presence in Cumberland and in the North Riding of Yorkshire. He was also able to extend his domination into Durham, once Bishop Lawrence Booth, who stoutly resisted all attempts to undermine his palatine powers, was promoted to the archbishopric of York in 1476. Richard reached an accommodation with the senior branch of the Neville family, whose head, Ralph Neville, Earl of Westmorland, became his retainer. And he persuaded Booth's pliant successor as bishop of Durham, William Dudley, to appoint his retainers to posts in the palatine administration. Such was the strength of his influence that in 1474 Henry Percy, too, became his retainer. But what was really happening was that Gloucester and Percy were establishing their respective spheres of influence and agreeing not to trespass. Percy was to be allowed to dominate Northumberland, where Gloucester's interests were slight, and the East Riding of Yorkshire, while Gloucester was to have a free hand in Cumberland, Durham and the North Riding of Yorkshire. Gloucester's superiority was confirmed in 1480, when he was made King's Lieutenant, a role which gave him overall command of the north. Nevertheless, there is no doubt that Percy power was formidable. Once in full control, Edward IV preferred making money to making war, but he did invade France briefly in 1475. Henry Percy's contribution to his army was ten knights, forty men at arms and 200 archers. Only two contingents were larger, those of the royal Dukes of Clarence and Gloucester, the latter contributing ten knights, 100 men at arms and 1,000 archers. When necessary, however, the Earl of Northumberland was capable of putting nearly 300 well-armed men into the field.

Edward IV's death (as the result of a chill caught while on a fishing expedition) in 1483 was premature and unexpected, and it created a serious political problem. Edward designated his brother, Richard of Gloucester, as Protector, that is, head of government during the minority of the new king, Edward IV's son, Edward V, who was only twelve years old. In order to exercise this role, Richard needed to secure the persons of the king, and his younger brother, Richard, Duke of York, and control of the machinery of government. These, however, were in the hands of Edward IV's widow and mother of the young king, Elizabeth, and her Woodville relatives. The two parties regarded each other with suspicion, dislike and distrust. Gloucester, who was in the weaker position, decided to strike first. On 30th April, he seized the young king and his relatives at Stony Stratford as they made towards London, and a few days later secured control of the capital. Eight weeks later, on 26th June, he usurped the throne, having persuaded a pliant bishop to declare Edward V and his brother illegitimate. (The two boys were imprisoned in the Tower, where they were subsequently murdered.) Richard III's successful seizure of power owed a great deal to Henry Percy, since it was he who raised an army in the north and brought it to London to overawe the capital to ensure that there was no counter-revolution. It was cynically appropriate that at Richard's coronation in Westminster Abbey on 6th July, the Earl of Northumberland carried *Curtana,* the pointless sword of mercy, known as Edward the Confessor's sword.

The reign of Richard III lasted for a little over two years, until August 1485, when he was defeated and killed in battle near Bosworth, in

Leicestershire. The victor was Henry Tudor, Earl of Richmond who, as a descendant of John of Gaunt and Katherine Swynford, was, after the deaths of Henry VI and his son, Edward, the Lancastrian claimant to the throne. Henry had been an exile in Brittany for fourteen years since 1471. His decision to bid for the throne was encouraged by some of Richard III's opponents who had fled abroad, but it was made possible by the French king, Louis XI, who loaned Henry a large sum of money and 4,000 experienced French and Scottish soldiers, led by a first-class commander, Philibert de Chandée. This small force landed in West Wales and advanced eastwards at great speed, gathering recruits as it did so. Richard III uncharacteristically reacted too slowly, and was forced to fight before he could mobilise his full strength. Among those who did answer his summons were two northern magnates, each of whom arrived at the battlefield with around 3,000 troops. The contingent sent by Thomas, Lord Stanley, was commanded by his younger brother, Sir William. The Percy contingent, however, was headed by the earl in person. Neither Stanley nor Percy joined the king, but instead held back, waiting to see what happened. At a critical moment, Stanley committed his troops, but to Henry Tudor, not to Richard. This intervention was decisive: it made Henry Tudor King Henry VII and Lord Stanley Earl of Derby.

Percy, however, made no move. His inaction, which many contemporaries saw as a betrayal, cannot be readily explained, particularly as he had displayed constant loyalty to Edward IV and then Richard III over a period of fifteen years. It is possible that he felt inadequately rewarded by Richard III: he had been made Great Chamberlain of England, but this was an honorary title without material benefits. He may also have come to recognise how dangerous a man Richard III was. He had seen at first hand how Richard ruthlessly disposed of men like Lord Hastings, whom he suspected of disaffection, and he had been directly involved in the judicial murder of another suspect, Henry Stafford, Duke of Buckingham. And he may have come to realise that Richard's grip on northern England was in no way loosened by his removal south on becoming king. There may also have been a more personal reason. Percy and Henry Tudor had been brought up together in the household of William, Lord Herbert, and in 1476 Percy married Herbert's daughter, Maud, who originally had been the intended bride of Henry Tudor before he fled abroad in 1471.

Percy's hesitation proved costly, since the new king was bound to regard him as a man of uncertain loyalty. His punishment involved the reopening of an issue which was thought to have been settled, the estate belonging to his mother. As well as being her grandfather's heir, by various twists of biological and legal fate Eleanor Poynings had also been the residuary heir of Sir Guy Brian, who had died as long ago as 1390. The Brian estate was substantial, comprising twenty-two manors in Somerset, Devon, Dorset, Gloucestershire, Kent and South Wales. Upon Eleanor's death in 1484, her son, the earl, inherited these properties. In 1488, however, three other men came forward with claims to the Brian inheritance: Thomas Seymour; Thomas Butler, Earl of Ormond; and Sir Edward Poynings. The resolution was not in Percy's favour: he was awarded only a quarter of the properties, the remainder being divided amongst the other claimants. The loss did not prove permanent, however, since on the deaths of the Earl of Ormond (1515) and Sir Edward Poynings (1521) their shares reverted to the Percy estate.

The fourth earl did not live to see this. On 28th April 1489, he was murdered at South Kilvington near Thirsk by a mob reckoned to have numbered around 700 men. The cause of this revolt was the exceptionally heavy taxation imposed by the government in 1487 and again in January 1489. The rebellion was a protest against its severity by yeomen and husbandmen, that is, by men who were wealthy enough to be in the tax bracket but for whom the financial burden could be crippling. They had looked to the Earl of Northumberland for 'good lordship'; in other words, they expected him to intercede on their behalf with the king, either for a reduction of their tax liabilities, or for an extension of the payment period. It seems likely that the earl did so, but without success. Instead, Henry VII had required him to enforce payment in full and on time. Consequently, it may have been an acute sense of having been let down that explains why the anger of the rebels was directed against the earl in person. What it does not explain, however, was what really caused the earl's death, namely, the desertion of his retinue, which was large and well armed, since the earl was well aware that the situation was dangerous and that he was expected to restore order, by the use of force if necessary. This failure of loyalty may well have stemmed from panic, although it is possible that it was the consequence of the earl's own betrayal of Richard III, who as Duke of Gloucester had been very popular in Yorkshire four years earlier. It has been suggested that Henry VII may have been behind a scheme or plot to contrive the earl's death, but recent research, while recognising Henry VII's anxieties and suspicions about the instability and uncertain loyalty of northern society, appears to undermine any conspiracy theory.

The 'Wars of the Roses' were not a happy time for the Percys in that all three earls and several of their brothers died in battle. But in spite of this, they survived with their estate largely intact, thanks to the eventual victory of the side for which they fought.

EIGHT

Self-Destruction

Henry Algernon Percy, Fifth Earl of Northumberland, 1478–1527
Henry Percy, Sixth Earl of Northumberland, 1502–1537

The first thirty-seven years of the sixteenth century saw the House of Percy reach its zenith, at least as regards wealth, and then again plunge rapidly to virtual extinction. The high point was achieved by the fifth earl, Henry Algernon, who was born on 14th January 1478 and was only eleven years old when his father was murdered. Being under age, he became a ward of the king and remained so until 1498, when he was allowed to end his minority a year early. Thereafter, he was head of the House of Percy for almost thirty years, until his death on 19th May 1527 at the age of forty-nine.

The fifth earl was renowned for his lavish lifestyle, which earned him the sobriquet of the 'magnificent earl', and was made possible by his great wealth. At the time of his father's death, the Percy estate yielded a gross annual income of just over £4,000, and this was increased when parts of the Brian inheritance lost in 1488 were returned in 1515 and 1521. Just how splendid the Percy lifestyle was is amply revealed in a document drawn up in the financial year 1512–13, which runs to no fewer than 409 printed pages. Entitled *The Regulations and Establishment of the Household of Henry Algernon Percy, the fifth Earl of Northumberland,* it sets out in meticulous detail the composition, costs and administrative apparatus of the earl's household when resident at Wressle and Leconfield, in the East Riding of Yorkshire. The personnel numbered 166 full-time staff, ranging from menials in the kitchen and the stable to men of knightly status, who were largely responsible for running the household and the estate: Steward, Treasurer, Chamberlain, Comptroller. In all, the annual stipends of these men and women came to £153 in cash plus bed, board and clothing. They included not only senior administrators and domestic servants, but also a chapel staff of a dean and ten priests, a schoolmaster and three musicians. Feeding this household and up to sixty guests and visitors a day was a complex and expensive business requiring very large quantities of a huge variety of foodstuffs, the total cost of which came to £427 13s 4d (= £427 67p).

The greatest outlay was inevitably on basics. Almost 2,400 bushels of wheat for bread were bought for nearly £79. For beer nearly 2,000 bushels of malt and 560 lbs of hops were acquired at a cost of £53 9s 10d (= £53 48p). Wine, too, was consumed in large quantity: over ten tuns, all from Gascony, were bought for just under £50. The main meats consumed were beef and mutton, which required the purchase and slaughter of nearly 150 cattle and over 800 sheep. Only small quantities of veal, lamb and pork were eaten, however. In all, the meat bill came to nearly £150. In contrast, only £32 10s 7d (= £32 53p) was spent on fish, partly because it was cheaper, but also because eating fish was largely confined to the period of the Lenten fast. As many as twenty-one different kinds of spices were bought at a total cost of almost £26. Other items included salt, crockery (mainly of wood and pewter), candles, wax, oil and wicks for lighting and nearly ninety yards of linen for table and sideboard cloths, napkins and towels.

The book also reveals the earl's household as a strictly ordered hierarchy. Not only was each man and woman graded and titled and his or her stipend specified, but it was even laid down what food each was entitled to at each meal. At breakfast in Lent, for example, while the earl and countess had large quantities of bread, beer and wine and three types of fish, the men in the porter's lodge and the stable had to make do with only a quarter of a loaf and a quart of beer. There were, however, "scrambling" days when the first-come, first-served principle operated.

The earl and his household were not stationary, at least not for long. In whole or in part, they were almost constantly on the move, either for business or pleasure, and consequently horses were needed in both quantity and variety. To meet these many and varied needs, the earl's stable contained not far short of a hundred animals, including gentle horses, palfreys, hobbies, nags, sumpters and the great trotting horse for the earl's coach, or chariot as it was called.

The earl's reputation was based not solely on the size of his household or the fact that it mirrored that of the king. Henry Algernon was also a literate man who bought and clearly enjoyed books. He also acquired a reputation, perhaps not fully deserved, as a patron of men of letters. He

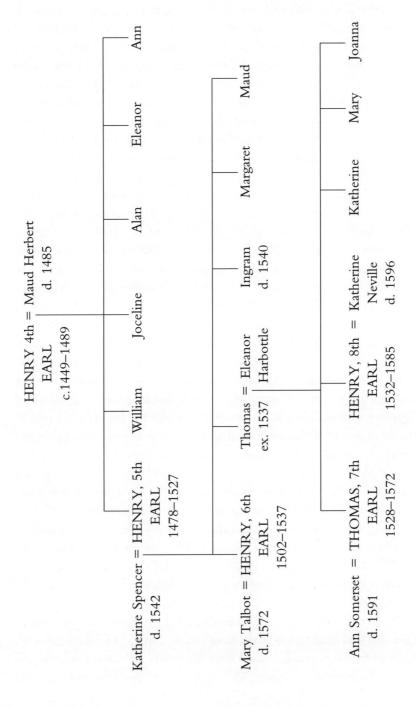

had married well, although this is not obvious at first glance. His wife, chosen for him by his guardian, Henry VII, was Catherine, daughter and co-heir of a Devonshire man, Sir Robert Spencer. Superficially, marriage to the daughter of a mere knight suggests that the earl was being demeaned. But the significance of the match is revealed in the person of his wife's mother, Eleanor, who was a daughter of Edmund Beaufort, Duke of Somerset. This meant that through marriage Percy became connected to the royal family. This, together with his investiture as a Knight of the Garter in 1499, when he was just twenty-one, suggests that he was considered a good prospect of whom much was expected.

But whatever this early promise may have been, it was never fulfilled. Under both Henry VII and his son, Henry VIII, who succeeded to the throne in 1509, the fifth earl played only a minor role in political and public life, and his contributions were confined to the sorts of diplomatic and military activity that great noblemen found difficult to avoid. His diplomatic service began in 1503, when he escorted Princess Margaret, Henry VII's daughter, from York to Lamberton in Berwickshire, where she was met by her husband-to-be, James IV of Scotland. As the leading nobleman in Northumberland and one of the great nobles of Yorkshire, not to have been asked to perform this duty would have been a slight. Four years later he was involved in the abortive negotiation for the marriage of Margaret's sister, Mary, to Archduke Charles, grandson of Emperor Maximillian I (Charles was to become the Emperor Charles V, the most powerful man of his generation as ruler of Germany, Spain and her empire which included the Low Countries, parts of Italy and much of central and south America, from 1519 until 1555). Percy's highest profile was at the Field of the Cloth of Gold, the fanciful name given to a series of summit meetings held near Calais in 1520 between Henry VIII of England, Francis I of France and the Emperor Charles V. As was often the case on such occasions, serious negotiating sessions were accompanied by festivities, including tournaments, at which Percy was the chief judge. It is clear from these incidents that the earl's diplomatic role was essentially ceremonial.

In military matters the earl, like other great magnates, was expected to raise and lead contingents in the king's armies. In 1513 he commanded a force of 500 light cavalry raised from his estates, his contribution to the army which invaded France. This was a short campaign that achieved little, although the English cavalry, which included Percy's contingent, defeated its French counterpart in what came to be called the Battle of the Spurs, which took place near Thérouanne. Ten years later, in 1523, the earl raised a larger force of 850 men during a period of tension between England and Scotland.

In all of these activities the earl's involvement was occasional, supportive and largely peripheral. He was never in a leadership role or at the heart of government. More significantly, he was never appointed to the traditional Percy post of Warden of the East and Middle Marches. It is worth noting that in 1513, when there was a large-scale Scottish invasion which ended in disaster at Flodden, he was not in Northumberland helping to defend the Border, but in France with the king. The victor of Flodden was a southerner, Thomas Howard, Earl of Surrey (second Duke of Norfolk, 1514). One view is that the earl's exclusion from Border affairs was the consequence of a royal policy of reducing the power of 'over-mighty' subjects, which meant developing an alternative to Percy power in the far north. The evidence seems clear enough: the appointment to the wardenship of southerners, such as the Earl of Surrey, or northern noblemen of lower standing, such as Lord Wharton; and the creation in 1525 of a Council of the North under the nominal chairmanship of Henry VIII's six-year-old illegitimate son, Henry Fitzroy, Duke of Richmond and Somerset, from which Percy was conspicuously excluded. On the other hand, it has been argued that the Crown would have preferred to entrust the East and Middle Marches to the fifth earl, since that would have been the simplest, cheapest and most convenient solution to the problem. That neither Henry VII nor Henry VIII and his chief minister, Cardinal Thomas Wolsey, felt able to do so was the result of their assessment of the earl as a person not fit for that office. Rather than new means of government to replace the Percys, the changes were expedients to which the Crown was driven because it dared not entrust the Border to a man in whom it had no faith.

And there is plenty of evidence to suggest that the fifth earl was indeed a man lacking stability and inclined to rashness. In the first decade of the sixteenth century, he was in serious trouble for three different offences. In 1504, he was engaged in a quarrel with Thomas Savage, Archbishop of York, which became so intense that he was required to give a recognisance of £2,000 to keep the peace. In the same year, he was indicted for illegal 'retaining', that is, maintaining armed men contrary to law. And two years later, he committed an even more reckless act by abducting Elizabeth Hastings, a young girl destined to be the sole heir of her father, Sir John Hastings, a wealthy Yorkshire knight. As to Percy's motive, we can safely assume that he intended to arrange a suitable marriage for the girl: suitable to him, that is. Tragically, his nefarious scheme was thwarted by Elizabeth's death soon after. By this act, Percy was not only guilty of the crime of 'ravishment', but he was depriving the king of his lucrative right of wardship. The earl's punishment was an enormous fine of £10,000, of which he paid half. The rest was excused in 1510 by the young Henry VIII, doubtless to ensure Percy loyalty in the early and uncertain days of his reign. This may have worked, but it certainly did not lead Percy to good behaviour, for in 1516 he was again in trouble, this time being hauled before the Court of Star Chamber to answer a charge the details of which have not survived. As a result, he was briefly in the Fleet Prison and on his release was subjected to a severe royal reprimand. It is impossible to be certain whether his wild actions were the cause or consequence of the Crown's disinclination to employ him on the Border. It is clear enough, however, that in some way and to some degree the fifth earl did not find royal favour.

The Crown's studied rejection of the fifth earl as a manager of the Border is thrown into sharp relief by the appointment of his son, Henry Percy, the sixth earl, as Warden of the East and Middle Marches late in 1527, only a few months after his father's death. What makes this all the more surprising is that the new earl's reputation had been blackened by his father, who had a very low opinion of him and more than once humiliated him in public. But the appointment was approved by Cardinal Wolsey, who must have known him well, since he had been one of the small but select group of noble youths who had been brought up in Wolsey's household.

One suggested explanation of the new earl's appointment to the wardenship concerns Sir William Lisle of Felton, a Northumbrian knight, who had broken out of prison in Newcastle early in 1527 and allied himself with some of the most notorious Border clans with whom he had then conducted a campaign of terror and mayhem in the county. As Lisle was a close associate of the Percys (he was constable of their castle at Alnwick), the argument is that the fifth earl deliberately contrived this episode in order to force the government to recognise that, without a Percy in charge, the Border region was ungovernable. This seems far-fetched, especially as most of Lisle's actions were directed against the Heron family, with whom he had a long-running quarrel, and the Sheriff of Northumberland, Sir William Ellerker, whom he believed was giving support to his enemy. It seems more likely that the younger Percy had been groomed by Wolsey to resume the traditional family role. And he did have instant success, as Lisle surrendered to him at Alnwick in January 1528, probably in the hope that Percy influence would save him from the ultimate fate. It did not, although Lisle's son, Humphrey, who had been fully engaged in his father's mischief, was spared.

Interest in the sixth earl's life centres less on his role as Warden of the East and Middle Marches than on his extraordinary and bewildering performance in disposing of his entire estate and so disinheriting his heirs, a feat he accomplished in exactly ten years. He succeeded to his huge inheritance in May 1527, when he was twenty-five years of age and therefore more than old enough in law to assume responsibility for its management. By the time of his death in June 1537, he had become a landless pensioner of the Crown.

Before attempting to describe and explain what he did, a number of significant facts about him need to be highlighted. The first is a fundamental antipathy between himself and his father. The reasons for this are not entirely clear, although two aspects are evident enough. One concerned finance: the fifth earl is said to have considered his eldest son to be utterly profligate and incompetent where money was concerned and to have called him to his face a thriftless waster. The other was the future sixth earl's marriage. It was long believed that in the early 1520s the young Henry Percy formed a strong attachment to Anne Boleyn, who was then sixteen and newly returned from an education in France to be one of the queen's (Catherine of Aragon) maids of honour. It was also believed that the romance was forcibly ended by Cardinal Wolsey and Henry's father, the Earl of Northumberland, because of the king's own interest in Anne. We now know that this version derives from an inaccurate account in a book entitled *The Life and Death of Cardinal Wolsey* written in the 1550s by George Cavendish. What is true is that Henry Percy and Anne Boleyn did form an attachment, the precise nature of which is not clear. It certainly fell far short of a consummated marriage, but it may have been a formal contract that needed the skills of a canon lawyer to break. But the reason why the marriage was prevented was not royal desire: this developed later; and indeed at that time the king's extra-marital attention was firmly focused on Mary Boleyn, Anne's sister. The real reason was that the king (who had a legitimate interest in the marriage alliances of his nobles), Wolsey and the Earl of Northumberland did not consider Anne a suitable bride for the earl's heir. In fact, since 1516 the earl had been discussing with another aristocrat, George Talbot, Earl of Shrewsbury, the possibilty of a marriage between his son and Shrews-bury's daughter, Mary. To remove any chance of a Percy-Boleyn union, arrangements were hurriedly made for the marriage of Henry Percy and Mary Talbot, which took place in late January or early February 1524. The marriage was a disaster. There were no children, and within a few years the couple's mutual dislike became so intense as to result in their separation. And for Henry Percy further agony was to follow: in 1536, by which time he was Earl of Northumberland and Anne was Queen of England, he was required to be one of the twenty-six peers who formed the jury at her trial on trumped-up charges. Each peer had to give his verdict separately, so that anyone who failed to pronounce Anne guilty would be clearly exposed as an enemy of the king. Some indication of the torment Percy must have suffered is revealed by the fact that, having spoken the word 'guilty', he fainted and had to be carried from the court.

The earl's failure to have children meant that his heir was his brother, Thomas, and failing him his younger brother, Ingram. Percy came to have a deep dislike of both men, although this seems to have developed fairly late in his life, and for reasons that are obscure. These antipathies may have been related to the earl's medical condition. For much of his life he appears to have suffered from indifferent health and he died of natural causes at the very early age of thirty-five. Here, too, there is uncertainty. What he suffered from is a mystery, but it may have been of such a nature and to such a degree as to affect his judgement. All these facts seem to come together to explain his addiction to favourites and his lavish generosity to them. That all of them were male raises the suspicion that he had a leaning towards homosexuality. On the other hand, given the failure of his family relationships, it is hardly surprising that he sought and bought the friendship of congenial contemporaries. The closest of them were three northerners: Sir Thomas Johnson, Sir Thomas Wharton and

Sir Reynold Carnaby, to whom a fourth man must be added, his doctor, Thomas Wendy.

What exactly did the sixth earl do with his inheritance? He appears to have started with the southern parts of the estate, substantial elements of which he disposed of between 1527 and 1531. In those four years he divested himself of all or most of the Percy properties in Devon, Somerset, Dorset, Sussex, Kent, Surrey, Norfolk, Suffolk and Leicester-shire: in all some thirty manors. The main beneficiaries were Thomas Arundel, one of the young men with whom he grew up in Wolsey's household, Henry, Lord Montagu, the Marquis of Exeter and Sir Edward Seymour. It has been suggested that there was a serious, perhaps pressing, purpose behind these disposals, namely, to extinguish annuities he had granted as the means of repaying debts he had contracted before he became earl. This may be correct, since it is known that one aspect of his father's abuse of him was the withholding of an appropriate income, even after his marriage. It is also worth remarking that these properties were from the Poynings and Brian estates, only recently acquired and in parts of the country where the Percys had no deep-rooted interests. But, as a counter to the charge of reckless profligacy, it has been noted that some of these sales were made subject to rent charges and that some grants included the possibility of reversion to the Percy estate. Similar reserva-tions apply regarding his generosity to his northern favourites. In many cases what he bestowed on them were lucrative offices in the manage-ment of the estate and beneficial leases, both of which were far from being outright or permanent alienations.

But the Crown also took a hand in the dissolution of the Percy estate. In 1531, the earl was required to hand over his property in Cumberland to the king as a means of extinguishing a debt of £8,000. However, this should not be seen as something exceptional. Almost all members of the aristocracy had long-standing debts to the Crown, which from time to time pressed them hard for repayment. And, as if to show that he was not intending the ruination of the Percys, in the following year Henry VIII forbade the earl to dispose of any more property. Three years later, however, he changed his mind when he returned to the earl the estate in Cumberland and took instead all the remaining Percy properties in Sussex, Wales, Lincolnshire, Gloucestershire and Middlesex. In return all Percy's debts were cancelled and he was paid £5,200 in cash. The effect of this was to reduce the Percy patrimony to its lands in Cumberland, Yorkshire and Northumberland. As well as suffering a sharp reduction in income, the earls would henceforth be regional not national figures.

This situation, which does have the look of a neat solution, rapidly proved to be the prelude to a cataclysmic *dénouement*. In January and February 1536, the earl wrote to the king's chief minister, Thomas Cromwell, informing him that he intended making the king his heir, and immediately the necessary legal paperwork was undertaken to put this into effect. But in the spring of the following year, Percy agreed to an immediate handover of his estates to the Crown in return for an annual pension of £1,000. This agreement was ratified on 2nd May. Seven weeks later, on 30th June, the earl died before any payment was due.

How is this to be explained? It is reasonable to believe that the Crown welcomed the situation arrived at in the early 1530s: a Percy family reduced in wealth and once more to regional status, although not to the extent that it could no longer perform its traditional Border role. That in the end the Crown got everything was probably due, not so much to royal wish or intention, as to the earl's extraordinary but personal decision: extraordinary in that the core of every nobleman's concern and ambition was the advancement of his family and the enhancement of his estate. Henry Percy, sixth Earl of Northumberland, with what appears to have been deliberate and utter perversity, contravened this most basic and vital instinct of his class. While it can be argued that the discharge of debt may explain why the earl sold his southern estates, this will not do for his decision of 1536. The explanation which must be considered is that, driven by the miseries of permanent ill health (and by this date he may well have sensed that he had not long to live), he resolved to take his revenge on those whom he felt had wronged him: his wife (whose dower would be reduced), his brothers (who would be disinherited) and, posthumously, his father. But some are more inclined to see the destruction of the Percys as part of a deliberate policy of Henry VIII's minister, Thomas Cromwell, to reduce the Crown's dependence on powerful regional nobles and to increase its control by the creation of regional government agencies, such as the Council of the North, and by reliance on less powerful and more reliable gentry. In the sixth earl, it is argued, Cromwell found an easy victim.

The tragedy of the Percy family was not solely that of the earl. On 29th June 1537, the day before his death at his former manor of Hackney near London, his brother, Sir Thomas Percy, was executed at Tyburn. The reason was the part he had played in the Pilgrimage of Grace, the rebellion which swept over most of northern England between October and December 1536. This was to a very large extent a spontaneous uprising of the lower strata of society, sparked by an outburst of anger in northern Lincolnshire. It was a protest against a wide range of government actions, particularly the closing of the smaller monasteries, changes in religious belief and observance, and high taxation. Added to what was actually happening were fears and rumours concerning further changes the government might introduce. The revolt spread rapidly, and within a few days nine 'armies', each numbering several thousand men, converged on Doncaster. In the end, Thomas Howard, third Duke of Norfolk, acting as the king's representative, was able to persuade the rebels to disperse on the guarantee of a general pardon and a promise that parliament would consider their grievances. The king never intended to honour this promise, and gave approval for the pardon only with reluctance. A fresh outbreak of rebellion on a smaller scale in the early weeks of 1537 gave him the excuse he wanted and needed for a crackdown, as the result of which 178 men were executed, including Sir Thomas Percy.

As the main centres of the revolt were in Percy country, the parts played by the three brothers are of interest. Throughout the five-month period the earl was ill and rarely left his manor house at Wressle, but even had he been in good health it seems unlikely that he would have taken part. Certainly he gave no response to the large crowd that came to the gates of his manor shouting 'thousands for a Percy' and expecting him at least to signal his approval. Sir Ingram's part was both more active and more disreputable. He spent most of the time in Northumberland, where he raised the gentry, ostensibly in support of the uprising, but in reality to inflict damage on Sir Reynold Carnaby and his brothers, the recipients of the earl's generosity.

About Sir Thomas Percy's actions, there is much greater uncertainty. Afterwards he claimed to have left his mother's house at Seamer near Scarborough in disguise, hoping to join his wife at Prudhoe Castle in Northumberland and so avoid involvement. But he was spotted and forced to change his mind by rebels, who threatened to destroy Percy property if he did not join them and assume a leadership role. Although this has a hollow ring, it is not entirely implausible, since it is evident that some of the wealthier gentry did try to remain aloof and joined only under duress. But the evidence of Thomas Percy's active participation, along with so many gentry who would normally follow the Percy lead, seems incontrovertible. And this was the view taken by Henry VIII's government: Sir Thomas Percy was attainted and executed. Two of the brothers were now dead. The third, Ingram, died two years later. Since neither the earl nor Ingram left any legitimate offspring, and those of Thomas were formally tainted by their father's treason, the Percy family was effectively dead.

ESPERANCE. EN. DIEV,
MA . COMPHORT : ∞

THOMAS. PERCY.
7 EARL. OF. NORTHVMBERLAND
ÆTATIS. SVÆ . 38 ,
AN DÑI: 1566 . ET. DIE. DEC.

1. THOMAS PERCY, 7TH EARL OF NORTHUMBERLAND 1528–1572 (ENGLISH SCHOOL 1566). He was the son of the 6th earl's brother, Thomas, executed in 1537 for his part in the Pilgrimage of Grace. He too was executed, at York in 1572, as one of the leaders of the northern uprising against Queen Elizabeth I in 1569. *The National Trust, Petworth House.*

2. HENRY PERCY, 9TH EARL OF NORTHUMBERLAND 1564–1632 (SIR ANTHONY VAN DYCK). The son of the 8th earl who died in unresolved circumstances in the Tower in 1585. Known as the Wizard Earl because of his interest in science, he too spent fifteen years in the Tower on suspicion of being involved in the Gunpowder Plot. *The National Trust, Petworth House.*

3. ALGERNON PERCY, 10TH EARL OF NORTHUMBERLAND 1602–1668 (SIR ANTHONY VAN DYCK). He was Lord High Admiral in the 1630s but became a committed although moderate opponent of Charles I throughout the Civil War. The portrait shows him with his first wife, Anne Cecil, and one of their daughters. *The National Trust, Petworth House.*

4. SYON HOUSE, MIDDLESEX (ROBERT GRIFFIER 1688–1750). Syon House was built in the 1540s on the foundations of a fifteenth-century monastery and acquired from the Crown by the 9th Earl of Northumberland. It is still the London home of the Percy family. The picture shows it as it was in the early eighteenth century. *The Northumberland Estates.*

5. JOCELINE PERCY, 11TH EARL OF NORTHUMBERLAND 1644–1670 (?SIR PETER
LELY). He succeeded his father in 1668, but died in Turin two years later at the
age of twenty-six. As his only son had died the previous year, he was the last in
the male line that began in the twelfth century. The heir to the Percy estate was
his infant daughter, Elizabeth. *The National Trust, Petworth House*.

6. Elizabeth Percy, 6th Duchess of Somerset 1667–1772 (John Closterman). She inherited the Percy estate on the death of her father in 1670 and in 1682 married the 6th Duke of Somerset as her third husband. She was a close friend and confidante of Queen Anne. The portrait shows her with her son, Algernon, the future 7th Duke of Somerset. *The National Trust, Petworth House.*

7. HUGH SMITHSON (PERCY 1750), 1ST DUKE OF NORTHUMBERLAND 1714 OR
15–1786 (SIR JOSHUA REYNOLDS). He acquired half the Percy estate through his
marriage to Elizabeth Seymour, the sole surviving child of the 7th Duke of
Somerset, who died in 1750. In the same year he became Earl of Northumberland
and changed his name to Percy. He became Duke of Northumberland in 1766.
English Life Publications.

8. Elizabeth Seymour, 1st Duchess of Northumberland 1716–1776 (Sir Joshua Reynolds). When her father the 7th Duke of Somerset died in 1750, she inherited half of the Percy estate; the other half passed to her cousin, Sir Charles Wyndham. By that date she was Lady Smithson, having married Sir Hugh Smithson in 1740. *English Life Publications*.

9. ALNWICK CASTLE (GIOVANNI ANTONIO CANAL KNOWN AS CANALETTO). Percy was a notable patron of Canaletto, who worked in England from 1746 until 1755. This picture of Alnwick was almost certainly painted in 1751. Canaletto also painted Syon House and Northumberland House in the Strand around the same time. *The Northumberland Estates.*

10. ALNWICK CASTLE (GRAEME PEACOCK). The Percys acquired Alnwick in 1309, but it did not become their main residence until the time of the dukedom in the late eighteenth century. Its present form is largely due to the restorations carried out by the 4th duke. *The Northumberland Estates.*

NINE

Recovery and Disaster

Thomas Percy, Seventh Earl of Northumberland, ?1528–1572

Although history does not repeat itself, Percy fortunes after 1537 were very similar to those they experienced in the early fifteenth century: the family seeming to be utterly ruined by attainder and execution, yet within a few years apparently recovering title and wealth in full measure. On both occasions, the member who made a comeback was the son of the dead earl's heir. In 1416 this had been Hotspur's son, Henry Percy; in 1557 it was Thomas Percy, son of Sir Thomas Percy executed in 1537 for his part in the Pilgrimage of Grace. The date of his birth is not known, but it is thought to have been in 1528, which meant that at the time of his father's death he would have been only nine years of age and therefore too young to be directly implicated or involved in his father's treason. Nor is much known about his upbringing although, initially at least, he appears to have been removed from the custody of his mother, Eleanor, sister of Sir George Harbottle of Beamish in County Durham, and placed in the care of another member of the Durham gentry, Sir Thomas Tempest.

The process of his rehabilitation began in March 1549 when he was 'restored in blood', that is, the taint of his father's attainder was removed from him and he became qualified in law to inherit property. The significance of this lay not simply in the removal of the stigma but also in the fact that, assuming his birth to have been in 1528, in 1549 he had reached the age of majority. By this time his father's executioner, Henry VIII, was dead (1547) and his nine-year-old son by his third wife, Jane Seymour, was on the throne as Edward VI. Government was effectively in the hands of the young king's uncle, Edward Seymour, first Duke of Somerset, a man whose seventeenth-century descendants were to play a crucial role in determining the fate of the House of Percy. The new regime was positively inclined towards a protestant solution of the religious issue and consequently Percy, who was a committed catholic, could expect no further favours. Indeed, his prospects became even bleaker in 1550 when Somerset and his associates lost out in a political power struggle to another faction led by John Dudley, Earl of Warwick, who shortly afterwards made himself Duke of Northumberland and awarded himself the estates lost by the Percys in 1537. Worse still, Dudley was intent upon driving the church even further in a protestant direction.

However, in October 1553 Edward VI died at the early age of fifteen, which brought to the throne his older half-sister Mary, daughter of Catherine of Aragon, Henry VIII's first wife. Naturally she was staunchly catholic, a commitment reinforced the following year by her marriage to Philip II of Spain. The change of monarch was ideal from Percy's point of view, and his hopes were turned to expectation as the queen began restoring some of the families crushed by her father. Percy's turn came in 1557. On the last day of April he was knighted and created Baron Percy, and the following day he was elevated to the earldom of Northumberland. A few weeks later, on 16th and 17th August, the new earl recovered not only all the lands held by his uncle in 1537, but he was also granted the lands of the suppressed Northumberland priory of Tynemouth. Earlier in the same month, he replaced a disgruntled Lord Wharton as Warden of the East and Middle Marches and was granted the keeperships of Tynedale, Redesdale and Berwick: in effect, he was given supreme authority on the eastern Border. In the following year, to complement his high status, he was granted permission to maintain 200 retainers over and above his necessary household servants. The Percys, it appeared, were back.

But the appearance was somewhat deceptive. The properties Percy acquired were the estates his uncle had willed to the Crown in 1536, which were recovered from John Dudley in 1553 after he was executed for attempting to prevent Mary's accession by intruding on to the throne his son's wife, Lady Jane Grey. This desperate gamble had little support, even though it had been approved by the dying Edward VI. The recovered estates included most of the old Percy lands in Yorkshire (the most notable exception being those in Craven, which had been acquired by the Earl of Cumberland), Northumberland and Cumberland. Also not regained were the properties the sixth earl had sold to other people. This meant that almost all of the estates in the southern counties were lost. Apart from the ancient Percy possession of Petworth in Sussex and the neighbouring manors of Sutton and Duncton, the only southern properties recovered were those centred on Storgursey and Batheaston in Somerset and Laugharne and Walwyn's Castle in Carmarthenshire and Pembrokeshire, together with the London house, Northumberland Place in Aldgate. Added to these was the manor of Hazelbury Bryan, which was restored to Percy out of friendship by the Earl of Arundel. Moreover, until the death of his aunt, Mary Talbot, in 1572, the actual value of the estate to the earl was diminished by her dower, which comprised several major Yorkshire properties.

The earl's position in the Marches was also weaker than it seemed, despite his appointment to almost all the important offices on the Northumberland Border. The fact was that, in the twenty years when the Percys were absent from the Border scene, other men had risen to fill the vacuum. The most prominent of them was Sir John Forster, initially a fairly minor member of the county gentry, who rapidly advanced in wealth by the acquisition of the former monastic estates of Alnwick, Hulne, Bamburgh and Hexham. He also gained a military reputation through his service in the war in Scotland during the 1540s, which the Earl of Huntley called the 'Rough Wooing', when the English government unsuccessfully tried to bully the government of Scotland into agreeing to the marriage of Henry VIII's son, Edward, and the infant Mary, Queen of Scots. Moreover, although far from being pious and moral in his business and political dealings, Forster was a committed protestant and also a staunch government man, willing to pursue an anti-Percy course of action on the eastern Border to his own and the Crown's advantage.

The new earl set out to undermine and reduce Forster's influence, but he was thwarted almost immediately by another shift in the political climate. On 17th November 1558 Mary I died and was succeeded by her half-sister, Elizabeth, Henry VIII's daughter by his second wife, Anne Boleyn. From being in favour, Percy rapidly found himself mistrusted as an adherent of the old religion, an attachment reinforced in June 1558 by his marriage to the pious Anne Somerset, daughter of the Earl of Worcester. The new sovereign, however, was determined to impose religious settlement, wherein the church would retain its ancient organisation and structure, albeit firmly under Crown control, while at the same time requiring the acceptance of protestant doctrines. Added to this was the determination of Elizabeth's closest adviser, Sir William Cecil (soon to be ennobled as Lord Burghley), to increase Crown control over areas of the country distant from the capital.

Percy soon felt the effects of these changes of policy. In 1559, he was required to relinquish all his Border posts. The wardenship of the East March was given to a southerner, Lord Grey of Wilton, together with the right to use Alnwick Castle, a privilege the Crown granted without bothering to ask Percy's permission. Wilton did not last long, but the change to incomers was permanent as he was replaced, first by Francis Russell, Earl of Bedford, and then by Henry Carey, Lord Hunsdon, the son of Anne Boleyn's sister, Mary, and thereby the queen's cousin. Hunsdon was to hold the post from 1568 until his death in 1597. Similarly, in 1560 Percy was deprived of the Middle March, which covered roughly three-quarters of Northumberland, including Alnwick. His replacement was none other than Sir John Forster, who also remained in post until the 1590s. These changes, and other pinpricks such as the confiscation of a copper mine discovered at Newlands in Cumberland, made it abundantly clear that Elizabeth I and her government, while prepared to accept Thomas Percy as Earl of Northumberland and a man of great wealth, were not willing to countenance his having the old-style lordship and control over the eastern Border region.

Percy languished in this state of rejection until almost the end of the decade, when he committed an act of political folly akin to that of his ancestor, the first earl, 250 years earlier. This was his decision to become involved in the rebellion known as the Rising of the Northern Earls. The earls in question were two only, Thomas Percy, Earl of Northumberland, and Charles Neville, sixth Earl of Westmorland. The origins of this ill-fated enterprise lay in the politics of the English court and the condition of northern England, which were linked to a certain extent. Events at court centred on two very different people. One was Sir William Cecil, whose closeness to, and apparent influence with, the queen aroused resentment and jealousy, and whose positively anti-catholic foreign policy was feared and opposed by those who wanted a peaceful resolution of the differences with France and Spain. England had become a protestant country only recently, and was by no means certain to remain one.

Indeed there was one very good reason to suppose it might not, namely, Mary, the ex-queen of Scots. Mary's catholicism was one of the reasons why she was deposed in 1567 in favour of her infant son, James. She was imprisoned in Loch Leven Castle, but escaped and attempted to regain her throne by military force. The attempt ended in failure. Her supporters were defeated at Langside near Glasgow, and she then fled across the Border to seek refuge in England. With Elizabeth unmarried and all her siblings dead, Mary was, as a great-granddaughter of Henry VII, the English queen's heir. Indeed, to anyone who was a catholic, Mary was already the rightful sovereign of England, since no catholic could recognise as valid Henry VIII's divorce from Catherine of Aragon and his subsequent marriage to Anne Boleyn. In catholic eyes, Elizabeth, daughter of Anne Boleyn, was a bastard, and as such, had no legal right to the throne. The presence of Mary in England was disturbing in all senses. A surprisingly wide range of people favoured the idea of her marrying Thomas Howard, fourth Duke of Norfolk, the wealthiest nobleman in England. This match was seen as likely to resolve the succession problem by producing an heir to the English throne, and perhaps to that of Scotland as well. Not surprisingly, it found no favour with the queen.

The result of these doubts and discontents was an atmosphere in which intrigue and conspiracy flourished, and rebellion was readily planned. The first hint of serious trouble came in September 1569, when the Duke of Norfolk suddenly left court and went to his estates in East Anglia without the queen's permission. This move, which was a serious breach of protocol, was almost certainly in preparation for rebellion. But he quickly took fright, and returned to court hoping to regain royal favour. As he did so, he wrote to the earls of Northumberland and Westmorland urging them not to rebel. Repentance did him no good: he was immediately thrown into the Tower and eventually executed.

The arrival of Mary from Scotland also had a disturbing and destabilising effect in the north as she immediately became the magnet for all those who hankered after the old religion. Among the lower ranks of society there was a widespread desire to continue with traditional ways and practices, while among the more educated gentry the influence of the reformed catholic church on the continent was beginning to be felt. Religious tension was especially high in Durham, where both the new bishop, James Pilkington, and the new dean of the cathedral chapter, William Whittingham, were leading an aggressive drive to impose new forms of worship in place of traditional practices, and to appoint strongly committed protestants to important church posts within the diocese. They were also equally aggressive in their counter-attacks against those gentry who had taken advantage of the disturbed and uncertain conditions of the recent past to encroach illegally upon church lands and mineral resources.

The rising ferment was bound to affect the two earls as the leaders of society. There is no doubt that both men and their wives were strongly catholic. Indeed, Percy had been among the first to greet Mary when she came into England, and thereafter he and Countess Anne regularly exchanged letters and gifts with her. He also expressed a wish to visit the ex-queen of Scotland, but permission to do so was denied by Elizabeth. It is perhaps an indication of the depth of Percy's religious conviction and commitment that he was among those who did not favour the marriage of Mary and the Duke of Norfolk, on the grounds that he was not a catholic. But it is certain that the two earls were engaged in communications that at the very least bordered on treason, and both were aware of the plots and rumours of plots at court. For good reason, therefore, they were under royal suspicion, despite their assurances of loyalty conveyed to the queen by the President of the Council of the North, Thomas Radcliffe, Earl of Sussex. Their guilt, however, was all but proven, at least in the queen's eyes, by their refusal to obey her demands that they come to court. The tension finally broke on 9th November when the Earl of Northumberland, rightly believing that an attempt to arrest him was imminent, fled from his home at Topcliffe near Thirsk to join the Earl of Westmorland at Brancepeth Castle, four miles south west of Durham. There the catholic gentry of Durham were assembling to urge the Earl of Westmorland to rebel.

It was at Brancepeth that the dynamic of the rebellion (or rather the lack of it) became clear. The fact was that neither earl wholeheartedly favoured rebellion, partly as a result of personal temperament, but also because of a sense of duty to his sovereign and an awareness of the personal consequence of failure. The earls' wives, whose necks were not at risk, were more eager: Anne, Countess of Northumberland, from deep piety, and Jane, Countess of Westmorland, because of her fiery, aggressive personality. And they were also pressed by their many followers, men such as Richard Norton and Thomas Markenfield from Yorkshire, the Earl of Westmorland's uncle, Christopher Neville and Durham gentry, such as John Swinburn and Robert Tempest. To a considerable degree the earls were trapped. Great and wealthy noblemen they might be, accustomed to lead and to be obeyed; but they were also prisoners of the social system they headed. To resist the widely and strongly held convictions and demands of their followers and clients would be to lose honour and influence.

The story of the uprising is one of aimless uncertainty and lack of direction. This became clear right at the outset in the discussions about what to do. The Earl of Northumberland's suggestions were at least positive: to raise more troops in Northumberland and to send a flying column to seize Mary of Scotland who was believed to be at Tutbury in Staffordshire (this would have been wasted effort as Mary had been moved to a more secure confinement in the walled town of Coventry). These proposals were rejected, and instead the rebels' first action on 14th November was to organise a symbolic but utterly pointless excursion to Durham where they paraded the famous Banner of St. Cuthbert and restored the altar in the cathedral in order to celebrate the old-style mass. A slow and meandering progress southward was then undertaken, during which they raised recruits, some volunteering through religious conviction, but others secured by threats to their property if they declined, or lured by promises of pay and booty. In the end, their army numbered around 4,000 foot and about 1,500 horse, of which only the latter could be regarded as having any serious military potential. By 22nd November, they had got no further than Bramham Moor near Wetherby, less than seventy miles from their starting point.

There another conference resulted in the decision to retreat. There were several reasons. One was the growing awareness of a large royal army being assembled in the midlands. Another was the fact that a small but effective military force was operating in Northumberland, under the leadership of Sir John Forster. A further cause for concern was the total absence of support from the west: Henry Clifford, Earl of Cumberland, was too ill (he was to die a few weeks later); Edward Stanley, third Earl of Derby, was too shrewd; and Leonard Dacre, the most powerful figure in Cumberland, was conveniently trapped in London engaged in a lawsuit. Finally, there was no encouragement from Scotland. Mary's deposition had divided the Scottish nobility into two camps: those who supported her and were prepared to work for her restoration; and those who had no wish to see her return. At this crucial juncture, the government of Scotland was in the hands of the Regent, James Stewart, Earl of Moray, who was strongly hostile to Mary. He therefore ensured by vigorous patrolling of the Border that no Scottish help could get to what he saw as pro-Mary rebels, who were a serious threat to his position.

Back north of the Tees, the rebel army forced Sir George Bowes, the Sheriff of Durham, who had organised the loyal gentry of his county, to surrender Barnard Castle. They also seized Hartlepool in the forlorn hope that the King of Spain's commander in the Netherlands, the Duke of Alva, would send professional troops to swell and stiffen their ranks. Alva did not oblige, recognising a lost cause when he saw one. Still moving north, the rebels at last came into contact with Sir John Forster's Northumbrian troops near Chester le Street. No battle ensued, but a slight skirmish was enough to bring the rebellion to an end. On 16th December, the earls dismissed what was left of their army, which was fast diminishing as the result of bad weather and no pay, and with a small escort made a dash up the Tyne valley. Their aim was to secure refuge in Leonard Dacre's castle at Naworth. But to their dismay they were refused admittance, and therefore they had no option but to turn northwards and cross into Scotland.

This desperate move gave the rebellion an international dimension. At first the two earls became captives of Hector Armstrong of Harlaw, a member of one of the most notorious Scottish Border clans or 'surnames'. Armstrong handed over the Earl of Westmorland and also the Countess of Northumberland (who had been stripped of her wardrobe and jewels) to Lord Home, a leading Border noble and a member of the Marian party. The Earl of Northumberland, however, he sold to the government of the Regent, the Earl of Moray, who recognised his value as a bargaining counter when dealing with the English government. Moray, however, did not live long enough to enjoy this windfall. In late January 1570, he was assassinated and the Marian party seemed set to assume control in Edinburgh. Elizabeth's response was to send an English army into Scotland, under the command of the Earl of Sussex, with orders to inflict maximum damage. Her purpose was to secure the return of the fugitive earls, and to ensure that Moray was replaced as Regent by another pro-English noble, Matthew Stewart, Earl of Lennox. By the autumn of 1570, she had achieved partial success in that the Marian

118

nobles were forced to accept Lennox as Regent. On the other hand, she lost the Earl of Westmorland and the Countess of Northumberland, who in August secured passage from Aberdeen to the Spanish Netherlands, thanks to the help given by the Marian nobles.

The Earl of Northumberland, however, who was regarded as the rebel leader, was still in the hands of the Scottish government. He remained so until the summer of 1572, when negotiations led to the Regent, now John Erskine, Earl of Mar, selling him to the English government. It says much for the earl's importance in international diplomacy that the money Mar accepted from Elizabeth was much less than that offered by Countess Anne, a sum she had raised with help from the Spanish and papal governments. Taken from Edinburgh, Percy was handed over to Lord Hunsdon and then to Sir John Forster to be led captive through his own 'country', Northumberland and Yorkshire. In the previous year he had been attainted in his absence, and consequently his execution at York on 22nd August was a formality. His widow, Anne, lived in exile for almost another twenty years, devoting her time to the pursuit of her religion and attacks on the woman responsible for her husband's death. She died of smallpox on 22nd September 1591 in a convent near Namur, in the Spanish Netherlands (modern Belgium).

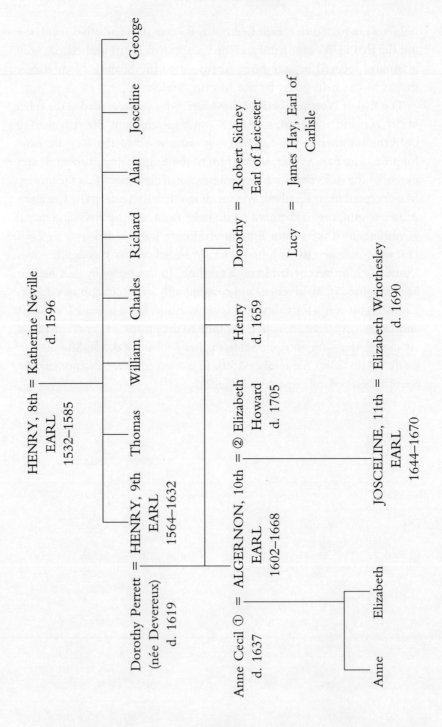

HENRY, 8th EARL 1532–1585 = Katherine Neville d. 1596

George
Josceline
Alan
Richard
Charles
William

Thomas

Dorothy Perrett (née Devereux) d. 1619 = HENRY, 9th EARL 1564–1632

Dorothy = Robert Sidney Earl of Leicester

Henry d. 1659

Lucy = James Hay, Earl of Carlisle

Anne Cecil ① d. 1637 = ALGERNON, 10th EARL 1602–1668 = ② Elizabeth Howard d. 1705

JOSCELINE, 11th EARL 1644–1670 = Elizabeth Wriothesley d. 1690

Anne
Elizabeth

TEN

The Political Tightrope

Henry Percy, Eighth Earl of Northumberland, 1532–1585
Henry Percy, Ninth Earl of Northunberland, 1564–1632
Algernon Percy, Tenth Earl of Northumberland, 1602–1668
Joceline Percy, Eleventh Earl of Northumberland, 1644–1670

In the hundred years between 1570 and 1670 there were four earls of Northumberland: Henry Percy, 8th earl 1572–85, Henry Percy, 9th earl 1585–1632, Algernon Percy, 10th earl 1632–68 and Joceline Percy 11th earl 1668–70. They were the last members of the Percy-Louvain line which began in the middle of the twelfth century. Apart from the last, who held the title for a very short time, they lived in a world fraught with danger, which required them to tread carefully to avoid the fate of the seventh earl and his father. The late sixteenth and early seventeenth centuries were a time of hatred and bitterness, aroused by religious differences and the belief in the principle of 'one state, one church'. This was in part responsible for the outbreak of three civil wars in Britain between 1637 and 1642 and a convulsed political situation which was to continue until 1660. As great noblemen, the Earls of Northumberland would have found it difficult to opt out of affairs of state; their wealth and status made some involvement in politics almost unavoidable. For them success, first and foremost, was to so arrange their involvements and commitments as to avoid losing life and inheritance. It was also in this period that they ceased to be, in any real sense, northerners: in these years their title belied their belonging. For all four men, home was Petworth House in Sussex, and to a lesser extent and after 1594, Syon House at Brentford in Middlesex. At first their residence at Petworth was enforced by the government; in the end, however, it became their natural home.

Henry Percy, the eighth earl, was the younger brother of the seventh earl, who was executed in 1572. When he was born is uncertain, but it was probably in 1532. Nor do we know anything of his upbringing and education, although it is fairly safe to assume that he enjoyed the same

121

straitened circumstances as his brother. By chance he reached his majority in the same year as Mary I became queen, and therefore it is not surprising to find him immediately becoming engaged in Border matters. In the 1554 parliament, he represented the Northumberland borough of Morpeth, enfranchised for the first time, and he probably became active militarily, since he was knighted in 1557. What is more surprising is his continued activity on the Border after Elizabeth's accession and the removal of his brother, the seventh earl, from his posts as Warden of the Marches and Keeper of Berwick. The reason for his retention, apart from his not being the Earl of Northumberland, is most likely to have been the crisis that enveloped England, France and Scotland at this time.

It began in April 1558, a few months before Elizabeth's accession, when Mary, Queen of Scots, married Francis, the French Dauphin, and, moreover, agreed to bequeath Scotland to France should she and her husband not have children. Not only was this development deeply disquieting to the English government, but it helped to trigger the protestant rebellion in Scotland spearheaded by John Knox, which erupted in May 1559. The crisis deepened a few weeks later when, as the result of the death of her father-in-law, Henry II, Mary's husband became King Francis II of France. Mary flaunted her rising fortunes at their coronation by displaying the arms of England and Ireland as well as those of France and Scotland, thus staking her claim to all four kingdoms.

Almost immediately a force of 3–4,000 seasoned French troops was sent to Scotland to suppress the rebellion there, which was being strongly resisted by Mary's mother, Mary of Guise, who was governing Scotland on her daughter's behalf. From England's point of view the situation was sufficiently serious to warrant a military intervention. In the summer of 1560, an English army under Lord Grey of Wilton advanced into Scotland and attacked the French garrison at Leith. This move was successful in two senses. It allowed the protestant nobles in Scotland to seize control of the organs of government, a task made easier by the death of Mary of Guise in June. It also resulted in the Treaty of Edinburgh, whereby the French and English governments agreed to withdraw their troops and Mary agreed to recognise Elizabeth as Queen of England. The situation was eased still further by the sudden death of Francis II in December, leaving Mary a young widow with no option but to return to a Scotland controlled by protestant nobles.

In all of these events Henry Percy took an active part. Militarily, he commanded the light horse (almost certainly men from the border regions of Cumberland and Northumberland) with distinction in the attack on Leith in April, and in the following month he was a member of the commission that negotiated the peace treaty. He continued to be active through the remainder of the 1560s. In 1561, he was given military responsibility as captain of the important castles of Tynemouth and Norham, one controlling the entrance to the Tyne, the other command-ing a major Border crossing. In the following year, civil responsibility was added when he was appointed Sheriff of Northumberland. In these roles he would have been required to co-operate with Lord Hunsdon and Sir John Forster, the men who had replaced his brother as Wardens of the Marches. When the crisis came in 1569 and 1570, he remained loyal to the Crown and co-operated with Forster and Hunsdon to ensure that Northumberland stayed quiet. Their success is measured by the fact that only four per cent of the rebel host that followed the earls of North-umberland and Westmorland came from north of the Tyne.

Why did he remain loyal? There are several answers to this question. Apart from not having to accommodate the wishes of followers and clients, which was incumbent upon the earl, Henry Percy may not have had his brother's depth of commitment to the old religion. Social situation and personal conviction therefore may have combined to make it easy for him to resist any temptation to rebel. Also, he may have been shrewder and more cautious, recognising that the odds against the revolt succeeding were very long. Then there was the nobility's age-old practice of 'divide and survive': having a member in each camp would ensure that, no matter what the outcome, the family was on the winning side. Although no evidence has yet come to light that the brothers were deliberately colluding to this end, the queen must have recognised the potent appeal of this idea when, in November 1569, she wrote to Henry Percy: 'considering your fidelity to us, we would have you well assured that, continuing your service and duty we will have regard to the continuance of such a house in the person and blood of so faithful a servant as we trust to find you'. This well phrased if rather convoluted assurance may or may not have been conclusive. But the fact is that Henry Percy did remain loyal, did not lift a finger to save his brother, and did live to reap the promised reward.

However, and inexplicably, having stayed clear of trouble in 1569 and 1570, Henry Percy was arrested on 15th November 1571 on suspicion of being involved in the Ridolfi Plot. The fiasco of the 1569 rebellion and the savage repression that followed its collapse did nothing to put an end to plots against Elizabeth. In February 1571, with papal approval, Roberto Ridolfi, an Italian financier with a network of international connections, began to put together another scheme for removing the Elizabethan regime and replacing her with Mary. English catholics were expected to rise in large numbers and to be assisted by an army of Spanish troops ferried from the Netherlands. However, the English government's intelligence network gradually became aware of what was afoot, and the full details of which were revealed under the threat of torture by the Scottish Bishop of Ross. Several English nobles were clearly involved, including the fourth Duke of Norfolk whose execution Elizabeth sanctioned, albeit with some reluctance.

Percy was among the suspects who were rounded up and incarcerated. However, he was lucky: although tried and found guilty in February 1572, his punishment was a heavy fine of 5,000 marks ($£3,333$ 6s 8d = $£3,333$ 34p); and following his brother's execution at York in August, Elizabeth kept her promise and allowed him to inherit the title. Full rehabilitation was gradual, however. He was not released from the Tower until May 1573, and only then did he recover the estates; and it was not until February 1576 that he was allowed to take his seat in the House of Lords.

Was the government's action against Henry Percy justified? It is hard to tell. The fact that his brother, the rebel earl, was still at large, albeit a prisoner of the Scottish government, must have been a cause of anxiety, and it is more than likely that, as acting head of the House of Percy, he would have been contacted by Ridolfi's agents. On the other hand, his involvement may have been deemed to be marginal, although the leniency shown to him could have been due as much to Elizabeth's reluctance to execute members of the nobility as to Percy's innocence.

Henry Percy may have recovered title and estates, but he did not fully recover his liberty. The condition of his release from the Tower was that he should not live in the north where the bulk of his property was located, but at Petworth in Sussex. Clearly, he was regarded by the government as a man on probation whose loyalty was not fully guaranteed. It is this continued suspicion of him that helps to explain his arrest on 15th December 1583 and committal to the Tower on 9th January 1584. The occasion was yet another plot against the regime known by the name of the man who under torture revealed its details, Francis Throck-morton. The formula was in essence the same as before: a rising of English Catholics timed to coincide with the landing of French and Spanish armies, which would result in the deposition of Elizabeth and her replacement as queen by Mary, and thereby the return of England and Scotland to the catholic camp. The immediate upshot was the expulsion of the Spanish ambassador, Bernadino de Mendoza, but it also began the train of events which led to Mary's execution in 1587 and the attempted Spanish invasion the following year.

How deeply, if at all, was the eighth earl involved in these schemes? The only certain evidence against him is that he received Charles Paget, a committed English catholic living in France, who paid a secret visit to Sussex to sound out his brother, Lord Paget, and the Earl of Arundel, and also to reconnoitre possible landing sites for a French invasion force. He protested that nothing treasonable occurred at this meeting and, in spite of torture, no proof to the contrary was extracted from several men who were interrogated. Consequently, there was insufficient evidence for Percy to be brought to trial with any real hope of conviction. Yet he was detained in the Tower. The likely reasons are that indiscreet remarks he made from time to time revealed that he had some sympathy for Mary, and that he was known to enjoy intrigue. It is also possible that Elizabeth was hoping to persuade him to confess and beg her forgiveness, an act which the earl was unwilling to perform.

The conclusion was then and still is a mystery. On the night of 20th–21st June 1585, the earl was found dead, lying on his bed, shot through the heart, with a small pistol known as a 'dag' lying by the bedside. An inquest concluded that he had committed suicide. The official version of events was that the earl had retired to his bedroom and bolted the door on the inside. Then, about midnight, a shot was heard followed by two groans. The door was immediately forced and the body discovered. This was all very neat and simple, and if true removed all possibility of foul play. Many contemporaries, however, and not only enemies of the regime, were sceptical and some were entirely convinced that the earl was murdered. How could he have acquired a firearm, and in any case was there any good reason for him to take his own life? On the other hand, his continued existence was a problem for the government in that, while he could not be proved guilty of treason, he was believed to be less than totally loyal.

The career of the eighth earl leaves many unresolved questions which merit fuller investigation than they have so far received. Happily, our knowledge of his eldest son and successor is much greater and more certain. Henry Percy was born in late April 1564 at Tynemouth Castle where his father held the office of Keeper. His mother was Katherine, the eldest of the four daughters and co-heirs of John Neville, Lord Latimer, who after her husband's death married one of his distant cousins, Francis Fitton, and lived until 1596. Although we have very little knowledge of the new earl's education, one fact is of great significance: its earliest stages were entrusted to the Vicar of Egremont in Cumberland, a conforming clergyman of the Church of England. Clearly, the eighth earl had decided that his heir should be trained to be religiously correct and consequently, given the beliefs of the time, politically correct. Precisely what effect this had on the future ninth earl is uncertain, since in later life he showed little interest in religion and may even have been an agnostic. The one other aspect of his education which is known is that in 1581, at the age of seventeen, he was sent abroad and did not return to England until a year after his father's death. The results of this extended stay on the continent were a good command of Latin, French and Italian and a deep and abiding commitment to academic and intellectual pursuits. Throughout his life he was an inveterate purchaser of books, all of which he would seem to have read, and a very supportive patron of scholars, particularly Thomas Harriott, the most outstanding mathematician and astronomer of his generation working in England. Nor was the earl's interest merely passive as his purchases of scientific instruments attests. In fact, his reputation for being interested in science earned him the sobriquet of 'the wizard earl', popular opinion assuming that he was attempting to find ways of converting base materials into gold.

But he was not easy to live with. There is no doubt that he was very conscious of being a member of the aristocracy, and as a result he was quick to take offence if he felt that he was being slighted or demeaned. Twice he came close to fighting a duel, first with the Earl of Southampton and then with Sir Francis Vere, the latter being prevented only by the queen's intervention. This incident occurred during a brief period of military service in the years 1600–1602 in the Netherlands, where Vere was in command of the English forces. Their presence there stemmed the revolt of the seventeen provinces that comprised the Netherlands, which began in the late 1560s and was to last until 1609. These provinces were part of the Spanish empire, but they became increasingly hostile to Philip II's centralising policy and adamant catholicism. The revolt was sustained by the military ability of William of Nassau, Prince of Orange, and, after his murder in 1584, that of his son, Maurice. The main rebel strength lay in the north, the future Holland, where protestantism had taken a firm hold. The south, the future Belgium, remained under Spanish control and thus catholic in religion. Naturally, ardent protestants in England were eager for Elizabeth to give full support to the Dutch cause, but she was cautious and anxious to avoid commitments which could be financially ruinous and diplomatically restricting. After 1588, however, English involvement was continuous, although never on a massive scale.

How did the earl become involved? One reason is that it was not unusual for members of the nobility to join campaigns as volunteers, and on this occasion Northumberland was one of a group who joined Vere's forces in the sieges of Rheinburg, Meurs and Ostend. As such they could have been regarded as dilettante, but there is some reason to believe that Northumberland had a more serious but surreptitious commission to sound out the Spanish authorities to discover whether there were any grounds for thinking that successful peace negotiations might be possible. The earl's quarrel with Vere was very much driven by Vere's requirement that the volunteer aristocrats submit themselves to military discipline and the earl's resentment at not being treated with the deference he believed was due to him. It has to be said that right was almost entirely on the side of Vere. The earl's only other military experience had occurred in 1599, when he was one of several noblemen who raised troops to defend London during an invasion scare, when it was believed that a Spanish army had landed on the Isle of Wight.

By the time these incidents took place the earl was married. His marriage in 1594 was to Dorothy, widow of Sir Thomas Perrott, who had died earlier in the year. The match had two important aspects. The first is that it prevented the marriage, which had been seriously mooted, between the earl and Arabella Stewart. She was the daughter of Charles

Stewart, younger brother of Henry Stewart, Lord Darnley, Mary Queen of Scots' second husband and the father of James VI. He, as everyone was acutely aware, was all but certain to become James I of England when the ageing Elizabeth died. Arabella, his cousin, was therefore, after him, next in line for the English throne. Added to this was the fact that a contemporary calculation put the earl himself eighth in line as the result of his being directly descended from the union in the fourteenth century of Lord Percy III and Mary Plantagenet. A Percy-Stewart marriage would therefore have had, potentially at least, serious political and constitutional implications. Consequently, the queen and her chief adviser, Robert Cecil (younger son of William Cecil, Lord Burghley, who had been groomed by his father as his successor), made sure that this marriage did not take place. (To avoid confusion, it should be noted that the correct spelling of the name of the Scottish royal family is Stewart. The corrupted version, Stuart, was adopted after 1603.)

The other significance was that the lady the earl did marry was the sister of Robert Devereux, Earl of Essex, Elizabeth's last favourite courtier, who was very actively engaged in building up a following, which he hoped would form a political power base. By his marriage, therefore, the earl allied himself with Essex, whose aim was to supplant Robert Cecil and his associates. In doing so, he joined the wrong party. In 1601, Essex, having failed disastrously to subdue a serious rebellion in Ireland, quarrelled with the queen and rashly attempted to rebel. It was a forlorn gesture, and it ended in his execution. By this time the earl had disengaged himself from the close association with Essex, and so was not implicated, although two of his brothers were involved. Nevertheless, he continued to be regarded by Cecil as a political opponent.

The earl's tactic to end his political isolation and to remove any suspicion of inordinate ambition arising from the notion of his marriage to Arabella Stewart was shrewd. In 1602, recognising that Elizabeth was unlikely to live much longer, he entered into a secret correspondence with James VI of Scotland, in which he assured the future king of his loyalty, supplied him with sound advice as to what he should do and avoid doing when he came to England and provided him with accurate assessments of the leading figures in English politics with whom as king he would have to deal. He also secured for his brother, Charles, the role of Privy Council messenger to convey the news of the queen's death to

Edinburgh. In the event Charles Percy was beaten by a few hours by an unofficial courier, Lord Hunsdon's son, Sir Robert Carey.

Elizabeth I died on 24th March 1603, and James VI of Scotland was accepted as her successor without opposition. There is almost certainly no truth in the story that the earl assembled a force of a hundred armed men and threatened anyone who opposed the succession. Nevertheless, when James arrived in London in May, the earl reaped a handsome reward. He was made a member of the Privy Council and Captain of the Gentlemen Pensioners, the sovereign's personal bodyguard. Having successfully extricated himself from the Essex entanglement, and firmly ingratiated himself with the new regime, the earl could look forward to a future of prestige, position and profit.

It was not to be. Late in 1605, disaster struck in the form of the Gunpowder Plot. It was the earl's great misfortune that one of the leading members of the conspiracy was Thomas Percy, a descendant of the fourth earl and therefore one of his distant cousins. This might not have mattered had not the earl appointed Thomas Percy as Constable of Alnwick Castle in 1596 and thereafter employed him as his factor on his northern estates. Despite numerous complaints from his tenants about Thomas Percy's abuse of his powers, the earl continued using his services to collect his rents and bring them south to him. Moreover, when he became Captain of the Gentleman Pensioners, the earl enrolled his cousin as a member of that elite corps. James, too, was familiar with Thomas Percy, since he had been the earl's messenger in his correspondence with the Scottish king. It was probably as a result of this contact that Thomas Percy was drawn into the Gunpowder conspiracy. Born about 1560 and therefore a few years older than the earl, he too had been brought up as a protestant, but at some stage he had converted to catholicism and had used his visits to Edinburgh to sound out James's intentions towards catholics in England, once he became king. In this delicate situation, with the old queen nearing death, James, ever the astute politician, was being all things to all men, with the result that he led Thomas Percy, inadvertently or otherwise, to believe that catholics would fare better under him than they had under Elizabeth. In the event, Percy and his co-religionists were disappointed: once on the English throne, James made it clear that the anti-catholic laws would not be repealed. Thomas Percy, the zealous convert, must have felt this to be a personal as well as a general betrayal.

On Monday 4th November 1605, around mid-morning, Thomas Percy arrived at Syon House where the earl was staying prior to going to Westminster for the state opening of parliament. The visit had an entirely innocent purpose: Thomas Percy had just arrived from the north with the earl's rents and to attend the annual audit of accounts. An hour later he dined with the earl and several other people, including Thomas Harriott, who had a house in Syon Park. The table-talk ranged over several matters, including the proposed arrangements for the union of Scotland and England, but it seems certain that there was no reference, open or coded, to what was planned for the following day. After dinner (then normally eaten around midday), Thomas Percy left and was followed some hours later by the earl, who went to spend the night at his London house.

In the event the plot was discovered and foiled. Most of the conspirators had already left for the west midlands, intending to raise the catholic gentry of that region once James's death was confirmed. When the news reached them that the plot had failed, they sought refuge in Holbeach House in Staffordshire, where they were besieged by the sheriff of that county. Percy was among those killed resisting arrest. His death removed the one person who might have saved the earl from the sudden downturn in fortune he now experienced.

The earl was arrested almost immediately, and on Friday, 27th June 1606, he was tried in the Star Chamber. He was not accused of treason, since none of the investigations and interrogations produced any evidence of his involvement or complicity in the plot. The composite accusation he faced amounted to misprision of treason, that is, having knowledge of treason but failing to disclose it. Here, too, the evidence was flimsy, although one fact was undeniable: the earl had admitted Thomas Percy to the ranks of the Gentlemen Pensioners, and, more damning, had failed to require him take the obligatory oath of supremacy. Almost inevitably, the earl was found guilty. His punishment was to be stripped of his public offices, fined £30,000 and sentenced to indefinite imprisonment. In 1613, after much haggling, the king accepted £11,000 and discharged the earl from the rest of the fine. He was not, however, at this stage prepared to release him from the Tower.

The earl's incarceration lasted sixteen years. It should not be thought, however, that he had to endure a harsh and unpleasant confinement. Far from it, although not initially: at first he was put in the Garden Tower, but there he was affected by the damp and the smells from the moat; and adding to his discomfort was the knowledge that it was in the Garden Tower that his father had died. His pleas for more congenial accommodation were answered. He was moved to the north side of the Tower complex, to the Martin Tower, where he had a spacious apartment, comprising a great chamber, a drawing room, a study, a library and two dining rooms. In addition, there was accommodation for the twenty servants who attended him. Not all could sleep in the Tower, however, and some were lodged in a house on Tower Hill rented for that purpose. Moreover, he improved his suite of rooms by paying for redecoration and refurnishing. The quality of the accommodation was matched by the richness of living. His annual expenditure on food and wine averaged £800 in the early years of his imprisonment but rose steadily in the later stages. These sums included an annual compensation to the Lieutenant of the Tower, one of whose perks was providing food for the prisoners at a profit, but not of course the titbits and delicacies sent to him by friends and well-wishers, while from his own gardens at Syon, he got grapes and other exotic delicacies. Among the many items purchased was tobacco, for the earl was one of the earliest addicts in England. Nor did he neglect his wardrobe, expending up to £150 annually on clothing.

This sumptuously appointed prison allowed him unlimited leisure to engage indulgently in his favourite pursuit, study. He spent on average £50 a year on books, which eventually grew to a library of very considerable size covering a very wide range of subject matter. In addition, he was able to receive virtually at will the scholars whom he patronised, notably Thomas Harriott and two other regulars, Walter Warner and Robert Hues, who collectively were known as the 'Earl of Northumberland's Magi'. And for thirteen years he had the intellectually stimulating company of a notable fellow prisoner, Sir Walter Raleigh. As well as the mind, the body also needed exercise, for which he had his own bowling alley and access to facilities for tennis and fencing. Indoors, he was able to play cards, billiards and shove ha'penny.

In fact, his way of life was so comfortable and congenial that it is said that he expressed reluctance to leave the Tower when at last he was released in July 1621. That this happened was owing in large measure to one of his sons-in-law, James Hay, one of James I's favourites, who persuaded his sovereign to grant an amnesty on his fifty-seventh birthday. By this time the earl was a widower, his wife having died in 1619, and he was complaining of deafness and poor eyesight. Clearly, for him, as for many long-term prisoners, the prospect of having to adjust to the outside world was not totally appealing.

Was his long imprisonment justified by the gravity of his offence? The investigations made in the immediate aftermath of 5th November, and others made subsequently, failed to come up with any evidence to link the earl with the plot. He was not a catholic, and his assiduous courting of James as King of Scotland and the rewards he received at his hands when James became King of England, make it impossible to see how he could have desired the outcome the plotters of 1605 had in mind. Against him, of course, was the Percy name, with its long history of rebellion. But perhaps of greater significance, was that the earl lacked political following and influence with which to counter the hostility of Robert Cecil, soon to be Earl of Salisbury, who became James's closest adviser as he had been for Elizabeth.

Undoubtedly one of the central concerns of the earl's life, both before and during his imprisonment, was his family, partly because of its size, but also because of the strained relations between him and so many of its members, particularly the females. It began early. It is quite evident that the earl and his mother had no great liking for each other. He considered her to be a grasping woman who had been too well provided for in widowhood. In return, she considered him to be a wastrel, which in his early years as earl was true. Consequently, for this if not other reasons, she settled the properties she inherited from her father, which were not included in the Percy entail, on her younger sons. With her second marriage in 1587, however, she ceased to trouble him.

Seven years later her role as the earl's female bugbear was assumed by his wife. Dorothy Perrott was by all accounts a good-looking woman, but with a biting tongue and a temper as short and as strong as his. Their domestic battles were notorious. The central issue seems to have been the smallness of the allowance he made her. One reason for this was that the earl believed his wife had cheated him by settling leases worth a great deal of money on her daughter by Sir Thomas Perrott. In addition to the financial squabble, the politics of the marriage were unravelling: she continued to support her brother, while he recognised that the Essex connection was becoming a serious liability. The upshot was that in 1599 the countess left the matrimonial home and rented a house in Putney, where she continued to reside until the end of 1601. Reconciliation may have been the consequence of the earl's return from the Netherlands, but it was also impelled by dynastic considerations. Prior to their separation, the couple had had four children, but while the two daughters survived, the two sons had died in infancy. The need for a male heir made renewed cohabitation vital, and their good sense was rewarded with two more sons, born in 1602 and 1605 respectively, both of whom survived to manhood. In spite of their differences, the countess strove hard to secure the earl's release from the Tower, and he appears to have been genuinely saddened by her death in 1619.

Conflict between husband and wife involved their daughters, both of whom as they grew into young women were often at court, thanks to the friendship of their mother and James I's queen, Anne of Denmark. The serious purpose was, of course, to contrive advantageous marriages, and in 1615 negotiations began between the imprisoned earl and Viscount Lisle aimed at securing the marriage of the earl's elder daughter, Dorothy, with Lisle's son, Robert Sidney. But the two fathers failed to reach an agreement, and therefore it seemed that the match was off. However, the countess, and presumably Dorothy, were determined women and the wedding took place without the earl's consent or knowledge. Paternal wrath at this act of defiance was understandable, and the earl felt justified in denying his daughter her dowry. Again, however, the women were victorious: faced with a threat of a recourse to law, the earl gave way and paid up in 1617 to the tune of £6,000.

Even before this had been settled, difficulties arose concerning the marriage of the earl's second daughter, Lucy, who was a woman of great beauty and sparkling wit. With these assets and the advantage of the Percy name, she was not short of suitors. Her choice was a Scotsman, James Hay, one of James I's favourites, whom he made Earl of Carlisle. Hay was already a widower with a well-deserved reputation for spending money carelessly and frivolously: when he died in 1636, it was said that he had got through no less than £400,000 and consequently left neither land nor money. This time both mother and father were opposed, the earl commenting that 'he would not see his daughter dance to a Scotch jig'. But the countess was eventually won round, and the couple were married late in 1617 in the presence of the king. The earl, however, never relented, and his second daughter did not get her dowry.

She went on to be one of the outstanding personalities at the court of James I's son, Charles I, the close friend and confidante of his French queen, Henrietta Maria, and the subject of verse by some of the leading poets of the day, such as Robert Herrick and Sir John Suckling. Given her beauty and vivacity, it is perhaps not surprising that there were rumours about her fidelity, especially as the court of James I was not noted for its moral rectitude. During the 1620s, Lucy's name was certainly linked with that of George Villiers, Duke of Buckingham, the last of James I's young male favourites who was, until his murder in 1628, the dominant figure at the court of James's son and successor, Charles I. These rumours remain unproven either way, although Buckingham's wife, Katherine Manners, daughter of the Earl of Rutland, whom he married in 1620, was intensely jealous of Lucy on account of her continuing close friendship with her husband. Later, in the 1630s and 1640s, Lucy's name was linked successively, and somewhat improbably, with Thomas Wentworth, Earl of Strafford, and then with his arch-enemy, John Pym. Although by then Lucy was a widow, neither rumour carries any proof, and both may stem from her undoubted involvement in political intrigue.

The earl was equally unsuccessful with his heir, even though his control over him had been greater during his formative years, which he spent with his father in the Tower. In spite of this, he defied the earl when it came to matrimony. In 1628, by which date he was twenty-six years old, and therefore entitled to make his own decisions, he became engaged to Lady Anne Cecil, granddaughter of Robert Cecil, Earl of Salisbury, the earl's political enemy, whose hostility may have been considerably responsible for his long incarceration. Naturally, the earl was horrified, but was eventually mollified by the size of the bride's dowry, £12,000.

As well as being burdened with the problems created by his children, the earl was also to quite a degree responsible for the fate and fortunes of his brothers. This was no light task, since the eighth earl and his wife had eight sons, only one of whom, the second, Thomas, did not survive to manhood. The earl grumbled that his brothers were envious of his wealth and wished for greater fortunes. This remark, however, may apply to the years before the death of the dowager countess in 1596, when the six younger men acquired the Latimer properties she had settled upon them.

Thereafter, the earl's relations with all his brothers were amicable and he helped and supported them when they ran into difficulties. In part this may have stemmed from the financial arrangements they made. All but one, the oldest, William, handed over their Latimer inheritances to the earl in return for guaranteed annuities. The sums were in the first instance equivalent to the income the properties were expected to yield, but over the years the earl appears to have awarded generous increases. The good sense of this arrangement is underlined by the case of William Percy, who elected to retain control of his property. Twice he was imprisoned for debt, and on both occasions the earl came to his rescue. Likewise, the earl helped two other brothers, Charles and Richard, to pay the fines they incurred by their involvement in the Earl of Essex's rebellion. All six men led separate and independent lives. None achieved fame, distinction or notoriety, except perhaps William, who was a minor poet and play-wright, and George, the youngest, who took part in the early attempt to found the colony of Virginia.

It is evident from all these internal family arrangements that the earl was very money conscious, which some of his family would have seen as a euphemism for meanness. His concern for money was the result of hard lessons learned during his early days as earl. On his own admission, he lived a riotous life in the 1580s, when he spent money with abandon and as a result ran up massive debts. This folly he attributed to the fact that, although he had been well educated academically, he was left woefully ignorant in the matters of estate management and financial administra-tion. He was even duped by his cousin, Thomas Percy, who used his position of trust to embezzle almost £2,000, which helped to finance the Gunpowder Plot. But the earl did learn his lesson. He worked up the necessary managerial and financial skills with which he set about extin-guishing his debts and increasing his income. He was totally successful in both exercises, especially the latter. At the time of his succession, the rents from the entailed estates realised almost £5,100 a year (£1,929 from Yorkshire, £1,759 from Northumberland, £390 from Cumberland, £588 from Somerset, £335 from Sussex and £93 from Wales). By 1603, the total had risen modestly to nearly £7,000, but by the time of his death in 1632, it was not far short of £13,000. This massive increase was achieved primarily by the application of three policies. One was the strategic purchase of land so as to round off and gain full control of key properties. Secondly, whenever possible and sensible, land was enclosed in order to create compact farms, which could be let at far higher rents. Lastly, again wherever and whenever possible, copyhold tenures, which were heritable and carried low, fixed rents, were extinguished and replaced by twenty-one year leases with economic rents. Underpinning all of these policies was a very detailed knowledge of the estate gained through scientific surveys. The earl was one of the first English landlords to commission these, and he was prepared to spend up to £200 a year on them in order to have the accurate data they provided. The results of his attention and concern have survived in the form of detailed surveys with well-drawn plans produced in 1624.

This did not mean that the earl ceased to borrow money, but the sums, individual and total, were much smaller than in the days of his wild youth, and their purpose was investment not consumption. Allied to this was a certain restraint in expenditure, particularly on servants. Compared with his ancestor the 'magnificent' fifth earl, who in the early sixteenth century had 166 persons on his payroll, the ninth earl's servants rarely exceeded sixty in number. In addition there was the unlooked-for benefit of imprisonment. Although his conviction resulted in the loss of lucrative state offices and the prospect of them, the earl was compensated by not having to face the expense involved in the life of a courtier with political ambition. Because of his successful financial management, he was able to undertake a substantial rebuilding of Syon House, and to enlarge Petworth House and provide it with magnificent stables, both projects costing over £5,000. The ninth earl's wizardry lay, not in the field of science, but in that of finance.

Henry Percy lived for eleven years after his release from the Tower. He died at the age of sixty-eight in 1632, ironically on 5th November. Throughout what may be seen as his retirement he lived at Petworth. This was probably through choice, although in fact he had none since it was a condition of his release that he did not venture more than thirty miles from Petworth. This meant, in theory at any rate, that he was denied the use of his other southern residence, Syon House. Apart from his enhancement of these two splendid mansions, his memorial is the book he wrote entitled *Advice to his Son*. The book is in two parts. The first was written in 1595, shortly after the birth of his first son who died in infancy, the second in 1609, when his heir, born in 1602, was seven years old and with him in the Tower. The second part, which is over twice the length of the first, is the more interesting. Described by its editor as 'an autobiography with comments', it could equally well be labelled a cynic's testament. The earl's three central precepts for a successful life were: understand your estate better than any of the people you employ to manage it; never entrust the running of your affairs to your wife; and when making gifts or decisions, do not be swayed by the arguments of others. He also added that his son should assume that all men love themselves better than anyone else and that groups invariably generate envy.

In contrast to the well-researched life of Henry Percy, the ninth earl, that of his son and successor, Algernon Percy, has been largely neglected. This is regrettable, since the tenth earl lived through the most turbulent period of British history, the civil wars and political disputes that convulsed the three kingdoms of England, Ireland and Scotland between 1637 and 1651 and resulted in the abolition of the monarchy and eleven years of republican government. But the tenth earl did not merely live through these events; he was at the centre of them until 1649, although he never played a decisive role. His involvement was natural, given his social status: as a great nobleman and a member of the House of Lords he was inevitably drawn into the political debates and disputes. But he was never a principal player, probably because he always held middle-of-the road views, his overriding concern being to reconcile Charles I and his subjects by means of compromise.

The earl was born in October 1602, two years after the future king, Charles I, with whose fortunes he was to become so deeply involved. His early life was closely supervised by his father, even though the earl was a state prisoner in the Tower. Until 1615, he was educated by private tutors, who, it has been proved, did not include Thomas Harriott. During this time, he lived close to his father in the house on Tower Hill, where he kept a pet fox. Then, at the age of fourteen, he went to Cambridge, where he spent a year at St. John's College, at a cost to his father of £500, followed by two years at Christ Church College, Oxford. After this experience, he was sent abroad to complete his education by an extended European tour, which gave him a fluent command of French and Italian, and also a refined appreciation of art, from which grew his patronage of Anthony Van Dyck. His education was to good effect, since he was widely recognised as an intelligent young man of serious outlook. Not surprisingly, he entered public life very soon after returning home. In 1624, he was elected as one of the members of the House of Commons for the county of Sussex, and in the following year he represented the borough of Chichester. In 1626, however, he became a member of the House of Lords as Baron Percy. By the time he succeeded to the earldom on his father's death in 1632, he was well educated, had gained useful experience of public life and was at an age when he could expect advancement to more important roles.

This came not in politics, however, but in the navy, where major developments were initiated during the 1630s. These stemmed almost entirely from Charles I's determination to make the North Sea and the Channel British-dominated waters. This policy involved forcing Dutch fishermen to buy licences and the suppression of Barbary (North African) and Dunkirk pirates, who were the bane of England's merchant shipping and the towns and villages along the south coast. It was also intended to serve notice to other naval powers, especially France, of Charles's intention of becoming a force to be reckoned with in international relations. To realise this ambition required a considerable outlay of money which Charles did not have, and since he had resolved in 1629 to govern and to finance his government without recourse to parliament, he had no obvious means of raising the necessary capital. The solution he adopted was Ship Money. This was based upon the king's ancient right, which was not disputed, to commandeer ships and levy cash for shipbuilding in coastal towns in the event of emergency. In 1634, however, a levy to finance a royal shipbuilding programme was raised in the coastal counties, and from the following year until 1639 in the inland counties as well. Financially, it was hugely successful, raising no less than £800,000, but it was clearly stretching royal rights to the limit and beyond. Naturally there were objectors who believed that Charles was in effect giving himself the licence to expropriate his subjects' wealth and property. This led to the famous test case, the trial of the Buckingham-shire landowner, John Hampden, for refusing to pay the tax. In the end, the judges of the Court of Exchequer gave a verdict in favour of the Crown, but only by the narrowest of margins. Charles may have won a victory in court, but it was hollow and tended to advertise the essential illegality of what he was doing.

In non-legal terms, however, the levy was justified, since all the money was spent on constructing warships, including the aptly named *Sovereign of the Seas,* which at 1,500 tons and with 100 guns was the largest warship of its day and the first genuine three-decker. In fact, the fleet built by means of Ship Money marks a major advance in the concept of a Royal Navy. The general failure to recognise this is in part due to the distraction of the Hampden case, but also to the fact that in the 1630s the fleet achieved no spectacular victories, basically because Britain was not at war with any of her potential rivals. Licensing Dutch fishing vessels and chasing pirates was not really suitable employment for great ships of the line, which spent most of their time riding at anchor at the Downs, the naval station off Dover.

It was in this potentially very important sector that the tenth earl found his first major public role. In 1636 and 1637, he was given command of the fleet, a duty he took very seriously. He certainly chafed at the enforced inactivity, particularly as he felt Charles should have been pursuing an anti-Spanish foreign policy. He was also appalled by the corruption and inefficiency that characterised naval administration: whereas the ships were new and up-to-date, their crews were abused and short-changed in a disgraceful and damaging fashion. The long memorandum he wrote on the subject had no effect, other than to make him vow not to waste his time in future on unsolicited proposals for reform. In 1638, he achieved the summit of his naval career, the post of Lord High Admiral, that is, head of the navy. The appointment, however, was not for life but 'at pleasure', since the king was reserving the post for his second son, James, Duke of York, when he came of age.

But by 1638 a political crisis was developing in which all members of the political nation were to be caught up. It began in July 1637 with an attempt to conduct a service in St. Giles Cathedral, Edinburgh, using the new prayer book which Charles had prescribed for the Church of Scotland. It had been prepared with almost no consideration for the known beliefs of that church, and was nothing more than a slightly modified prayer book of the Church of England. Its attempted imposition had been long expected, and when it came it triggered what proved to be a revolution. Early in 1638, the National Covenant was drawn up and signed by a wide range of Scotsmen. It bound the signatories to resist the king's innovations and gave legitimacy to the group of nobles and ministers of the Kirk who seized control of the government in Edinburgh and began to raise an army to defend their cause.

Almost at once the earl became involved in the crisis. In July 1638 he became a member of the Scottish Committee, a group of eight members of the Privy Council created to consider the Scottish problem, and he immediately recognised how threatening it was. Charles resolved to fight force with force, and in March 1639 he went north with such troops as he could muster to attempt to suppress the revolt. In his absence, the earl was placed in command of all forces in southern England, that is, south of the Trent, and was made a member of the Council of Regency, which would take charge of the government in the event of the king's death. It is clear, however, that the earl had serious doubts about Charles's policy and had little confidence in or respect for most of his ministers. He was right, for the expedition was a fiasco. The king's forces comprised contingents supplied by the nobility and the trained bands (a select militia that had been developed since 1573) of the northern counties. Neither was enthusiastic, and they were no match for the Scottish army, which had been drilled into an efficient fighting force by highly experienced Scots officers with recent mercenary service in continental armies. Consequently, there was no battle, and Charles had to sign the humiliating Treaty of Berwick, which gave the Scottish leaders freedom to press on with their revolution.

The solution to the king's problem was obvious: to coerce Scotland, he had to have a proper army; this meant money, which could be raised only by taxation; and for this he had to have parliamentary consent. The upshot was what came to be known as the Short Parliament. Elected in March 1640, it immediately proved to be totally intractable, refusing to vote taxes until the grievances of its members had been addressed. As a result the king dissolved it in May. The earl was disappointed. He had welcomed the re-introduction of parliament to the process of government, but he believed that the Commons had adopted an unproductive strategy. He was convinced that, had they pursued a more conciliatory and less strident line, they would have got most of what they wanted.

The crisis deepened. Charles tried to raise the necessary money by borrowing, both from wealthy men at home and from foreign governments, but without significant success. The militias of the southern counties were called out, but they proved unwilling to go north, to the point of mutiny and desertion. Finally, in August 1640, the Scottish army crossed the Tweed and Charles was obliged to agree to the Treaty of Ripon, whereby the Scots would occupy Northumberland and Durham and be paid £850 a day for doing so until an agreement was reached. The recall of parliament was now unavoidable, and on 3rd November 1640, what became known as the Long Parliament began its life. Initially it was almost entirely an opposition body, such was the pent-up dissatisfaction with Charles and his conduct of government. There was an almost universal determination to get rid of the king's ministers and to bring about changes in the government of both state and church, which would restrict the power of the Crown to act unilaterally and without the involvement of parliament. Although virtually all members of the Commons favoured change, debates were dominated and business was driven by the more radical members and above all by John Pym, who led the opposition until his death in 1643. He was primarily responsible for what amounted to a revolution in the course of 1641 with Charles on the sidelines as a virtually helpless spectator.

In the course of this tumult, the earl gradually moved from being a member of the king's government, as a Privy Councillor and Lord High Admiral, to being a member of the opposition. In February 1640, however, he was still on the king's side and Charles appointed him commander of the army he was attempting to create for the invasion of Scotland, which meant that for the time being the earl was head of both land and sea forces. Moreover, at this point he was amongst the few men prepared to advance money to the king to finance military action against the Scots. In August, however, he resigned his command of the army on the grounds of ill health, although whether his indisposition was genuine or diplomatic is not clear. Then, early in 1641, when the king's most able and energetic minister, Thomas Wentworth, Earl of Strafford, was impeached on a charge of treason, the earl gave an equivocal performance. On the one hand, he refused to corroborate the charge made by Sir Henry Vane that Strafford had advocated using the army he had raised in Ireland while Lord Lieutenant there in the 1630s to crush the Scottish rebellion and restore Charles to full authority in England. At the same time, he declined to deny that in the meetings of the Scottish Committee Strafford had urged the use of arbitrary measures to deal with the crisis. In the end the impeachment failed through want of evidence, and Pym, who had an implacable hatred of Strafford, had to resort to judicial murder through the device of an act of attainder. Although the earl opposed this extreme solution, the more so since he and Strafford had agreed about many aspects of policy, it was clear that he had entered the opposition camp, where he immediately performed a service of important though generally unrecognised value. He was still Lord High Admiral, and when the king refused to appoint a notable opposition peer, the Earl of Warwick, as commander of the fleet, he obeyed parliament's order by appointing Warwick as his vice-admiral and allowing him to take command of the ships anchored off Dover. When in June 1642 the king belatedly dismissed Percy from office, it was too late. The navy that Charles had created was now firmly in the service of his opponents, and the royal fighting capability was thereby significantly reduced.

The civil war in England formally began on 22nd August 1642, when Charles unfurled his standard, the traditional signal for announcing hostilities, at Nottingham. But weeks before that parliament had begun to form its own army under the command of the Earl of Essex and had created a number of executive committees, most notably the Committee of Safety, whose main purpose was to ensure that the army had the resources it needed. The earl was immediately made a member of this crucial body. Why had he so firmly allied himself to the opposition cause? The cynical view would be that he rowed with the tide, and it is true that he always appeared on the very moderate edge of the parliamentary opposition, so that when the monarchy was restored in 1660, he was readily forgiven by the new regime. But if this cynical view is rejected, then we should accept that his expressed concern to find a peaceful, compromise solution was genuine. As he said in May 1642, a few weeks before the outbreak of war, 'God forbid that either king or parliament should by power and force go about to cure the present distempers, for that course can produce nothing but misery, if not ruin, both to king and people'. It is also clear from his speeches and writings that he had no wish to see the king's prerogative destroyed or curtailed. Yet at the same time, he was equally clear that the privileges and rights of parliament and the rights in law of the subject should not be infringed. The fact that he came to range himself with the opposition would seem to indicate that he saw Charles's actions and beliefs as threatening this desirable and necessary balance. And he presumably continued in this belief since, unlike many

9. ALGERNON PERCY, 6TH DUKE OF NORTHUMBERLAND 1810–1899 (GUSTAV POPE).
A deeply religious man, he became committed to the Catholic Apostolic Church
(wrongly called the Irvingite Church) through the influence of his wife's father,
the banker, Henry Drummond. *The Duke of Northumberland. Photograph:
Photographic Survey, Courtauld Institute of Art. Also Plates 10–16.*

10. HENRY PERCY, 7TH DUKE OF NORTHUMBERLAND 1846–1918 (SIR EDWIN POYNTER). He had an undistinguished political career, serving as MP for North Northumberland and briefly as Treasurer of the Household. His eldest son, Lord Warkworth, showed much greater promise, but died in 1909 at the early age of thirty-eight.

11. Alan Ian Percy, 8th Duke of Northumberland 1880–1930 (Philip de Laszlo 1927). After a military career in which he saw action in South Africa, Sudan and the First World War, he became an outspoken and controversial political figure in the 1920s.

12. HENRY GEORGE PERCY, 9TH DUKE OF NORTHUMBERLAND 1912–1940 (SIR OSWALD BIRLEY 1947). His promising political career was cut short by the outbreak of the Second World War. Tragically, he was killed in May 1940 during the withdrawal of the B E F to Dunkirk.

13. HUGH PERCY, 10TH DUKE OF NORTHUMBERLAND 1914–1988 (SIR OSWALD BIRLEY 1946). He inherited the title in 1940 as the result of his brother's death in action. After 1945 he successfully undertook the restoration of the estates after the neglect and disruption of the war years. He was the last Duke of Northumberland to be buried in Westminster Abbey.

14. HELEN, 8TH DUCHESS OF NORTHUMBERLAND 1886–1965 (PHILIP DE LASZLO 1916). She was the youngest daughter of the 7th Duke of Richmond. She outlived her husband by thirty-five years and did much to sustain the family during the difficult years of the 1930s and 1940s.

15. ELIZABETH, 10TH DUCHESS OF NORTHUMBERLAND (SIR OSWALD BIRLEY 1947). Lady Elizabeth Montague-Douglas-Scott, the elder daughter of the 8th Duke of Buccleuch, married the 10th Duke in 1946. She and the Duke had three sons and three daughters. As dowager duchess she continues to be active in Northumbrian life.

16. THE SONS OF THE 10TH DUKE (MOLLY BISHOP 1977). At the top is Henry, later 11th Duke of Northumberland, who died aged forty-two in 1995. Below are (left) Ralph, the present (12th) duke and his brother, Lord James Percy.

17. RALPH AND JANE PERCY, 12TH DUKE AND DUCHESS OF NORTHUMBERLAND. They succeeded to the title in 1995 on the death of his elder brother. They have two sons and two daughters. *The Northumberland Estates*

members of the Long Parliament who began by opposing the king and then became staunch royalists, the earl remained a committed opponent of Charles I.

The civil war lasted for almost four years, until June 1646, when the king's defeat was signalled by the surrender of his last stronghold, Oxford. Until late 1643, however, his armies were in the ascendant and at one stage he seemed close to victory. One consequence of this was the visit to the royal court at Oxford of a parliamentary commission with a remit to seek a negotiated settlement. The earl was a member of this group and his commitment to a peaceful solution was at this stage so evident as to arouse the suspicion that he was a covert royalist. In April, a letter he had written to his wife was opened illicitly by Henry Marten, an M.P. who was convinced that it would reveal evidence of the earl's duplicity. It did not. But Marten refused to apologise, presumably still convinced that he was right, and for once the earl's temper snapped and he laid about the trespasser with his cane, even though they were in the precincts of parliament. A few weeks later the earl again fell under suspicion of being party to a royalist plot, but here too there was no evidence, and his name was cleared. Nevertheless, the earl was sufficiently upset or unnerved to feel it wise or necessary to retire to his estate at Petworth. This too raised doubts about his loyalty and fears that he was about to change sides. Whether he seriously contemplated doing so is unclear. What is certain is that he did not do so, and after a few months he returned to political life at Westminster.

Meanwhile, the threat to the parliamentary cause had become sufficiently serious for John Pym and the leadership to enter into an alliance with the Covenanter government in Scotland which they styled the Solemn League and Covenant. One consequence of this was that Scottish members were added to the Committee of Safety, whose title was changed to the Committee of Both Kingdoms. When the earl returned from his brief, self-imposed exile he became a member of this body. More important, however, was that in January 1644, under the terms of the alliance, a large and well-equipped Scottish army invaded England. In the course of that year it played a significant role, firstly, in the parliamentary victory at Marston Moor near York in July, which destroyed the northern royalist army commanded by the Marquis of Newcastle; and then in October, by forcing the surrender of Newcastle upon Tyne, which effectively ended the king's hopes of controlling the north of England.

In the following month, another effort was made to persuade the king to agree to a peaceful solution, and almost inevitably the earl, as a member of the Committee of Both Kingdoms and a committed advocate of negotiation, was appointed to the commission that met with Charles at Uxbridge. But again the king could not be pinned down, and the negotiation was aborted. Failure to obtain a settlement resulted in a hardening of attitudes, one momentous consequence of which was the reorganisation in the spring of 1645 of parliament's three main armies into a single, national, professional force, the New Model Army. Its commander-in-chief was Sir Thomas Fairfax, with Oliver Cromwell as Lieutenant-General in command of the horse. It is clear that the earl supported this move, which probably indicates that after the failure of the Uxbridge talks he too had become more pessimistic about the prospect of getting Charles I to agree to any sort of compromise settlement. Also in the spring of 1645 the earl was appointed guardian of the younger royal children, whom he lodged at his house at Syon. This may explain the rumour that Charles was to be deposed and that his young son, Henry, Duke of Gloucester, was to be made king with the earl acting as Lord Protector during the minority. Behind this rumour may have been a recognition of the earl's rising impatience with the king, but also of his good standing and reputation for disinterested honesty in the eyes of all parties.

The formation of the New Model Army had disastrous consequences for the royal cause. In the twelve months that followed, the king's forces were beaten on all fronts, and in early May 1646 Charles conceded defeat by giving himself up to the Scottish army camped near Newark. The end of the fighting did not mean peace, for it did not produce a political settlement. Charles remained determined to avoid making any concession that would restrict the Crown's authority and his enemies were hopelessly divided. There were now three distinct groups opposed to the king: the Scottish government in Edinburgh, with its army controlling northern England; the English parliament in Westminster; and the New Model Army, which was rapidly emerging as a separate political force with its own agenda. Making the situation doubly complex were disunity and the disputes that deeply divided all three groups. The confusion this caused is reflected in what happened to the king. He was held by the Scottish army until February 1647, when the Scottish government handed him over to the English parliament in return for the money they needed to pay their troops. As a result, he was transferred from Newcastle to Holdenby House in Northamptonshire as a prisoner of the English parliament. Then, in early June, he was seized by a force of five hundred horse of the New Model Army led by a very junior officer, Cornet (2nd Lieutenant) George Joyce, who was probably acting under secret orders from Oliver Cromwell. He was taken first to Newmarket, where the Army was encamped, and then to Hampton Court. There, the watch on him was so slack that in November he was able to abscond to the Isle of Wight where, although a prisoner of the governor of Carisbrooke Castle, he had considerable freedom of action.

The king's captivity at Hampton Court meant more frequent contact between him and the earl, who had to accompany the royal children when they made the short river journey from Syon House to visit their father. It was on one of these occasions that Charles is reputed to have tempted the earl to change sides by offering to arrange for his second son, James (the future James II), to marry one of the earl's daughters. The offer was declined, but the fact that it was made is testimony to the earl's standing and reputation. The earl, however, was unhappy with his role and asked parliament to relieve him of it even though it was worth £7,500 a year. This lack of enthusiasm probably explains the escape of James from the earl's custody and thence to Holland.

The equally loose supervision of the king made it possible for him to negotiate an agreement known as the Engagement with the Scottish government, which was becoming increasingly alarmed by the military power of the New Model Army and its hostility to the presbyterian form of church government, to which the Covenanters fiercely and firmly adhered. By the terms of this agreement, the Scots undertook to invade England, and in conjunction with royalist uprisings, to restore Charles to his thrones, in return for which he would allow the Church of England to have a presbyterian government for a three-year trial period. The consequence was the second civil war, which was a total disaster for the royal cause. The uprisings in England and Wales were put down without great difficulty, and in August 1648, the invading Scottish army was comprehensively defeated at Preston by the New Model Army commanded by Cromwell.

It was now the turn of the English parliamentary leaders to try yet again to reach an accommodation with the king, and this time they met with success. Both parties were by now fearful of the growing power of the army, and this served to concentrate their minds. As usual, the earl was a member of the commission that held talks with the king in late September and early October 1648 in the grammar school at Newport on the Isle of Wight. The main clauses of the agreement are not only of national importance, but also interesting in that they probably represent the core of the earl's thinking about the needs of the constitution. They were: a fresh parliament every three years; parliamentary control over the militia and the appointment of ministers of state for twenty years (in effect the remainder of Charles's reign); and the abolition of bishops for a trial period of three years, after which a committee of sixty clergy would settle the form of government of the Church of England.

But it was too late. To the New Model Army and some of the more radical members of parliament, the renewal of war by Charles I was an inexcusable act. For them their victory over him was a sign of God's judgement, and therefore in restarting the war he had defied the Divine Will. King Charles I had become in their eyes 'Charles Stuart, that man of blood' who must be punished. Consequently, in December 1648, the New Model Army occupied Westminster, purged parliament of its known opponents and created the machinery for trying the king. Charles I was duly tried in January 1649 on a charge of flouting the law of the land and ruling in a tyrannical manner. It was inevitable that he would be found guilty and condemned to execution, which was carried out on 30th January.

These events brought Oliver Cromwell to power and drove the tenth Earl of Northumberland out of public life. He strongly opposed the trial and execution of the king, and during the 1650s he remained in retirement at Petworth, declining all invitations to sit in the parliaments created under the several constitutions that were devised for governing what was styled the Commonwealth of England, Scotland and Ireland. The events of 1649 and after were too extreme and radical for the earl's stomach, and he appears to have remained firmly wedded to the ideal of a monarchy restrained by law and parliament, or better still perhaps, self-restrained by respect for the law and the ancient constitution.

The Commonwealth was not a success. It became little more than the thinly disguised rule of Oliver Cromwell, and when he died in 1658, his place was taken, for want of better, by his son, Richard. He, unlike his father, had little appetite or capacity for government, and he resigned in May 1659. With the political situation sliding towards chaos, General George Monck, commander of the army in Scotland, intervened to restore order. This in turn paved the way for the restoration of the monarchy in the person of the exiled Charles II, which was increasingly accepted as the only possible answer to what had become a constitutional and political nightmare. The earl was among those who accepted the necessity of this solution, but he did not favour the idea of an unconditional restoration. Rather, he wished to see Charles II required to accept the conditions his father had agreed to at Newport twelve years earlier. To the end, it would seem, the earl retained his conviction that the power of the monarchy needed to be hedged about with restraints.

Despite this less than wholehearted welcome, Charles II signalled his lack of hostility to the earl by appointing him to membership of his Privy Council, making him Lord Lieutenant of Northumberland and giving him a prominent role at his coronation. This was not, however, the prelude to the earl's resumption of an active political and public life. He was now nearing sixty years of age and had no wish to leave his pleasant retirement at Petworth, where he continued to live until his death in October 1668. The fact that he was honoured in 1660 and 1661 and was allowed an undisturbed retirement is a testimony to the respect in which he was held, even by his opponents. In his *History of the Great Rebellion*, Edward Hyde, Earl of Clarendon, the leading adviser of Charles I and of his son, said, 'though his notions are not large or deep, yet his temper and reservedness in discourse, and his unrashness in speaking, got him the reputation of an able and a wise man'. And something of the same comes though in a letter written by Sir William Temple to the earl's son after his father's death. 'There was no man perhaps of any party but believed, honoured, and would have trusted him.' These would seem to be fitting and well merited epitaphs to what appears to have been an almost entirely honourable political career. That career had been spent largely in the south and concerned with events in the south. As a postscript it is worth noting that the tenth earl was not unmindful of his interests in the county from which he derived his title. Between 1635 and 1640 he took the opportunity of securing the estate of the dissolved monastery of Tynemouth where his fifteenth-century ancestors had founded a chantry. This comprised Tynemouth itself, seven adjacent townships and the fishing port of North Shields. It was there that he provided land on which a new parish church was built between 1654 and 1658 to replace the dilapidated building in the old priory precincts. This church, which is still in use, although substantially altered, is a very rare example of an Anglican place of worship built during the Commonwealth period.

ELEVEN

The Long Interlude

Charles Seymour, Sixth Duke of Somerset, 1662–1748 and
Elizabeth Percy, Countess of Somerset, 1667–1722
Algernon Seymour, Seventh Duke of Somerset, 1684–1750

When the tenth earl died in October 1668, the future of the House of Percy looked to be assured. Yet, less than two years later their world had fallen apart and the Percy name disappeared below the surface of the British aristocracy, not to re-emerge for eighty years, by which time their great estate had been broken up.

The tenth earl married twice. By his first wife, Anne Cecil, the girl to whom his father had shown such animosity, he had five daughters, only two of whom survived infancy. The countess herself died of smallpox in 1637, at the early age of twenty-five. For the next five years the earl remained a widower, but this condition could not be permanent since the only other possible source of an heir was his younger brother, Henry, who was still a bachelor and apparently without any inclination to marry. (In fact, he remained a bachelor until his death in 1659. He was also a staunch royalist throughout the civil wars, but it is uncertain whether this was a genuine case of divided loyalties within the family, or a deliberate move to ensure its survival.) The earl's second countess, whom he married in 1642, was Elizabeth, daughter of Theophilus Howard, Earl of Suffolk. She was ten years his junior, but was destined to outlive him by nearly forty years and to play a crucial role as his widow in directing Percy fortunes. This second marriage was successful in the way the first was not: in 1644, Countess Elizabeth gave birth to a boy, Joceline. Three years later, she had a daughter, Mary, but this child died in 1652 at the age of five.

Joceline Percy, however, survived the perils of childhood and in 1663 at the age of nineteen he was married to Elizabeth, the sixteen-year-old daughter of Thomas Wriothesley, Earl of Southampton. At the time of the tenth earl's death, Joceline Percy and his wife had already produced a daughter, Elizabeth, born in 1667, and the new countess was pregnant with what proved to be a son, Henry, born in February 1669. Thus, within a period of a few weeks, the old earl was replaced by what should have been his next but one successor. Before the year was out, however, the infant Henry was dead. In all respects this was a tragedy. But as high infant mortality was expected and accepted in the seventeenth century, and as the new earl and his countess were still in their early twenties, there was every reason to hope and expect that they would have many more children, including another heir. This did not happen, however, for in May 1670 the young earl, too, died of a fever while on a visit to Turin. With his death the earldom of Northumberland and the barony of Percy, which had been revived in 1557, became extinct. The estates of course remained, inherited by the earl's surviving child, Elizabeth, who was only three years of age.

In this situation it was almost inevitable that at least one male Percy would claim to be related to the dead earl and therefore to be the legal successor to his titles and his properties. The man who did so was a London trunkmaker, James Percy, who claimed descent from Sir Ingram Percy, third son of the fifth earl. His claim was heard by the House of Lords in June 1689, but was totally rejected as 'groundless, false and scandalous'. For his impudence he was to spend the remaining years of his life in prison.

Long before James Percy was condemned, however, the title 'Earl of Northumberland' was back in use. The recipient was George Fitzroy, the youngest of the illegitimate sons Charles II had by his mistress, Barbara Palmer (née Villiers), Countess of Castlemaine and later Duchess of Cleveland. George was born just after Christmas 1665, curiously and improbably, in the rooms of a Fellow of Merton College, Oxford. In 1674, Charles II, who looked after all his bastards well, created George Fitzroy, Baron Pontefract, Viscount Falmouth and Earl of Northumberland. Nine years later, in 1683, the last title was raised two rungs up the ladder of nobility to Duke of Northumberland. George Fitzroy was reckoned to be the best of Charles's illegitimate offspring and the one most like his father. He died in 1715 aged fifty, having enjoyed a successful career in the army and as a courtier. These facts, although perhaps of general interest, are of little relevance to a history of the House of Percy. What is important is that neither of his marriages, to Catherine,

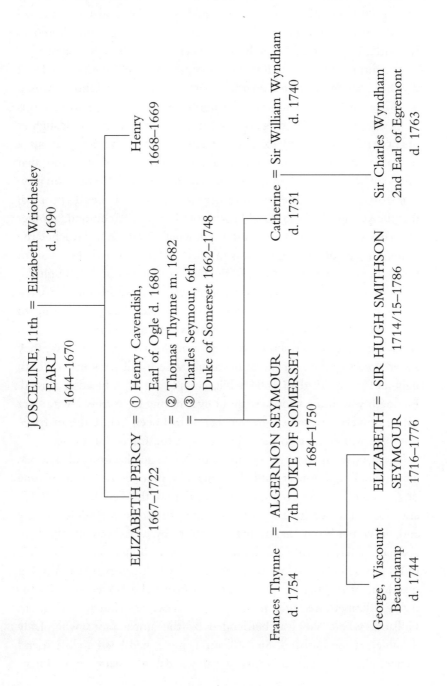

widow of Thomas Lucy of Charlecote in Warwickshire in 1684, and to Mary Dutton in 1714, produced any children. Had he had a son, and had that son grown to manhood, he would have inherited the Northumberland title, which would thereby have been lost to the Percy family.

The future of the Percy line now rested with the eleventh earl's infant daughter, Elizabeth, whose guardian was not her mother, who remarried in 1673, but her grandmother, the tenth earl's dowager. This lady was ruthlessly determined to ignore whatever wishes her granddaughter might have had and to exploit the girl's eligibility to bring about a revival of the Percy fortunes. As a result, the course of events that unfolded between 1679 and 1683 read like the plot of a Restoration play. The story began with the grandmother's rejection of Charles II's proposal that the young Elizabeth should marry the Duke of Richmond, another of his bastard sons. Instead, in June 1679, when Elizabeth had reached the minimum age of twelve, she was married to Henry Cavendish, Earl of Ogle, the sixteen-year-old heir of the Duke of Newcastle. Although this was a contract between families of apparently equal wealth and status, the Cavendishes agreed that the bridegroom should change his name to Percy. However, because of the extreme youth of the bride, it was also agreed that the couple should be kept apart for two years. In fact, they never lived together, for the bridegroom, who by all accounts was both ugly and sickly, died in 1684 while completing his education abroad. Elizabeth was thus a widow without ever having been truly a wife. Her value, however, was even greater than it had been before the marriage since she was entitled to her jointure from the Cavendish estate.

There now entered the villain of the piece in the form of Thomas Thynne of Longleat near Bath. Although a commoner, he had an income of £10,000 a year, hence his nickname 'Tom of the Ten Thousand'. He also was renowned for his profligacy; but at least he was adult, healthy and, it would seem, handsome. In 1681, by what was in effect an abduction, Thynne married Elizabeth in his own house using the services of his private chaplain, and without the knowledge or permission of her guardian, or making any of the normal financial arrangements. Fortunately, Elizabeth managed to escape from Thynne's clutches and get to Holland, where she was befriended by the ambassador's wife, Lady Temple, whose husband, Sir William Temple, had been a close friend of her father and grandfather. How this scandalous situation would have been resolved cannot be known, since in February 1682 Thynne was shot dead by a gang of three ruffians, two of whom were Swedes and the third a Pole. It emerged that they had been hired by a rival, a Swedish nobleman, Count Charles von Königsmarck, who also had designs on Elizabeth and her fortune. The hired assassins were caught, tried, convicted and executed, but their employer was acquitted, thanks to biased summing up by the judge at his trial, behind which almost certainly was the hand of Charles II. A rumour circulated that Elizabeth was privy to Königsmarck's plot and may indeed have been his accomplice; but there is no evidence that this was so and it seems highly improbable.

In a good play this should have been the cue for a happy ending for the abused heroine. But life was not quite so kind as the dramatist's pen. Late in 1682, Elizabeth, by now fifteen years of age, was married, although with considerable hesitation on her part, to Charles Seymour, sixth Duke of Somerset. Contrary to appearances, this was not a match between equals since, although the duke had a grander title, most of the Seymour estates belonged to the senior branch of his family, the Seymours of Berry Pomeroy in Devon. Consequently, for him, marriage to Elizabeth Percy was the route to a much needed fortune. The price he had to pay, which her family demanded, was that he change his name to Percy. Once married, however, Seymour reneged on his promise: in 1688, when Elizabeth attained her majority, her husband persuaded her to release him from his undertaking.

Although our interest must lie primarily with the duchess as the former Elizabeth Percy, her life cannot be properly understood in isolation from that of her husband. Born in 1662, Charles Seymour, sixth Duke of Somerset, was a prominent courtier and politician throughout the reigns of James II (1685–88), William III and Mary II (1688–1702) and Anne (1702–14). He first came to prominence in the reign of James II when he took an active military part in 1685 in putting down the rebellion of Charles II's illegitimate son, James, Duke of Monmouth, whose opposition to his uncle was based on the king's catholicism. As a reward for his contribution, Somerset was appointed Lord Chamberlain. His tenure, however, lasted only until 1687 when he was dismissed for refusing to carry out one of the duties of his office, formally presenting at court a newly appointed foreign ambassador, the papal nuncio, Count Ferdinand D'Adda. It is said that Somerset pointed out to the king that were he to do so, he would be breaking the laws against Roman Catholicism, and when James told him that this did not matter, Somerset retorted that breaking the law might not be a seroius matter for the king, but it was for him. In the light of his stand, it is not surprising that he was among those who signed the letter inviting William, Prince of Orange, the ruler of Holland and husband of King James's elder daughter, Mary, to come to England.

William's invasion and James's flight to France resulted in the so-called Glorious Revolution, which wrought significant changes in the constitutions of both England and Scotland. For the next twenty-five years, Somerset was at the heart of political and court life as the holder of numerous state offices, most notably Master of the Horse, which he held with only a short break from 1702 until 1715. The Master of the Horse was the third most senior officer in the royal household and was responsible for all matters relating to horses, carriages and hounds. The office was always held by a peer and he was a member of the ministry and the Privy Council. Throughout his time at Westminster and Whitehall, he was almost totally unswerving in his commitment to two causes. One was the continued exclusion from the throne of James VII and II, and after his death in 1701, of his son, James the Old Pretender, James VIII and III to his Jacobite supporters. As a result, he was loyal to William and Mary, and after William's death in 1702, to Mary's sister, Anne. Safeguarding the protestant succession became one of the central issues in politics following the death of Anne's last surviving son, William, Duke of Gloucester, in 1700. By the Act of Succession passed in the following year, it was laid down that the childless William III (his wife Mary had died in 1697) should be succeeded by Anne. After her death, the crown was then to pass to Sophia, the granddaughter of James I, who became Electress of the German state of Hanover upon her husband's death in 1698, or failing her, her son, Georg Ludwig. In the end Sophia died a few weeks before Anne, thereby opening the way for her son to become George I (1714–27).

The days following Anne's death were very tense, since some politicians and many others in the country would have preferred to have the Old Pretender as James VIII and III. It used to be thought that, together with the Duke of Argyll, Somerset saved the Hanoverian succession by bursting into a meeting of the Privy Council and forcing it to appoint the pro-Hanoverian Duke of Shrewsbury as Lord Treasurer. This is now known not to be true, although Somerset was nominated as one of the Regents, the group of ministers and leading politicians appointed to rule the country pending George I's arrival from Germany.

Somerset's other solid commitment was to the war against the France of Louis XIV. This had been the prime concern of William III whose native country, Holland, was threatened by French imperialism. But behind this was a greater problem: what would happen to Spain and her huge empire in Europe and in central and south America after the death of the childless Carlos II, especially as one of the two main claimants was Louis XIV's grandson, Philippe, Duc d'Orléans. When Carlos II died in 1700, Louis XIV recognised his grandson's claim to the Spanish throne, and the next year, following the death of James VII and II, the Old Pretender's right to the thrones of Great Britain. The consequence was the formation of the Grand Alliance of Britain, Holland, Austria and several smaller states against France and the outbreak of the War of the Spanish Succession, which lasted from 1702 until 1713. From the British angle the war was militarily successful, initially brilliantly so, thanks to the abilities of John Churchill, Earl (later Duke) of Marlborough. But as it dragged on without achieving its objective, it became politically divisive. In the end, the Peace of Utrecht, signed in 1713, was a peace of exhaustion that allowed Philippe, Duc d'Orléans, to become Felipe V of Spain.

Somerset retired from public life in 1715, although he lived for another thirty-three years. He was known as 'the proud duke', thanks to his highly inflated self-esteem, which was so great as to make him appear utterly ridiculous. Numerous tales were told of his insufferable pride and pomposity. For example, he would not allow his servants ever to have their backs to him, and on one occasion he even reproved his second wife when she playfully tapped him on the shoulder with her fan, with the words 'Madam, my first duchess would not have presumed to do that, and she was a Percy'. His high opinion of himself extended into public life, but alas it far exceeded that held of him by his political associates. His arrogance was such that he even entertained hopes of becoming head of the ministry during the political crisis of 1710, when the then Lord Treasurer and Marlborough's close political ally, Sidney, Lord Godolphin, was ousted. The duke was bitterly disappointed at being passed over. No one else, however, thought him worthy of consideration. Nevertheless, he retained high office longer than anyone and was in the cabinet for all but eighteenth months of Anne's reign. The fact was that he was an inveterate mischief-maker whom it was dangerous to ignore. He was seen as a man 'who acted more by humour than by reason' and who 'was rather a ministry-spoiler than a ministry-maker', and 'very troublesome if kept out of secrets, but more so if let into them'. In spite of, or perhaps because of, these adverse judgements, his fellow politicians clearly decided that it was safer to have him in the team than to leave him out. But this alone does not explain his permanent presence at the heart of politics, as will become apparent when we consider the parallel career of his duchess, Elizabeth Percy.

Elizabeth Percy, Duchess of Somerset, was equally involved in court and political life, especially with its female dimension. At the heart of this were the relationships between Princess, later Queen, Anne and her older sister, Queen Mary II, and two other women, Sarah Jennings, who married John Churchill, the future Duke of Marlborough in 1678, and Sarah's younger cousin, Abigail Hill, who by her marriage in 1707 became Abigail Masham. These relationships were of considerable moment politically, especially after Anne became queen, since Abigail Hill's second cousin was the ambitious politician, Robert Harley (later to become Earl of Oxford), who replaced Lord Godolphin as head of the ministry in 1710.

Sarah Churchill was without doubt one of the most beautiful women of her generation and was endowed with a keen intelligence and an acid wit, but also with an unquenchable thirst for power. Her great flaws, which were to prove fatal to her ambition, were an ungovernable temper and an inability to conceive that she could be wrong. Her friendship with the Princess Anne began in childhood, when Anne was five and she was ten, and it lasted until Anne became queen. Then their relationship began to cool and it gradually became so bitter and acrimonious that in 1711 Anne dismissed Sarah as First Lady of the Bedchamber, Groom of the Stole and Keeper of the Privy Purse. The core of the problem was Sarah's determination to run the queen's life and dictate her opinions and decisions. To that extent she was the author of her own downfall, but her removal from office also owed something to the intrigues of Abigail Hill, for whom she had secured a lowly post in the queen's household and who gradually insinuated herself into the queen's favour. It is a measure of Sarah's arrogance and lack of self-control that she had the temerity, verging on treason, to write to the queen accusing her of having a lesbian relationship with Abigail.

In the end it was Elizabeth Percy who gained from this three-sided quarrel. Her close relationship with Anne was not of recent origin either, but went back to the early days of the reign of William and Mary when, as the queen's sister, Anne, with her Danish husband, Prince George, occupied the apartments in the Palace of Whitehall known as the Cockpit. Princess Anne's friends included John and Sarah Churchill, now ennobled as the Earl and Countess of Marlborough, who took up residence at the Cockpit once Sarah became a member of Princess Anne's household. In 1692, however, William III dismissed Marlborough, his ablest general, on suspicion that he was in contact with the deposed James II, now living in France. This was probably true since Marlborough, like his wife, was extremely ambitious and so not prepared at that stage to discount the possibility of a Stuart comeback. Dismissal of the husband by the king was soon followed by the queen's demand that the wife too be dismissed, and that both she and her husband be required to leave the Cockpit. This was a gross insult to Anne to whom the apartments had been given by Charles II at the time of her marriage, as well as an infringement of her right to choose the members of her own household. In protest, she decided to withdraw from court, a symbolic act of defiance. It was in this difficult situation that the Duke and Duchess of Somerset came to her rescue by offering her the use of the great Percy house at Syon.

This act of kindness cemented what proved to be a lifelong friendship between Anne and Elizabeth Percy. She served in the queen's household throughout Anne's reign and upon Sarah Churchill's dismissal became First Lady of the Bedchamber and Groom of the Stole. More than that, it was she rather than Abigail Masham who was the queen's favourite companion in the last years of her reign. The secret of Elizabeth's success was simple: unlike Sarah Churchill, she did not try to dominate, but exercised her talent to influence and persuade in a far more subtle and tactful way. And there seems little doubt that she was able to influence the queen. Certainly, her political opponents were so convinced of this that they hired the poet and novelist Jonathan Swift to use his acid wit in an

157

attempt to undermine her reputation. In a piece entitled *The Windsor Prophecy,* published at the end of 1711, Swift produced the following lampoon:

> Beware of *Carrots* from Northumberland.
> *Carrots* sown *Thyn* a deep root may get
> If so they are in *Sommer set*
> Their *Conyngs mark* them, for I have been told
> They assassine when young and poison when old.

'Carrots' was an allusion to Elizabeth's red hair, but the main aim of the lines was to blacken her reputation by reviving the suspicion that she was in some way involved in the murder of Thomas Thynne nearly a quarter of a century earlier, and also to spread the idea that she was poisoning the queen's mind against her ministers. The queen was unmoved, and Elizabeth Percy remained close to her sovereign until Anne's death in 1713. Indeed, such was the queen's affection that she intended to leave Elizabeth half her jewels, a gift prevented only by the queen's failure to make a will. In the light of this closeness between the monarch and the duchess, it is not surprising that the duke was tolerated by those who had scant regard for his talents and his ridiculous airs. It was she, not he, who was politically important.

Elizabeth outlived her sovereign by eight years, dying of breast cancer on 23rd November 1722, at the age of fifty-five. As Lord Onslow said of her, 'she was in all respects a credit and ornament to the court', and because of this and of her undoubted political importance, her life deserves more serious attention than it has received. It is therefore a great pity that, following her death, her husband the duke chose to destroy all her correspondence with Anne, since this must have contained a great deal of revealing detail about court life and politics during the first decades of the eighteenth century.

Elizabeth Percy and her husband were also successful in producing children: in the course of the 1680s and 1690s they had seven sons and five daughters. However, such was the vulnerability then of human beings to disease and illness that only half of them survived. Happily, one survivor was their second son, Algernon, born in November 1684. From the time he reached his majority in 1705 until he succeeded his father as duke in 1748, he enjoyed a full and active life in the sort of roles a nobleman expected and was expected to play. He was elected to the House of Commons in 1705 for the Wiltshire borough of Marlborough, but in 1708 he secured a more prestigious county seat for Northumberland. In 1723, however, as a consequence of his mother's death in the previous year, he became Baron Percy and thereby able to become a member of the House of Lords. His elevation was based upon the false belief that he had inherited the title created in 1299; strictly speaking, that title was extinguished by the attainder of the first Earl of Northumberland in 1406.

Coming to his majority in a time of war, it was almost inevitable that he should have embarked upon a military career. He was present at two of the Duke of Marlborough's victories in the Spanish Netherlands, Oudenarde in 1708 and Malplaquet in the following year, when he acted as the duke's ADC. In the same year he was made colonel of the 15th regiment of foot (the future East Riding Regiment), but in 1714, the year after the end of the War of the Spanish Succession, he was given command of the 2nd troop of the Horse Guards, a post he held until 1740, when he assumed command of the entire regiment as colonel. Eventually, he got to the top of the army ladder: he was made brigadier in 1727, major-general in 1735, lieutenant-general in 1739 and finally general in 1747. He also held a variety of other government posts. In 1706 he was made Lord Lieutenant of Sussex and in 1710 Governor of Tynemouth Castle, posts he retained until his death. He was also Governor of Menorca (the Mediterranean island conquered by Britain in 1708 and not finally returned to Spain until 1782), from 1737 until 1742, when he became Governor of Guernsey, an office he held for the rest of his life.

In March 1715, Algernon Seymour, who as heir to the dukedom of Somerset bore the title Earl of Hertford, married Frances, granddaughter of Thomas Thynne, Viscount Weymouth who, ironically, was the heir of the notorious 'Tom of the Ten Thousand' who had so abused his mother. The new Countess of Hertford, however, was a very different character, having the reputation of being a morally upright bluestocking with a keen interest in literature: she wrote poetry herself and patronised such writers as William Shenstone and James Thomson. Because of this, and therefore more significant for the future of the House of Percy, her father-in-law, the sixth Duke of Somerset, developed an irrational but intense dislike of her.

The Earl and Countess of Hertford had two children. The elder was a daughter, christened Elizabeth but always known as Lady Betty, who was born on 26th November 1716 and was destined to be the central character in the inheritance crisis that blew up in the late 1740s. This followed the premature death of her brother, George Seymour, Viscount Beauchamp, who was ten years her junior and who, had he survived, would eventually have become the eighth Duke of Somerset in succession to his father and grandfather. But this was not to be. In September 1742, he embarked with his tutor on the Grand Tour to complete his education. Almost exactly two years later, at the age of nineteen, he died of smallpox at Bologna in Italy. Naturally, this caused his parents deep distress, but unnaturally, it threw his grandfather into an apoplectic rage, wherein he cast all the blame for the young man's death on to Lord and Lady Hertford. Although his attitude and behaviour were totally unwarranted and reprehensible, it has to be recognised that behind them lay an acute awareness that there was no direct male heir to the dukedom after his own death and that of Lord Hertford, whose wife was now too old to have more children. For a man with his overweening pride this was almost beyond endurance.

In this mood of anger and frustration, the ageing duke secretly approached the king, George II, and persuaded him to grant him the earldom of Northumberland with the right to settle his entire estate upon his other grandson, Sir Charles Wyndham, the son of his daughter, Catherine (by his second wife Charlotte Finch), and her husband, Sir William Wyndham, both of whom were dead. The effect would have been to disinherit his granddaughter, Lady Betty Seymour, who since 1740 had been the wife of Sir Hugh Smithson, the subject of the next chapter. The duke's plot was foiled at the last minute by Lord Hertford and Sir Hugh, who were able to convince the king that the duke's proposal contravened an earlier settlement, whereby the Northumberland estate, together with the title Baron Percy, had to go to Lady Betty. The king promptly withdrew his agreement to the duke's request, a position he maintained despite the duke's renewed application.

There the matter rested, much to the sixth duke's annoyance and frustration, until his death on 2nd December 1748. The following year, it was settled by two patents issued by George II in favour of the seventh Duke of Somerset, the former Lord Hertford. By the first, issued on 2nd October, the duke became Earl of Northumberland and Baron Warkworth, to which titles were attached the estates in Northumberland and Middlesex, including Syon House. Assuming that he had no male children (which was a certainty), upon his death both titles and estates were to pass to Sir Hugh Smithson and his wife, Lady Betty, and thereafter to their male descendants. The following day, a second patent created the duke Earl of Egremont and Baron Cockermouth. To these titles were attached the estates in Cumberland, Yorkshire and Sussex, including Petworth. Again, assuming that he had no male children, these titles and estates were to pass when he died to Sir Charles Wyndham and his male descendants. The dukedom of Somerset, however, was not involved in these arrangements: as a consequence of a much earlier settlement, it was inherited by Sir Edward Seymour, a direct male descendant of Edward Seymour, first Duke of Somerset, who was executed in 1552, and his first wife. There was one other important element in this complex solution: the title Baron Percy was to be inherited by Lady Betty in her own right.

These arrangements were accepted by all parties, and they came into force four months later upon the death of the seventh duke, on 7th February 1750. Shortly thereafter, by private act of parliament, the new Earl and Countess of Northumberland, the former Sir Hugh and Lady Smithson, changed their name to Percy. The House of Percy was in business again after an eighty-year vacation, but with an estate significantly different from its earlier structure.

PART THREE

Dukes

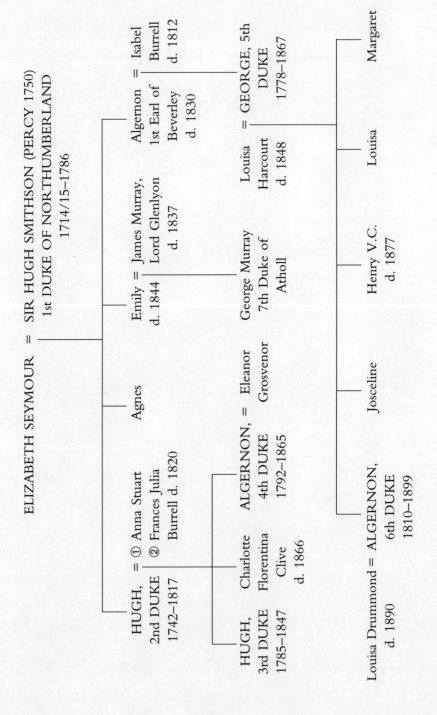

ELIZABETH SEYMOUR = SIR HUGH SMITHSON (PERCY 1750)
1st DUKE OF NORTHUMBERLAND
1714/15–1786

HUGH, = ① Anna Stuart
2nd DUKE   ② Frances Julia
1742–1817   Burrell d. 1820

Agnes

Emily = James Murray,
d. 1844   Lord Glenlyon
          d. 1837

Algernon = Isabel
1st Earl of   Burrell
Beverley   d. 1812
d. 1830

Charlotte
Florentina
Clive
d. 1866

HUGH,
3rd DUKE
1785–1847

ALGERNON, = Eleanor
4th DUKE   Grosvenor
1792–1865

George Murray
7th Duke of
Atholl

Louisa = GEORGE, 5th
Harcourt   DUKE
d. 1848   1778–1867

Louisa Drummond = ALGERNON,
d. 1890   6th DUKE
                   1810–1899

Josceline

Henry V.C.
d. 1877

Louisa

Margaret

164

TWELVE

Attaining a Dukedom

Hugh Percy (Smithson), First Duke of Northumberland, 1714/5–1786 and Elizabeth Percy (Seymour), First Duchess of Northumberland, 1716–1776

In 1740, the name of Percy had disappeared from view, absorbed into the stock of the Smithson family. Twenty-six years later, it not only re-emerged along with the ancient title of Earl of Northumberland, but it had been elevated to the highest rank in the social scale, a dukedom. This revival was the achievement of two people, Elizabeth Seymour, daughter of the seventh Duke of Somerset and granddaughter of Elizabeth Percy, and her husband, Sir Hugh Smithson Bt. Although much of the credit should be accorded to this couple, chance and accident also played significant parts.

Sir Hugh Smithson was of comparatively humble origin. Until the 1660s, the Smithsons were a family of landowners in the North Riding of Yorkshire, whose wealth did not permit its head to style himself more than esquire. Their social advancement began with the marriage of the then Hugh Smithson Esq. and Eleanor, the daughter and heir of George Catterick of Stanwick, which thereafter was the Smithsons' family seat. Equally important was the title 'baronet', conferred upon Hugh Smithson in 1663 by Charles II as a reward for Smithson loyalty to the royalist cause during the civil war and the years of the Cromwellian regime.

Sir Hugh was the third baronet. He was born on 19th December in 1714 or 1715, but at that point he was not destined to inherit either the title or the estates, since his father, Langdale Smithson, was a younger son. However, Langdale's elder brother, Hugh, died unmarried, followed soon after by Langdale himself. Consequently, when his grandfather, the second baronet, died in 1733, Hugh inherited both title and estate at the age of eighteen. At that time his income was reckoned to be around £4,000 a year, but it was soon to be almost doubled as the new baronet was the heir of an aged, distant relative, another Hugh Smithson, of

165

Tottenham in Middlesex. As a result of his good fortune, Sir Hugh Smithson, the third baronet, was able to enter the marriage market with a respectable income and attractive prospects. And, by all accounts, he was also extremely handsome in appearance and had polished manners. These assets proved to be sufficiently attractive to the young Elizabeth Seymour, and equally important, acceptable to the head of her family, the aged sixth Duke of Somerset, who showed very little interest in his granddaughter's marriage. Union with a mere baronet might seem to have been a mismatch, but it needs to be remembered that in 1740, when the marriage took place, Elizabeth's brother, Viscount Beauchamp, was still alive and well and guaranteeing the continuation of the Seymour male line. As we have seen, however, fate in the form of smallpox intervened, and ten years after her marriage Elizabeth Seymour became Elizabeth Percy, Countess of Northumberland.

Elizabeth's husband, the new earl, was thirty-five years of age and already much involved in public life. In 1738, he had been pricked as High Sheriff of Yorkshire and two years later he was elected as Tory MP for the county of Middlesex. His success in securing the necessary votes in what by eighteenth-century standards was a large electorate was in fair measure due to the active canvassing of his young and attractive wife. Smithson retained the seat for ten years, relinquishing it on becoming Earl of Northumberland and so entitled to a seat in the House of Lords. With his new status and great wealth he could look forward to advancement at court and in politics, provided he displayed the right qualities of character and discretion. By 1753, he had clearly passed muster, since in that year he was made a Lord of the Bedchamber by George II and Lord Lieutenant of Northumberland; and three years later he became a Knight of the Garter.

After 1760, however, he came more to the fore in public life, largely as a result of the upheavals following the death of George II and the accession of his twenty-two-year-old grandson as George III (George II's eldest son, Frederick, Prince of Wales, the new king's father, had died in 1751). The politics of the 1760s were the turbulant and convoluted workings of the political system that had evolved since the Hanoverian succession in 1714 following the death of Anne. In the last quarter of the seventeenth century, politics had gradually taken the form of a struggle between two clearly identifiable parties, Whig and Tory. During Anne's reign the Tory party had been dominant, but since 1715 it had been permanently out of office and in opposition. The fundamental reason for this was that the Whigs 'captured' the king in that they were able to convince both George I (1714–27) and George II (1727–60) that, as the unreserved champions of the Hanoverian succession, they were the only safe political option. They also portrayed the Tories as a Jacobite party. Although this was an over-simplification, there was sufficient truth in it to make both monarchs cautious, especially as the Jacobite threat was real enough. The uprisings of 1715 and 1745 were both intended to coincide with the invasion of Britain by a French army, and even without this aid, that of 1745 came very close to success. Most Britons probably had little liking for the prospect of 'James VIII and III', but this did not mean that they had great enthusiasm for the Hanoverians.

Through their influence over the Crown, the Whig ministers were able to control the patronage system, thereby ensuring that most state employment, whether at Westminster or in local government, was in the hands of men of Whig allegiance. It has been calculated that by 1760 no fewer than 260 MPs were 'placemen', that is, they were the holders of Crown posts and were therefore tied to the ministry which dictated the way they spoke and voted in the Commons. Whig control of power was further assisted by the Septennial Act of 1716, which extended the life of that and subsequent parliaments from three to seven years, thereby reducing the Tory party's opportunities for regaining power through victory at the polls. The Whigs, however, were never a monolithic party, but rather a coalition of groups, each centred on a leader, who was in most cases a magnate able to control or strongly influence elections in many constituencies. Jealousy, suspicion and rivalry tended to make the links between these groups tenuous and temporary, and this underlying tendency to fissure became more pronounced after the retirement in 1742 of Sir Robert Walpole, who had dominated political life since the 1720s, and the end of the Jacobite threat in 1746.

The other significant feature of the period between 1740 and the early 1760s was war. Throughout these years, Britain was at war for two-thirds of the time in what are known as the War of Austrian Succession (1739–48) and the Seven Years' War (1756–63). They were phases in an ongoing European conflict and at the same time world wars. On the continent of Europe they were essentially contests between three major powers: France, Austria and Russia. Britain was less involved physically, although she did provide her allies with immense financial support. In both wars there was some tension between Crown and ministry. George II's primary concern was for the safety of his other 'kingdom', the Electorate of Hanover, and with good reason since one major consequence of the fighting was the emergence as a great power of a rival German state, Prussia. The king's ministers, on the other hand, were increasingly convinced that Britain's war aims should be directed towards expanding her overseas empire, which meant conflict with the two other imperial nations, France and Spain. In the second of these wars, under the leadership of William Pitt the Elder, Britain was to have spectacular success, virtually eliminating French influence and presence in both India and North America.

The accession of George III in 1760 threw what was a basically unstable system into turmoil. Young and idealistic, George loathed his grandfather and the politicians of the 1750s, on account of what he saw as their cynical and unscrupulous manipulation of the system for their own ends. His ambition was a government free of corruption and party strife run by men disinterestedly devoted to the public good. This high-flown attitude was fostered and enhanced by John Stuart, third Earl of Bute, one of his father's close friends, who was appointed as his tutor in 1755. Bute, who was devoid of political experience, gave his future sovereign a pedantically academic education. Although valid in its own terms, this was a poor preparation for a man of the world, which any king needed to be. This might not have mattered too much had George not been so attached to Bute and looked to him for guidance, and had Bute not harboured political aspirations above his qualifications.

The first decade of the reign was therefore a time of political upheaval and short-lived ministries. The great war leader, Pitt, resigned in 1761 and was replaced as the king's first minister by Bute. After holding office for less than two years, he resigned in 1763 on the verge of a nervous breakdown. His replacement was George Grenville, an astute political operator and an able administrator, but unfortunately a man given to lecturing the king, which induced mounting royal irritation. George soon found the situation so intolerable that his foremost concern became Grenville's removal and the return of Pitt. Grenville, however, was not so easily shifted, and it was not until the summer of 1766 that the king succeeded in his aim. Unfortunately, by that time Pitt was in poor health, and he further reduced his scope for controlling the Commons, which he had been able to dominate earlier in his career, by taking a peerage as Earl of Chatham.

From this turmoil the Earl of Northumberland at first gained considerably, particularly from his close association with Bute, whose daughter, Anna, married the earl's heir, Hugh, in 1764. In 1762, he was made a member of the Privy Council, Lord Lieutenant of Middlesex and Chamberlain of the Queen's Household (George III had married Charlotte of Mecklenburg-Strelitz in September 1761). The following year, 1763, he was appointed Lord Lieutenant and Viceroy of Ireland, a prestigious post then worth £20,000 a year, and none too arduous in that the holder was required to reside in Dublin only during the sessions of the Irish parliament. As this met for about six months every other year, the Viceroy could expect to spend much of his time in Britain. The earl reputedly discharged his duties, many of which were social and ceremonial, with due magnificence, but his tenure lasted only two years.

In the spring of 1765, he became a casualty of a clumsy and bungled attempt by the king to get rid of his hated first minister. Failure meant that Grenville, who had disliked the earl's appointment in the first place, was able to use his knowledge of the earl's involvement in the intrigues against him to insist upon his dismissal. It was at this time that the political game was so convoluted that in one of the many schemes that were mooted, the earl was considered as a possible head of the ministry in place of Grenville. Had this happened, his lack of political experience would have meant that his leadership would have been little more than nominal, but that he was considered at all testifies to the political instability of the time and to the king's desperate dislike of his first minister. A few months later the king was able finally to rid himself of his incubus. The new ministry was ostensibly headed by an even younger man than the earl, Thomas Wentworth, Marquess of Rockingham, but the real power lay with the king's uncle, William, Duke of Cumberland, the victor of Culloden. However, one of the conditions laid down by all who agreed to serve in this ministry was that Bute and his associates should be totally excluded from office, and this included the earl, who was widely regarded as nothing more than Bute's front man.

The Rockingham ministry lasted only until the summer of 1766, when the king at last persuaded Pitt to return to office in a ministry nominally headed by Augustus Fitzroy, Duke of Grafton (who was descended from another of Charles II's bastard sons by Barbara Palmer). One of Pitt's aims was to achieve the king's ideal of a broadly based ministry embracing men from all political groups, including those linked with Bute. As a result the earl returned to the political fold and was proposed for the office of Lord Chamberlain of the Royal Household. But this was blocked and the post was given to a slightly younger contemporary who had succeeded the earl as Lord Lieutenant of Ireland, Francis Seymour, Earl of Hertford, a cousin of Sir Edward Seymour who became eighth Duke of Somerset in 1750 upon the death of Lady Betty's father. The earl protested vehemently, arguing that his services entitled him to preferential consideration. To no avail, for the very basic reason that Hertford's wife, Isabella, was daughter of the previous Duke of Grafton: clearly the old rules of the political game were still in force.

The earl's anger and injured pride were considerable, and they had to be assuaged lest he become an active opponent of the ministry. The sweetener, conferred on 22nd April 1766, was the titles of Earl Percy and Duke of Northumberland. The king was far from happy at being pressed into conferring such an exalted title and proposed the lower rank of marquess. Percy declined to accept this compromise, arguing that the Percy name was far older than the proposed title which had first been used in the reign of Richard II. There was a certain cheek in this, seeing that until 1750 the earl's name had been not Percy but Smithson, and that his then title, baronet, was the most recent of all hereditary titles, having been introduced by James I. Nevertheless, Percy got his way, although not entirely. His real desire was to have the title Duke of Brabant, an ambition fanned and informed by his wife's detailed knowledge of and immense pride in her Percy ancestry. This title, which would have emphasised Percy links with the high nobility of Europe, was too much for anyone to stomach and he was persuaded to drop the idea.

As duke, Hugh Percy was to live for another twenty years, but he made little further impact on public life. In 1778, he was appointed Master of the Horse, and in the following year he laid claim to the office of Hereditary Great Chamberlain of England upon the death of Peregrine Bertie, Duke of Ancaster, basing his case on a descent on his mother's side from John de Vere, Earl of Oxford, who died in 1625. The claim was rejected in favour of that of Ancaster's two daughters, but five years later, in 1784, the duke did acquire the additional titles of Viscount Lovaine and Baron Alnwick, the first perhaps being some consolation for failing to become Duke of Brabant. There was more to this than mere aristocratic pride and hunger for honours, although these were real enough. Their serious purpose was to secure entry into the ranks of the nobility for the duke's younger son, Algernon Percy, on whom they were legally settled at the time of their creation, together with the Smithson lands in Yorkshire. Therefore, when the duke died in 1786, his younger son was handsomely provided for. Four years later, in 1790, his status rose still further when, as a reward for his support for the government, he was made Earl of Beverley. The separation of the Yorkshire estate was a significant move. The Smithson marriage had had the effect of reuniting the Percys with their county of origin. The duke's decision to use his lands there to endow a younger son and hopefully to found a cadet branch meant that the senior branch of the family would be firmly anchored in the county from which it took its title.

Out of this came the decision by the duke and duchess to make their main seat at Alnwick. This was not inevitable, since they could have elected to continue to be absentee landlords like their predecessors since the sixteenth century, using Syon as their country house and North-umberland House in the Strand as their London residence. Nor was the choice of Alnwick inevitable, since they owned two other notable castles in Northumberland, Warkworth and Prudhoe. Indeed, serious consid-eration was given to the former, but in the end location and history dictated that Alnwick should prevail. As a result, the great medieval castle, which had been allowed to fall into a dilapidated condition, was restored and refurbished to ducal standards. This included a splendid range of paintings, of which the duke and duchess were avid collectors, even to the extent of employing as their purchasing agent Sir Horace Mann, the British Minister-Resident in Florence, then the capital of the Grand Duchy of Tuscany. The duke also devoted a great deal of time and capital to raising the value of his Northumberland estates. Between 1750 and 1780, the annual income they generated rose from under £9,000 to around £50,000, although this included profit from the expanding coal industry as well as increased land rents.

The duchess died on 5th December 1776, her birthday, at 8pm, the hour of her birth: she was exactly sixty. In her heyday, she had been one of the grandest figures in London society, a Lady of the Bedchamber and (perhaps more importantly) a close friend of Queen Charlotte. She was a patron of writers, including Oliver Goldsmith and James Boswell, and wrote poetry herself. She had a reputation for enjoying the company of a wide range of people, while also being extremely fond of high ceremony and grand formal display. From 1752 until her death fourteen years later, she was an inveterate diarist, and what she recorded illustrates not only the life and personalities of the courts of George II and George III, but also the many places and events she saw during her frequent travels on the Continent. Among the highlights were a visit to Voltaire and witnessing, in May 1770, the marriage of the future King Louis XVI of France and the Austrian princess, Marie Antoinette. These travels were not solely for pleasure, but also on account of declining health.

The duke outlived her by almost ten years, dying in June 1786, aged seventy-one. He had lived most of his life at the centre of events, but he was more of a courtier than a politician. Although he was identified with the Bute group, he was never really a party man, having the wealth and social status that enabled him to act according to his own inclinations and convictions. This was particularly evident in 1767 when, even though he had only recently been made a duke, he voted against the Stamp Act, the government's first move to tax the American colonists, which was to have such momentous consequences. Educated at Oxford, he was a man with wide interests, including science and history as well as art. As early as 1736 he was elected a Fellow of the Royal Society and of the Society of Antiquaries, and from 1753 until his death he was a trustee of the British Museum. His greatest achievements, however, together with his wife, were the resurrection of the Percy name and the rooting of the family in Northumberland; and in so doing he laid the foundations of the modern House of Percy. In the course of his life Sir Hugh Smithson had come a long way: at birth he was the son of a younger son destined for London, where he was expected to train and then seek his fortune as an apothecary; he died a duke and one of the wealthiest men in Britain.

THIRTEEN

The American Connection

Hugh Percy, Second Duke of Northumberland, 1742–1817

In the late eighteenth and early nineteenth centuries, the Percy family twice became involved, although in very different ways, in the British colonies that became the United States of America. The first of these involvements concerned the second Duke of Northumberland, who was born Hugh Smithson on 28th April 1742, but became Hugh Percy eight years later, when his father changed the family name on becoming Earl of Northumberland. Upon the death of his mother in 1776, he inherited as her heir her personal title, Baron Percy, and he became the second duke on his father's death ten years later, a title he was to hold for thirty-one years, until his death in 1817 at the age of seventy-four. His career fell broadly into two phases.

The first of these, which lasted until the late 1770s, was military. After spending five years at Eton College between 1753 and 1758, he did not proceed to university or embark upon the Grand Tour. Instead, the Seven Years' War having broken out, he sought military experience with the British contingent sent to Germany in 1758 to reinforce the army of Prince Ferdinand of Brunswick, whose prime duty was to prevent George II's other 'kingdom', Hanover, being overrun by the French. He was almost certainly attached to John Manners, Marquis of Granby, who commanded the British contingent from the summer of 1759 until 1763. Granby was in fact a distant relation by marriage, being the husband of Frances Seymour, a daughter of the sixth Duke of Somerset by his second wife, Charlotte Finch. Percy is known to have been present at the great victory at Minden on 13th April 1759, and he may have taken part in the famous cavalry charge led by Granby, which was a major factor in another victory fourteen weeks later at Warburg. Granby was an outstanding divisional commander, who must have had a considerable influence on the young Percy, who was still in his teens. Among other things, Granby was renowned for his concern for the welfare of his troops, an aspect of command Percy was to copy.

Percy's enthusiasm for the military life was not shared by his father, however, since the duke was bound to be anxious for the safety of his heir, especially as he was not yet married. As a result, Percy did not get a commission in the army until 1762. His commitment, however, was genuine and he appears to have made a serious study of army organisation and the art of war. Because of this, but also because of his high social status, his advancement was rapid, much to the annoyance of equally competent but less well connected officers. He was immediately made colonel of the 11th regiment of foot and two years later, in 1764, he became ADC to George III. Then, in 1768, he became colonel of the 5th regiment of foot, a post he was to hold until 1784. The consequence of this long association was that when the seventy foot regiments of the British army were assigned county titles in 1782, the 5th became the Northumberland Fusiliers.

It was in these years that Percy again saw serious military action, this time in America. Following the end of the Seven Years' War, the thirteen colonies along the eastern seaboard of America gradually became a serious problem. In large part this stemmed from the victories of that war, whereby Britain acquired Canada, thereby removing the French threat to the American colonies and to their future westward expansion. The war had been expensive, and consequently the British government of the 1760s resolved to require the American colonies to contribute through taxation to the cost of imperial defence. But the population of the colonies was expanding and third and fourth-generation colonists felt that they were more than merely Britons abroad. Most significant of all was the stubborn determination of the king and his prime minister from 1767 until 1783, Frederick, Lord North, to subordinate the colonies to British rule, by force if necessary. But attitudes were not totally polarised. Many Americans remained staunchly committed to the British connection, even to the extent of migrating to Canada when the thirteen colonies achieved independence as the United States of America. In Britain, several leading politicians, most notably the Earl of Chatham, and a number of senior army and navy officers, were horrified by the prospect of using force against those they regarded as fellow countrymen.

Among those hostile to the drift of government policy were the first Duke of Northumberland and his son, although Colonel Hugh Percy was not prepared, as some others were, to resign his commission rather than serve in America. Consequently, although with considerable reservations, he sailed with his regiment late in 1774 to join the small British army at Boston under the command of General Thomas Gage, who shortly after was made Governor of Massachusetts. Percy arrived just in time to play a prominent part in the first military action of the War of American Independence, the Battle of Lexington, fought on 19th April 1775. In purely military terms, this was little more than a skirmish, but its symbolic significance was considerable. The event began on the previous day as an attempt by a detachment of 400 men sent by General Gage to seize the weapons the rebels had been accumulating at Concord, a town twenty miles west of Boston. Although the troops got through, most of the arms had been removed and they found themselves in a desperate plight with little ammunition and their retreat to Boston blocked by a growing number of American militiamen. The situation was saved by Percy (now Brigadier General), who was ordered to advance with 1,400 men to Lexington, some fifteen miles from Boston. Having met the exhausted survivors, Percy conducted a skilful retreat, harassed all the way by American sharp-shooters, who inflicted 273 casualties on the British force for a loss of only 93 of their own men. Their success in the face of professional troops gave American confidence a major boost.

Five weeks later, British strength was substantially increased by the arrival of reinforcements commanded by three major-generals, William, Viscount Howe, Sir Henry Clinton and John Burgoyne. Their first task was to secure Boston by removing the Americans from the high ground on the opposite (northern) bank of the Charles River from which, if not dislodged, they would be able to bombard the town. The engagement, which is known as the Battle of Bunker Hill, although it was actually fought on the neighbouring Breed's Hill, took place on 19th June and was another setback for the British forces. Although they succeeded in driving the Americans off the hill, the British suffered 1,054 casualities. These amounted to more than forty per cent of those who had taken part in the assault, a totally unsustainable casualty rate.

For some reason Percy was not present, but his regiment, the 5th, suffered more heavily than any other unit, losing 158 men. It is a measure of Percy's professional and humanitarian concern that he paid for the return home of the widows of the members of the regiment killed in the battle and gave them a sum of money when they landed in Britain. (His

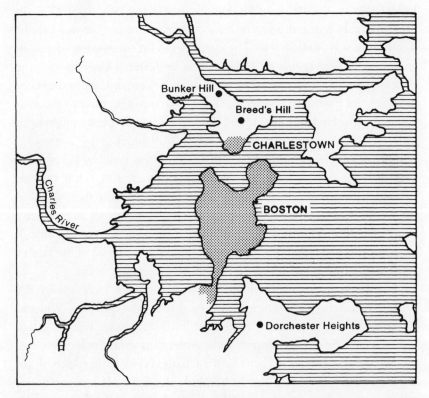

4 & 5.   Sites relating to the future 2nd Duke's role in the American War
of Independence

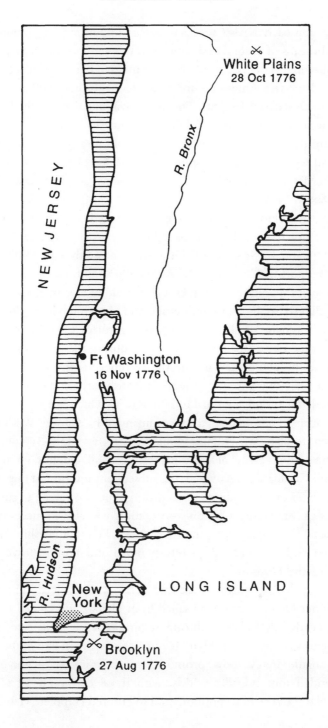

humane approach is also revealed by his opposition to flogging, the standard means of enforcing discipline in the eighteenth-century army.) The following March, he nearly became involved in a similar action, this time to drive the Americans from the high ground south of Boston known as Dorchester Heights. The assault was initially cancelled because of bad weather, but then abandoned as militarily impossible. American control of this ground made Boston untenable, and consequently Howe (who had replaced Gage as Commander-in-Chief) had no option but to abandon Massachusetts, at least for the time being, and withdraw his army to Halifax in Nova Scotia.

From there Howe planned a three-pronged assault by which he hoped, if not to win the war outright, at least to force the American rebels to negotiate. Sir Henry Clinton was sent south with 2,000 men to secure the port of Charleston, South Carolina, and then to re-establish control over the southern colonies with the aid of loyalist elements, who were believed to be both numerous and determined. In the north, General Burgoyne's task was to regain control of Canada, which had been occupied by a small American army during the previous summer. This done, he could then invade the colonies via the Hudson valley. Between these two extremes, the main British force was to secure New York and the mouth of the Hudson River, which were held by the newly formed Continental Army commanded by George Washington. If all went to plan, Washington would be defeated and the colonies split into three more easily defeated sectors. But all did not go to plan. Although Canada was recovered, the subsequent invasion of upper New York in 1777 ended in disaster when Burgoyne was forced to surrender at Saratoga. Sir Henry Clinton's expedition was also unsuccessful, but immediately: in failing to capture Charleston, he lost a warship and over 200 men and was obliged to return north and rejoin Howe at the mouth of the Hudson.

It was with this central thrust that Percy was involved. The British force under Howe's command sailed from Halifax and landed on Long Island in early July and on 27th August comprehensively defeated part of Washington's army at Brooklyn Heights at the western end of the island. In this battle Percy, now promoted to the rank of major-general, commanded four brigades which, with those of Sir Henry Clinton, outflanked the American positions and so ensured complete victory. But the victory was not conclusive, as Howe allowed the bulk of the American army to escape across the river to Manhattan Island.

Howe's next move was to advance with most of his forces northwards up the valley of the River Bronx, with the aim of cutting off Washington from the New England colonies, one of his main sources of supply. Washington had no option but to respond to this threat, and in the last days of October the two armies clashed briefly and inconclusively at White Plains. Percy was not engaged in this move as he had been left in command of a force to contain the American garrison in Fort Washington, a strongly fortified camp near the northern tip of Manhattan Island. This had to be eliminated, and on 16th November Percy commanded one of the four columns that assaulted the fort. The attack was a complete success, the Americans losing well over 3,000 men, mostly prisoners, at the expense of 458 British casualties.

These successes forced Washington to retire into New Jersey on the western bank of the Hudson River, leaving Howe in control of New York, Long Island and Manhattan Island. With his army depleted by desertions, Washington was pursued by Howe, who hoped to capture Philadelphia, the 'capital' of the rebel colonies. He was thwarted, however, partly by the onset of winter, but also by two surprise counter-attacks by the Americans which secured them victories at Trenton and Princeton, setbacks which caused him to abandon most of New Jersey. Overall, Howe had the better of the fighting, which is not surprising, given that his army was larger and made up of professional troops. But it was Washington who could claim real success. In spite of considerable difficulties, he had managed to keep his army in being and had avoided overwhelming defeat and annihilation. That he had done so was in part due to his determination and skilful handling of his limited resources, but his survival also owed something to the performance of the British commander. Howe was a competent general, but his approach was slow and methodical, so that on several occasions he allowed Washington to slip away when rapid and decisive action might have secured the total victory that would have put the American cause in serious jeopardy.

The war was to last for another five years, but Percy was not involved. By the end of 1776 he had developed a personal dislike of Howe, as well as having a poor opinion of his military ability. He therefore asked to be relieved, a request granted with some reluctance by the Secretary at War, Lord George Germain, and he arrived back in Britain in June 1777. It is difficult to apportion blame, but much must fall on Percy who, in George III's words, was a man of 'peevish temper' whose prickly pride made it hard for him to accept a subordinate role. His resignation did not end his military career, however. Shortly after his return he was promoted to lieutenant-general, and in 1793 he attained the rank of general. He also moved from the infantry to the more prestigious cavalry, becoming colonel of the 2nd Troop of Grenadier Horse Guards in 1784, then of the 2nd Troop of Life Guards in 1788, and finally, in 1806, colonel of the Horse Guards. But these were essentially honorary roles. He never again saw active service, although during the invasion scare in 1798, as Lord Lieutenant of Northumberland he raised the Percy Yeomanry from amongst his tenants.

His resignation did not affect the course of the war in America, which became increasingly international in 1778, 1779 and 1780 with the intervention of France, Spain and Holland on the American side. These countries recognised in Britain's difficulties an opportunity to regain some of the losses they had sustained at British hands in the Seven Years' War. Their interventions proved to be decisive: Britain's temporary loss of control of the sea off the coast of America in 1781 brought about the surrender, on 19th October, at Yorktown on Chesapeake Bay, of the British army commanded by Lord Cornwallis. Thereafter there remained only the protracted peace negotiations in Paris, which lasted until 1783 and from which the United States of America emerged as an internationally recognised independent state.

Although Percy's involvement with America had ended on a discordant note, it did have three small but agreeable by-products. One was the visit to Britain of the Mohawk chief whose Indian name was Thayandanegea but who also, because he was of mixed parentage, had an English name, Joseph Brant (1742–1807). He was known to Percy during the American war when he was the leader of the Iroquois Confederacy (also known as the Six Nations) who fought on the British side. After the war, he and his people settled in Ontario in Canada, where the town of Brantford was named in his honour. He subsequently visited Britain and stayed with the duke, as he had then become, at Syon House. It was here that the portraits of both the duke and Joseph Brant were

180

painted by the distinguished American artist, Gilbert Stuart (1755–1828), the son of an emigrant from Perth. Stuart came to Britain in 1775 and lived there until 1787, gradually building up a reputation as a portraitist until he was considered second only to Thomas Gainsborough and Sir Joshua Reynolds. The duke was also the dedicatee of a book, *Journey of 1000 Miles down the Ohio in 1809,* describing the Indians of that region. It was written by a Major John Norton who, although a British officer, had lived among the Indians, married an Indian wife and acquired an Indian name, Teyoninhokarawen.

After 1777, Percy's public life was in politics, although in contrast to his military career he was largely ineffectual. He returned to Britain shortly after the death of his mother, which meant that he had to vacate his seat in the Commons, where he had represented Westminster since 1763, and take his seat in the Lords. He did not become politically important, however, until he became the second duke on the death of his father in 1786. This gave him, under the unreformed arrangements for parliamentary elections, control over several seats in the House of Commons. Nominally a Tory, he nonetheless developed a deep dislike of William Pitt the Younger who, with a brief interlude between 1801 and 1804, was prime minister from 1783 until his death in 1806, and a liking for Pitt's leading Whig opponent, Charles James Fox. Consequently, he was seen as belonging to the opposition. In reality, however, he was not by nature a party politician with a great thirst for power. He never held any ministerial office, although it was thought that, had Fox become prime minister in 1789, the duke would have become either Lord Lieutenant of Ireland or Master General of the Ordnance. The occasion was the onset in November 1788 of George III's insanity, which provoked a constitutional and political crisis. Had the bill to make the king's eldest son Regent during his father's incapacity been passed, it is all but certain, given the son's well-known hatred of his father, that Pitt would have been replaced as prime minister by Fox. This did not happen, thanks to the king's return to health in February 1789. Pitt was saved, and the duke denied office. In normal times, the duke's chief concern seems to have been to see that the political world acknowledged his importance by consulting him on important matters. When this did not happen, he was highly displeased and complained bitterly. This was particularly the case in 1806 when, following the death of Pitt, the so-called Ministry of All the Talents was formed. In all of this can be seen the same personality traits he displayed in the army: prickly pride and an unquestioning sense of his own worth and importance.

If he failed to play any significant role in national politics, he was at least active in the affairs of his native county of Northumberland. He was Lord Lieutenant from his accession to the dukedom until 1803, when he resigned because of his disapproval of the government's military arrangements, although this did not deter him from raising a regiment of 1,500 men from his tenantry at his personal expense. And he was a good landlord, entertaining his tenants regularly when he was in residence at Alnwick and lowering their rents when farm prices fell sharply after the end of the Napoleonic War in 1815. In gratitude, his tenants raised the money to erect a tall column surmounted by a lion, which is still a prominent landmark in Alnwick. The lion's tail is straight, as is that on a similar statue now at Syon House, but originally on the pediment of Northumberland House in London. The idea for this feature is said to have been derived from Michaelangelo, but the statue is in fact a recognised heraldic device, a lion statant tail extended, that is, facing forward with all four feet on the ground. A very similar device, the lion passant tail extended, that is, facing forward with one leg raised, appears on several medieval Percy pennons. The story has an ironic ending: the duke concluded that, if his tenants could afford to pay for the column, they could afford higher rents, and he acted accordingly.

The duke had two wives. The first, whom he married in 1764, was Anna Stuart, a daughter of his father's early political ally, John Stuart, third Earl of Bute. How the marriage fared in its early years is unclear, but there were no children, and in 1779 Percy secured a divorce by act of parliament on the grounds of his wife's adultery with a Cambridge student, William Bird. For her he was clearly a bird of passage, since a few years later she married a German nobleman, Baron von Pöllnitz, the King of Prussia's chamberlain. The couple settled in New York, but not for long, for she then took up with a new lover, an American, Stephen Sayre. (It is possible that this was the same man who had been Sheriff of London and who had been thrown into the Tower for a brief period in 1775 on account of his violent anti-monarchical views.) Whatever Percy's faults as a husband may have been – and it is clear that he was not an easygoing man – the divorce must be seen as stemming largely from his wife's emotional instability. His second wife, whom he married a few weeks after the divorce had been granted, was Frances Julia, daughter of Peter Burrell of Beckenham in Kent, whose sister was already married to Percy's younger brother, Algernon. This marriage was successful in that it lasted until Percy's death in 1817 and produced what was expected of all such marriages, an heir to the inheritance.

The other link between the Percy family and the United States of America takes us back to the first duke, who in addition to his children by the duchess, had an illegitimate son, James, born in 1765. His mother was Mrs Elizabeth Macie, the granddaughter of Sir George Hungerford, who at the time of the birth had been widowed for the second time. Until 1800, James was known by his mother's name, but in that year he changed it to Smithson. He was an intelligent man with a strong leaning to scholarship. After an education at Pembroke College, Oxford, he became an internationally renowned chemist and mineralogist who published twenty-seven scientific papers. One of his main interests was calamines, as a result of which, in 1832, the name *smithsonite* was given to the mineral zinc carbonate. He spent most of his working life on the Continent and died in Genoa in 1829 at the age of sixty-four. In his will he bequeathed his estate to his nephew, Henry James Hungerford, with the stipulation that, should he die without issue, it should be sent to the United States to found the Smithsonian Institution, whose purpose was to be 'the increase and diffusion of knowledge among men'. When Hungerford died childless six years later in 1835, his estate was valued at £104,960. Surprisingly, perhaps, Smithson's generosity was not well received by everyone in America. In particular, acceptance was opposed by the southern politician, John C. Calhoun, who doubted the right of Congress under the constitution to accept such a gift. As Calhoun had been Vice-President, his argument carried some weight. It was successfully countered, however, by the man under whom he had served, John Quincy Adams, President of the United States from 1825 to 1829. The argument won, Adams and another leading politician in favour of acceptance, Richard Rush, came to Britain in 1838 to secure the right of the United States government to the bequest by means of a suit in the Court of Chancery. The money was then taken to Washington, where it was recoined into $505,318. This sum became the foundation endowment of the Smithsonian Institution, which finally came into being in

August 1846, when President James Polk signed its Act of Organisation.

Why did James Smithson choose to benefit the United States rather than his native country? Although there is no certain answer, there are several strong clues. One is that he lived much of his life, not in Britain but on the Continent in places such as Berlin and Paris, where he was able to meet and work with men who shared his scientific interests. And he is known to have had definite republican leanings, possibly as the result of his most impressionable years coinciding with the French Revolution, when monarchy was abolished, as it had been in America. Also, and perhaps more significantly, he is reputed to have said that he intended that the name Smithson should outlive the titles Northumberland and Percy. It would seem that the man born as James Macie was determined to get back at the family to whom he owed nothing save his birth. (The only money Smithson is known to have received from the Percy side was a bequest of £3,000 from Dorothy Percy, another of the first duke's illegitimate offspring.) To a considerable extent he succeeded since, although the titles are still very much alive, the Smithsonian Institution is more widely known as one of the world's pre-eminent scientific organisations. It is fitting that his remains were taken to the United States from Genoa for reburial at the Smithsonian in 1904 by Alexander Graham Bell.

FOURTEEN

The Nineteenth Century

Hugh Percy, Third Duke of Northumberland, 1785–1847
Algernon Percy, Fourth Duke of Northumberland, 1792–1865
George Percy, Fifth Duke of Northumberland, 1778–1867
Algernon George Percy, Sixth Duke of Northumberland,
1810–1899

Between 1817 and 1899, there were four dukes of Northumberland. Each was a unique person, but there were many aspects of their lives held in common, which makes it possible to consider them collectively as well as individually. All were educated, firstly at Eton College and then, with one exception, at St John's College, Cambridge; and all in later life had honorary degrees conferred by the Universities of Cambridge and/or Oxford, and in the case of the sixth duke, by Durham as well. All married the daughters or female relations of fellow aristocrats, none being tempted to marry actresses or American heiresses. But perhaps the most significant feature was their diminished involvement in central government: although all of them became members of the Privy Council, only one, and then for only a brief period, held cabinet office. Otherwise, their contributions to national life took the form of such things as trusteeships of the British Museum, the presidency of the Royal Institution and fellowships of the Royal Society and the Society of Antiquaries.

Their absence from political office should not be seen as part of a general lessening of aristocratic involvement in national government: a glance at the composition of any nineteenth-century cabinet reveals a prominent contingent from the ranks of the long-established nobility. Nor does it imply a total withdrawal from or lack of interest in politics: all four were members of the House of Commons prior to their succession to the dukedom, which removed them to the Lords. Until 1832, they had no difficulty in becoming MPs, as the result of their control of seven constituencies: one of the two seats for the county of Northumberland and three boroughs – Bere Alston in Devon, and Launceston and

185

Newport in Cornwall – each of which returned two members. All seven were in the first duke's patronage, but on his death Bere Alston passed to his second son, who became Earl of Beverley in 1790. This situation, which undoubtedly bestowed political influence, lasted until 1832, when the Reform Act of that year totally disenfranchised fifty-six of the smallest and most notorious 'pocket' boroughs and removed one member from thirty others. In this slaughter, Percy patronage was virtually wiped out: Bere Alston and Newport lost both members and Launceston was reduced to one, which is hardly surprising given that prior to the 1832 act these six West Country members were returned by electorates that averaged less than ten per member. Thereafter the sons of the dukes of Northumberland represented the county constituency of North Northumberland.

The ability of the senior members of the Percy family to enter one or other house of parliament, virtually at will, means that their failure to attain high office and to play leading roles in the direction of the nation's affairs must be put down to other factors. Of prime significance is that none was at heart a politician, and, partly because of this, none appears to have possessed in sufficient measure the abilities and capacities needed to gain and hold the highest political offices. In addition, there was also a certain lack of opportunity: the Percys were Tory (Conservative after 1835), but from 1830 until the end of the century, political power was in the hands of the Whigs (and their successors from 1868, the Liberals) for all but twenty-eight years. Above all, there was little material incentive, since their wealth was so great that the emoluments of public office were only marginally attractive to them. They were inclined therefore to find assured provincial dominance more attractive than competing for power nationally. Their circumstance and the outlook it induced are well summed up in a letter written by the second duke in 1797: 'my own situation in this country is much above what any office in the kingdom can give me. I have ample fortune and the general good opinion of my county to satisfy me, if I wish to be quiet; an anxious and hardy race of men, my tenantry, to back me and support me in troublesome times; and so far from wishing to seek office, it would require much persuasion indeed to prevail upon me to accept . . .'

This statement, suffused as it is with an air of comfortable self-satisfaction, is nonetheless an accurate portrayal of the standing enjoyed by the dukes for much of the nineteenth century. Evidence of their commanding social status in the region is perhaps most clearly revealed by what happened when they died. On the death of the third duke in 1847, the shops in Alnwick and Newcastle closed and respectful crowds lined the streets of the towns and villages through which the funeral procession passed on its way to join the special train that was to take the coffin to London for burial in Westminster Abbey. At the edge of the Town Moor, it was met by the Mayor and Corporation of Newcastle and the tenants of the southern district of the estate, who escorted it across the Tyne to the station at Gateshead. Similarly, when the fourth duke died in 1865, it is estimated that 7,000 people (which must have represented most of the population of Alnwick) filed past his coffin, while the announcement in a black-bordered *Newcastle Journal* averred that gloom and sorrow had descended on the North. By this date, the railway traversed Northumberland, and so the special train could start its journey at Alnwick. Nevertheless, crowds still came out, standing on station platforms at Newcastle, Durham and Darlington, while at York the passing of the train was signalled by the tolling of the minster bells.

The following lines uttered on the occasion of the tenants' dinner in 1859 are revealing:

> Those relics of a feudal yoke
> Still in the North remain unbroke:
> That social yoke, with one accord
> That binds the peasant to his lord . . .
> And Liberty, that idle vaunt,
> Is not the comfort that we want;
> It only serves to turn the head,
> But gives none their daily bread.
> We want community of feeling
> And landlords kindly in their dealing.

The tone may seem obsequious, but the sentiments express a clear-sighted appreciation that, of all the freedoms, freedom from want is the most basic, and that co-operation between landlord and tenant was to their mutual advantage.

It is clear, therefore, that the nineteenth-century dukes were more involved than their predecessors had been with their vast estate in Northumberland, which the third and fourth dukes enlarged, and in the life of the county. All of them held the office of Lord Lieutenant, which gave them great influence at elections, until the introduction of the secret ballot in 1872 and the widening of the franchise in 1884, and in the running of the county, until the removal of the monopoly of nominating justices of the peace in 1910. However, although all of them died at Alnwick, they restated their national stature by electing to be buried not there, but in the family vault in St. Nicholas' Chapel in Westminster Abbey, which they had inherited from their Seymour forebears.

The third duke was, like his father and grandfather, named Hugh. He was the fourth child but eldest son of the second duke and his second wife, Frances Burrell, and he succeeded to the title upon his father's death in 1817. Earlier in that year, he married Charlotte Florentia Clive, a daughter of Edward Clive, Earl of Powis, the son of Robert Clive, the famed conqueror of India. Although duke for almost thirty years, he did not contribute a great deal to national life. In 1825, he was the Extraordinary British Ambassador and the personal representative of George IV at the coronation of Charles X as King of France. His selection for this ceremonial role arose from his being a Lord of the Bedchamber and from his having carried the second sword at George IV's own coronation in 1821, although his willingness to bear the expense of this duty may also have been influential. He is said to have spent the enormous sum of £40,000, which allowed him to outshine some of the European royalty who also attended the ceremony. His reward from Charles X was a huge Sèvres vase, which is now at Syon House.

Four years later in 1829, he was appointed Viceroy of Ireland. Again financial considerations may have been significant, since he offered to do the job for a salary of £20,000 a year instead of the usual £30,000. His tenure of office was brief, lasting only until the following year. It was terminated by the political change resulting from the 1830 election. For over forty years government had been in the hands of the Tory party, but they proved incapable of responding to the rising demand for reform, not only of parliament, but of other institutions of government. From the beginning of 1828, the prime minister was the Duke of Wellington, an outstanding soldier and the hero of Waterloo, but in other respects an arch reactionary. It was his dated views that helped to ensure the victory of the Whigs, who were committed to reform, in the 1830 election.

The year 1830 also saw the death of George IV and the accession of his brother, the Duke of Clarence, as William IV. The change of monarch had interesting consequences for the Percy family, in that the duke ceased to be a Lord of the Bedchamber, while his duchess, Charlotte Florentia, came to prominence. The new king (who was already sixty-five) and his wife, Adelaide, had had two children, but both had died. Consequently, the heir to the throne was Princess Victoria, the daughter of the third of George III's sons, Edward, Duke of Kent, who in middle life had been persuaded to discard his mistress and to marry a German princess, Victoria of Saxe-Coburg-Saalfeld, the widow of Prince Charles of Leiningen. Victoria was born in 1819 and was therefore only eleven years of age when her uncle became king. The duchess was appointed to the post of Official Governess, the duties of which were to oversee the future queen's education and to accompany her when she attended court functions. However, the discharge of these duties was made difficult by the tension between the king, who expected to have some say in the upbringing of his successor, and Victoria's mother (her father had died the year after she was born). She not only intended to exercise complete control over her daughter's upbringing, but demanded, and got, formal recognition as Dowager Princess of Wales (with suitable remuneration) and the right to be sole Regent in the event of the king dying before Victoria attained her majority, which for royalty was the age of eighteen. Added to her ambition was that of her secretary, Sir John Conroy, who, it was widely believed, was also her lover: certainly the Duke of Wellington, when asked, 'supposed he was'. Conroy's aim was nothing less than to be the power behind the throne as Victoria's adviser, once she had become sovereign.

The Duchess of Northumberland was caught in the cross-fire. At first, Victoria's mother was delighted that the duchess accepted the role, since it was she who had put forward her name, believing it would enhance the status and dignity of the princess's little court at Kensington Palace. What she expected was that the duchess would adopt a passive role and regard her office as nominal. Charlotte Florentia, however, was of no mind to be a cypher, but was intent on playing an active part in Victoria's education, including attending her lessons and reporting her progress to the king. In the end, the two duchesses were at such odds that Kent refused to communicate with the king through Northumberland. The impasse was resolved in 1837. On 24th May, Victoria became eighteen and so slipped beyond the control of Conroy, for whom she had developed a considerable dislike on account of his influence over her mother. Her majority came just in time, for less than a month later on 20th June, William IV died. It was probably with some relief that the duchess was able to resign her commission.

After 1830, the only office of note the duke held was that of Chancellor of Cambridge University from 1840 until his death in 1847. He spent some of his time at Syon House, but he also resided at Alnwick, where his impact appears not to have been notably beneficial. The testimony of George Tate, a near-contemporary and native of the town, who in the late 1860s published a two-volume *History of Alnwick*, was not especially favourable. His recollection of the duke was of a man who lived magnificently but exclusively in the castle. Moreover, Tate considered that the duke had done little to improve conditions on his estate and felt that his reactionary views had harmed Alnwick in two respects. One was the deletion of the town from the original list of 250 boroughs whose systems of government were to be reformed under the terms of the Municipal Reform Act of 1835. The effect of this act, which in the end applied to 179 boroughs, was to replace their ancient constitutions, which in many cases fostered corrupt practice and were, even by the standard of the time, undemocratic, with councils elected by rate-paying householders of three years' standing. The duke used his influence to have Alnwick removed from the list, which meant that it continued to be under ducal control until later in the century.

The other development hindered by the third duke was the railway. The late 1830s and 1840s saw the rapid expansion of railways, inspired by the success of the Liverpool–Manchester line opened in 1830 and that between London and Birmingham completed five years later. In the later 1840s, one of the most important schemes, promoted by the man *Punch* portrayed as 'The Railway King', the flawed business genius, George Hudson, aimed at linking London and Edinburgh. Under the terms of an act of parliament of 1845, a line engineered by George Stephenson was built between Newcastle and Berwick. Its natural route would have been, like the main road used by the mail coaches, through Alnwick. But the duke did not relish the idea of this new and noisy means of transport coming so close to his castle, and as a result, despite the expressed wishes of the commercial interests in the town, the main east-coast line was made to pass, as it still does, through Alnmouth, three miles east of Alnwick. The most he would allow was a branch line linking his town with the main line at Alnmouth. He was not alone in this concern for his comfort. Many other aristocrats sought to dictate the route taken by the railway, including the duke's neighbour, Lord Howick, who backed a rival, and from his point of view more convenient, proposal designed by the other great engineer of the day, Isambard Kingdom Brunel. It was the Hudson/ Stephenson scheme, however, that secured parliamentary approval. The whole episode illustrates the conflicts of interest that characterised the development of Britain's rail system: between aristocratic owners of land, whose concern was their own comfort and convenience; growing commercial and industrial as well as agricultural interests, who recognised the economic value of this new and faster means of transport; and railway companies, which were not only in competition but were looking to lay their lines along the most direct routes and at the lowest cost.

The third duke, then, who died in 1847, did not enjoy a high reputation. As one contemporary remarked, he was 'a man whose intellect and attainments procured for him a modest degree of respect'. He and his wife, who survived him by almost twenty years, had one still-born child the year after they were married. He was succeeded therefore as fourth duke by his fifty-five-year-old younger brother, Algernon, who proved to be a man of far higher calibre.

As a younger son, Algernon, who was born on 19th December 1792, did not go to Cambridge after his years at Eton, but in 1805, the year of Trafalgar, at the age of thirteen he became a midshipman in the Royal Navy. The war against the France of Napoleon Bonaparte continued until 1815, during which time the Royal Navy was permanently on active service, much of it the arduous, monotonous and unglamorous routine of blockading the Atlantic and Mediterranean ports and naval stations of France and her ally, Spain. In the course of these ten years, Percy rose from midshipman to post captain, a promotion which undoubtedly owed a great deal to his social status and connections, but which he could not have achieved without mastering the complexities of a naval officer's duties. The rank of post captain indicates that by the age of twenty-three he was in command of a 5th or 6th rate warship, that is, a single-deck frigate of between twenty-four and thirty-six guns. It also meant that, under the rules then governing the promotion of naval officers, he would rise automatically in rank, whether he was in service or not, which explains why he eventually attained the rank of admiral, even though he had not been to sea for over thirty years.

Percy left active service soon after the Napoleonic war ended and was granted the title Lord Prudhoe. In the thirty years between then and becoming duke, he became a man of wide and serious interests, which he supported at considerable personal expense. In the 1830s, he accompanied the astronomer, Sir John Herschel, to Cape Colony to study the southern constellations, and ten years later he financed the publication of Herschel's calculations. For these services, he was made a Fellow of the Royal Society and of the Astronomical Society. Earlier, he undertook a similar task in connection with Arabic studies: in 1826, he began to support Edward Lane, whose aim was to produce a comprehensive Arabic lexicon, a commitment he maintained for the next twenty-three years. His other great interest was also centred in the Middle East, namely, Egyptology. This too began in 1826 with a visit to Egypt, where he met the French scholar, Champollion, who was responsible for deciphering the hieroglyphic script. In that year, and on other occasions, he journeyed up the Nile, accompanied by a draughtsman, to make serious and detailed studies of ancient sites. Over the years that followed, he gradually built up a hugely valuable and informative collection of artefacts, mainly of the New Kingdom (the later part of the second millennium BC), although largely from auctions in Britain rather than by means of on-site purchases in Egypt. The final total, which exceeded 2,500 items, remained in ducal possession until 1950, when the tenth duke sold the collection for its valued price of £12,000 to Durham University, where it forms a major element in the Oriental Museum.

As duke, he briefly played some part in national politics, and he was the only nineteenth-century Duke of Northumberland to enter the cabinet. He did so in the short-lived minority Conservative administration formed by the Earl of Derby in February 1852, which lasted only until December of that year. (It was facetiously dubbed the Who? Who? Ministry from the reported response of the aged and almost deaf Duke of Wellington to the list of ministers read to him by Lord Derby.) The duke was made First

Lord of the Admiralty, an office appropriate to his earlier interest and experience and into which he threw himself with great enthusiasm, but insufficient discretion. Not being at heart a politician, he made appointments on the basis of professional competence, ignoring political considerations. This led to loud complaints from his secretary, Augustus Stafford, and the duke came to feel that his colleagues did not sufficiently support him against a subordinate. He also insisted on pressing for an increase in the navy estimates against the wishes of the Chancellor of the Exchequer, Benjamin Disraeli. After the fall of the ministry, he experienced a further rebuff. Several colleagues wished to launch a periodical to be called *The Week,* the aim of which was to explain and promote Conservative views. The duke enthusiastically supported the idea, to the extent of offering to put up £2,000 if four other men would do likewise. The proposal, however, came to nothing, as the result of Lord Derby's opposition.

These experiences, together with the fact that the Conservatives remained out of power, except for a few months in 1858 and 1859, until after his death, help to explain why the duke largely abandoned political life and concentrated on Northumbrian matters. The research of his contemporary, the great Scottish agriculturalist, Sir James Caird, who published a monumental survey of English farming in 1852, and of the modern historians, has revealed the fourth duke as one of the most energetic and forward-thinking landlords of his day. Consciously or otherwise, he followed the wise precept of the ninth earl in knowing more about his estate than the men he employed to run it. Four aspects of his work stand out.

The first was a highly efficient and effective management structure. In charge at the centre was the Duke's Commissioner, an office held throughout the fourth duke's time by Hugh Taylor, a man of exceptional ability and outstanding loyalty. Under his command were five major officers: the Colliery Agent, the Surveyor, the Clerk of Works, the Drainage Surveyor and the Wood Bailiff, who were assisted by a staff of clerks in the estate office. Local administration was in the hands of thirteen bailiffs, tenant farmers of long experience and proven loyalty, whose role was to collect rents, see that tenants farmed correctly, recommend repairs, settle disputes between outgoing and incoming tenants and generally act as channels of communication between their bailliwicks and the estate headquarters. This close inspectorial attention might have been a recipe for disharmony, but in fact landlord-tenant relationships were excellent. The underlying reason for this was that, almost alone among Northumberland landlords, the duke let his farms on an annual basis, so allowing the tenants the opportunity of applying for an annual rent revaluation. These assessments were carried out by two knowledgeable local men of good standing, whose decisions were binding on both landlord and tenant. Such was the appeal of this arrangement that only a handful of tenants preferred leases, which were granted to them if they so wished.

The duke's success as a landlord also owed a great deal to his commitment to improvements, on which he was reckoned to have spent around £650,000. Here it should be recognised that, quite by chance, the duke took over responsibility for the estate the year after the repeal of the Corn Laws by the Conservative government of Sir Robert Peel. The removal of protective import duties on corn, which exposed the farming industry to free trade and foreign competition, had the effect of forcing landlords to look closely at their estates and to reassess how they could be more effectively and profitably managed. The result was an almost universal commitment to improvement without which, it was appreciated, rent income would decline. The key to the whole process was the laying of under-soil tile drainage pipes, which would allow heavy clay land to be cultivated for cereal production. The recognition of how critical drainage was to better farming was a major feature of agricultural thinking in the 1840s and 1850s, to the extent that, by the Drainage Act of 1846, the government made low-interest loans available to encourage farmers to act. The duke was wealthy enough not to need this assistance; nor did he need to buy in pipes, since he had his own tileries. The benefit to his tenants was considerable and at the cost of only small rent increases. The lot of the tenants was also greatly improved by the duke's programme of reconstructing and modernising farm steadings, this time without any attendant rent increases. In part, this was a response to developments in arable farming described above and to the need to accommodate larger herds of cattle. The capital outlay could be considerable: on one 500–acre farm, for example, it was reckoned that expenditure on new buildings came to £1,800. One aspect of this policy, which particularly impressed Sir James Caird, was the duke's efforts to provide farm labourers with better accommodation, the condition of which he declared to be appalling throughout the county, with humans and animals commonly living under the same roof.

The repeal of the Corn Laws and the improvement in farming that followed brought to an end a prolonged period of depression in agriculture, which had persisted since the end of the bonanza years of the French wars between 1793 and 1815. There now began a period of rising prices and consequently of rising rents, which was to last until the late 1870s. Although the duke's huge investment, which amounted to around £10 an acre, yielded only a modest return of less than three per cent, it prevented a certain fall in rents and made possible their almost continuous rise from the mid-1850s until, by 1875, they were on average twenty-five per cent higher than they had been in 1847. The duke may have enjoyed favourable circumstances, but this advantage should not detract from his performance as a landlord and an estate administrator.

If the fourth duke's performance in estate management was impressive, his record in supporting developments in transport and industry was rather less so: like many other landed aristocrats, he was reluctant and cautious when it came to investing in such enterprises. This was certainly true of railways, despite his claim that since 1829 he and his predecessor had encouraged and promoted railway development. If anything the opposite was true, even though the estate had benefited to the tune of £23,000 in compensation from railway companies. In the 1850s, however, the duke did invest in railways, but only on a modest scale and only when he felt confident that direct benefits would accrue to his estate. His first venture, amounting to £15,500 worth of shares and an interest-free loan of £40,000, was the Border Counties Railway built to link the Newcastle-Carlisle line at Hexham with the Edinburgh-Carlisle line across the Border. The potential benefit to the duke was the easier exploitation of the iron ore and coal reserves on his land in Tynedale and Redesdale. It was calculated that the railway would facilitate the transport of coal to the developing mill towns of the Scottish border region, and also help to sustain the iron-making enterprises that had been started a few years earlier at Bellingham and Ridsdale. What the duke was not prepared to do, however, was to invest in either of these latter enterprises, both of which failed due to the adoption of out-of-date technology and to financial incompetence and not, as is commonly thought, through the exhaustion of reserves.

He was equally cautious in his approach to the various proposals for the Northumberland Central Railway, which dragged on through the 1850s and 1860s. These were promoted by two distinct interests: local land-owners, who wanted better transport facilities to get their produce to market and to bring in the materials needed on their estates; and the North British Railway Company, which was seeking to develop a central line between Scotland and England to rival the existing east-coast and west-coast lines.

The duke also made only a modest investment in the Northumberland Dock, a major development promoted on the north bank of the Tyne in the early 1850s by the recently created Tyne Improvement Commission: the most he was prepared to venture was £10,000 of the required £135,000. At first glance his caution or lack of enthusiasm is surprising, given that the dock was to be built on his land, and that its prime purpose was to capture coal exports from the expanding coalfield in south-east Northumberland, much of which came from his collieries. If successful, it would protect the duke's wayleave rents (payments by mining concerns to landowners for permission to transport coal across their land) which amounted to £8,500 a year. In the end, the duke accepted a scheme devised by Hugh Taylor, whereby the dock was built by the Commission, while the duke guaranteed that coal from his collieries would be exported though it for forty years and undertook to lower his wayleave charge from 10s 6d (53p) per 'ten' to 6s (30p). (The 'ten', i.e. ten score corves or baskets of coal, was the traditional measure upon which royalty and wayleave payments were made. By this date, it amounted to around fifty tons.) This reluctance may well have been connected with the ducal policy, which had been pursued since 1799, of not being directly involved in mining, but of leaving the risks to others and securing a more certain income from royalties on coal mined and wayleave rents. Although he kept himself fully informed about his mineral interests, which yielded an income of around £25,000, the duke showed no inclination to veer away from the line followed by his two predecessors. And partly this may have been due to his recognition that, although great, his financial resources were not unlimited and that therefore the sensible policy was to concentrate on the business he knew best.

The duke was also much concerned with the welfare of the people for whom he felt responsible. A rapidly expanding population created a need for additional churches. For the Church of England, this meant dividing ancient parishes, a difficult process until the passing of facilitating legislation by Sir Robert Peel's government in 1843. Again the duke, who was a sincerely religious man, was fortunate in living in easier times, but this does not lessen the credit due to him for spending around £40,000 on the erection and endowment of five churches in Northumberland and providing land for five others. The 1850s and 1860s were also a time of growing concern about public health, particularly how it was affected by sanitation. In 1848 a new government department, the Board of Health, was set up in response to the recognition of the importance to health of sewage disposal and clean water provision, following the discovery in the early 1850s of the true causes of cholera, the disease that had killed thousands in a series of epidemics since the early 1830s. The duke gave the Board of Health his full support and encouragement in implementing the measures needed to remove waste and refuse in Alnwick and to provide the town with a supply of clean water. In addition he made his parks, which virtually surrounded the town, available to its inhabitants on two days every week, a philanthropic gesture he repeated at Syon. Almost inevitably, given his early naval career, he was concerned for the health and safety of mariners. He took a great interest in, and gave great support to the development of, lifeboats, to the extent of providing some of the stations along the Northumberland coast with boats at his own expense. And to provide for the physical and spiritual welfare of seamen on land, he built at a cost of £8,500 The Sailors Home at North Shields.

Finally, it needs to be recognised that the duke's antiquarian interest was not confined to the Near East. He spent around £320,000 on Alnwick Castle, restoring it as far as was possible to its medieval form, so that what can be seen today is very largely the result of his work. Having done so, he and the duchess preferred the less medieval atmosphere of Stanwick Park, where they had lived and built an extension as Lord and Lady Prudhoe, their title before he became duke. They also enjoyed the solitude of Kielder Castle, the hunting lodge built by the first duke close to the Border in North Tynedale. He also gave active support and encouragement to the growing interest in the history and archaeology of Northumberland, which led to his becoming Patron of the Newcastle Society of Antiquaries in 1848 and financing the monumental surveys of

Hadrian's Wall and Watling Street by Henry MacLauchlan, published between 1857 and 1864.

The fourth duke died, greatly and genuinely mourned (the *Newcastle Journal* lauded him as 'Algernon the Benevolent, the greatest of all the Percys') on 25th February 1865. He had not married until 1842 when he was fifty. His wife, Eleanor, a daughter of Richard Grosvenor, Marquess of Westminster, was twenty-eight years his junior and was destined to outlive him by nearly fifty years until 1911. The marriage did not produce any children, however, a fact which had serious consequences when the duke died. The first was the extinction of the title Baron Prudhoe, which had been conferred on him in 1816, when he left active service in the Royal Navy. Secondly, the Percy barony devolved on George Murray, seventh Duke of Atholl. This barony always passed to the heir general, that is, through and to females in the absence of a male heir. The seventh Duke of Atholl was the son of Emily Percy, the eldest daughter of the second Duke of Northumberland to survive, marry and have children. This would have meant the break-up of the estate had not a reversion been purchased some years earlier, when it was foreseen that the problem might arise. The other titles, that is, those created in 1749 and 1766, passed to the heir male, the dead duke's cousin, George Percy, second Earl of Beverley, whose father, Algernon, was the first duke's younger son. This man now became the fifth Duke of Northumberland.

He was born in 1778 and therefore was fourteen years older than the man he succeeded. It is not surprising that he was duke for only a little over two years, dying in 1867 at the age of eighty-nine. In his early years he had been active in politics, and between 1804 and 1812 he was successively a Lord of the Treasury and a member of the India Commission. Like his cousin, the third duke, he was a Lord of the Bedchamber of George IV, but after that king's death in 1830, which coincided with his succession to the earldom of Beverley, he withdrew from public life. The only office he held thereafter was the captaincy of the Yeomen of the Guard from 1841 until 1846, the one true period of Conservative government between 1830 and the year after the duke's death.

In contrast to his predecessor, the fifth duke married early, in 1801 at the age of twenty three. His wife was Louisa, a daughter of James Stuart, the younger brother of John Stuart, third Earl of Bute, a marriage which reinforced the links between the two families. They had five children, including three sons, one of whom, Henry, was one of the first men to be awarded the Victoria Cross, which he won on 5th November 1854 at the Battle of Inkerman, one of the major battles fought by the armies of the Franco-British alliance against the Russians in the the Crimean War. The citation recorded that Percy, who was then aged thirty-seven and a colonel in the Grenadier Guards, although wounded himself and under heavy fire, managed to extricate fifty men who were out of ammunition and virtually surrounded and then get them back into action. But it was not he but his eldest brother, Algernon, who succeeded their father as sixth duke and who, like his father, was no longer a young man at the time of his succession, having been born in 1810.

Early in his life he had a brief military career between 1829 and 1837, reaching the rank of captain in the Grenadier Guards. Later, in 1852, he became MP for North Northumberland, a seat he occupied until he entered the House of Lords on becoming Earl Percy in 1865. During the brief Conservative ministry headed by the Earl of Derby in 1858 and 1859, he was a junior Lord of the Admiralty and then Vice-President of the Board of Trade. But his enjoyment of office was brief, terminated in June 1859 by the return of the Whigs to power. When the Conservatives regained office for another brief period between 1866 and 1868, the duke, as he had then become, was passed over. He was, however, made Lord Privy Seal in 1878 in Disraeli's 1874–1880 ministry. But it is clear that he was regarded as a man who lacked the qualities or abilities necessary for high office, and after the Conservatives were defeated in 1880, he appears to have completely abandoned political life.

He married in 1845 Louisa Drummond, the eldest daughter and co-heir of Henry Drummond, a successful banker, whose wife was a daughter of the Earl of Kinnoull, who built up an estate in Surrey centred on Albury Park. It was through his wife's influence that the duke became a member of the Catholic Apostolic Church, a sect founded in 1835, which had its headquarters at Albury, where his father-in-law built a church for it in the 1840s. This church is sometimes called the Irvingite church, but this is an inaccuracy based upon the erroneous belief that its founder was Edward Irving (1792–1834), a minister who was expelled from the Church of Scotland in 1833, many of whose ideas foreshadowed those of the sect. The Catholic Apostolic Church placed great emphasis on ceremonial, the celebration of the eucharist, ancient and mystical aspects of worship and the literal truth of the Bible. Its teachings were to have a considerable influence on members of the Percy family for two generations, although this did not lead to their leaving the Church of England. The other monument to the duke's piety is the splendid church commissioned by him as a memorial to his father and designed by one of the greatest architects of the Gothic Revival, John Loughborough Pearson, which dominates the seafront at Cullercoats near Tynemouth. Duchess Louisa died in 1890, but the duke lived on until 1899, dying in his eighty-ninth year.

During the fifth and sixth dukes' time the estate was affected in two important ways. One was its enlargement by the acquisition of the Albury estate on the death of Henry Drummond in 1860, and then five years later of the Stanwick estate in Yorkshire after the Earl of Beverley became the fifth duke. The other was the onset of the agricultural depression caused by the unrestricted import of cheap wheat from America and Canada and of wool and refrigerated meat from New Zealand, Australia and Argentina. This competition forced down the prices of almost all farm produce, which in turn led to a lowering of rents: it has been calculated that by the time of the sixth duke's death, rents on the Northumberland estate were around eleven per cent lower than the average for the years 1874–78. Fortunately, this decline in income from land was compensated by rising income from minerals.

FIFTEEN

The Twentieth Century

Henry George Percy, Seventh Duke of Northumberland,
1846–1918
Alan Ian Percy, Eighth Duke of Northumberland, 1880–1930
Henry George Percy, Ninth Duke of Northumberland,
1912–1940
Hugh Algernon Percy, Tenth Duke of Northumberlnd,
1914–1988
Henry Alan Percy, Eleventh Duke of Northumberland,
1953–1995
Ralph George Percy, Twelfth Duke of Northumberland, 1956–

During the present century, which generally has not been kind to the landed aristocracy, there have been five dukes of Northumberland, including the present holder of the title, Ralph, the twelfth duke, who succeeded in 1995. In style and pattern of life, they have largely continued the trends set by their nineteenth-century predecessors, devoting much of their time and energy to the care and management of their estate and the affairs of the North-East of England, particularly of Northumberland, while at the same time having a serious interest in aspects of national life. All have had their schooling at Eton, but for university education they have deserted Cambridge for Oxford.

Henry Percy, who succeeded as seventh duke in January 1899, was the eldest son of the sixth duke. He was born in May 1846 and was therefore fifty-three years old on his succession. Like his predecessor, in his early years he had experience as MP for North Northumberland between 1868 and 1885. During that time he became a member of the Privy Council, and in 1874 he was briefly Treasurer of the Royal Household. He lost his seat in the Commons at the 1885 election, basically because of the 1884/ 85 Reform Act, which doubled the size of the electorate and fundamentally restructured the electoral constituencies. The overall effect of these changes was to make Britain genuinely, although far from completely,

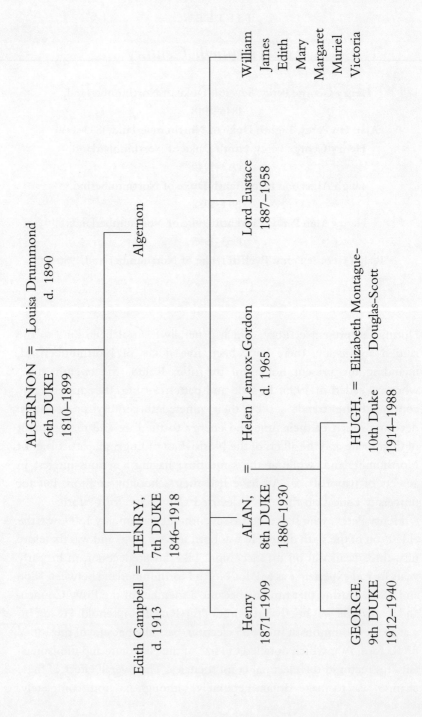

democratic. In Northumberland, the old constituency of North Northumberland disappeared and was replaced by a new division, which included Berwick upon Tweed. Previously, while North Northumberland had been reliably Conservative, Berwick was strongly Liberal, which, together with the enlarged number of voters, made for a hard contest and an uncertain outcome. In the event, Percy was defeated by the Liberal candidate, the son of another Northumbrian landowner, Sir Edward Grey, the future Lord Grey of Fallodon, who was to be Foreign Secretary for ten years between 1906 and 1916 in the governments of Sir Henry Campbell-Bannerman (1905–8) and Herbert Asquith (1908–16). After the declaration of the result, such was the cosiness of Northumberland politics, the two rivals went fishing together. Percy's electoral defeat occasioned only a temporary interruption to his political life, for in 1887 he was allowed to enter the House of Lords as Lord Lovaine. His only other services to the Crown occurred in 1892 and 1901 when, as a member of the militia, he acted as ADC to Queen Victoria and to King Edward VII.

Also like his predecessors, he was President of the Royal Institution, a Fellow of the Royal Society and a trustee of the British Museum. In 1904, he was appointed Lord Lieutenant of Northumberland, a post he held until his death, and in 1913 he became the first elected Chancellor of Durham University under its revised constitution of 1908. In 1868, he married Edith Campbell, the eldest daughter of George Campbell, eighth Duke of Argyll. She died in London in 1913, following a gallstone operation. He survived her by five years, dying in 1918.

The seventh duke and duchess had thirteen children, six of whom died prematurely, including their eldest son, Henry, who was known as Lord Warkworth until 1899, when he was styled Lord Percy. This was a tragedy, obviously for his parents, but also for the Conservative party and perhaps for the country, in that Henry Percy was a man of outstanding intellect, who seemed certain to attain high political office. He was at Eton between 1884 and 1889 and then at Christ Church College, Oxford, where he took a First in Classics in 1893. Two years later, he was elected Conservative MP for South Kensington, a seat he retained until his death. The ten years following his election were a period when the Conservative party was in power, initially under Robert Cecil, Marquess of Salisbury (1895–1902), and then under Arthur James Balfour

(1902–5). Percy was one of the administration's most promising young men, and from 1902 he held the junior offices of Under Secretary of State for India (1902–3) and then Under Secretary of State for Foreign Affairs (1903–5). In December 1905, however, following several by-election defeats, Balfour resigned as Prime Minister in favour of the leader of the Liberal Party, Sir Henry Campbell-Bannerman. In the general election held a few weeks later in January 1906, the Liberals won a landslide victory. Percy retained his seat, but with only 156 fellow Conservatives, his prospects of an early return to office were almost nil. In fact, he never again held office, for at the end of 1909 he died of pneumonia in the Gare Du Nord Hotel, Paris.

Henry Percy was unmarried, and therefore when his father died in 1918, it was his next brother, Alan, who was born on 17th April 1880, who succeeded as the eighth duke. Like his brother, Alan was educated at Eton and then Christ Church, but he was a vigorously physical man, whose inclination was far more towards the military than the academic life. In January 1900 he became an officer in the Grenadier Guards and immediately went on active service to South Africa where, late in the previous year, war had broken out. The aim of the Boers, or Afrikaners, of Transvaal and the Orange Free State was to liberate South Africa from British rule. Initially, their forces won a string of impressive victories (Stormberg, Magersfontein, Colenso, Spion Kop, Vaal Krantz) against inept British commanders. In the course of 1900, however, their field armies were defeated by the able Lord Roberts and they were forced to lift the sieges of Kimberley, Mafeking and Ladysmith. But the war was far from over. Due to the highly effective guerrilla tactics adopted by the Boers, it dragged on until March 1902. In the end, British success stemmed from the determination and ruthlessness of Sir Herbert Kitchener, who herded women and children into concentration camps (where nearly 20,000 of the 120,000 died of disease) and cornered their menfolk by means of blockhouses linked by barbed wire. Winning this war cost Britain nearly 20,000 dead and £222m.

Percy was seconded to the Egyptian army in 1908. He became a member of the Camel Corps, reaching the rank of *bimbashi* (captain), and saw active service in Kordofan Province in the Sudan in the campaign to subdue the Nubas. These were a fiercely independent people, much given to raiding, who lived in very difficult mountain country on the border between the Arabic, Muslim north and the African south of the country. They remained a serious problem for the authorities in the Sudan long after the defeat of the rebellion inspired and led by the fanatical Islamic religious leader, Mohammed Ahmed, known as the Mahdi, [guide]. This uprising, which had begun in 1884 and resulted in the famous death of General Charles Gordon in Khartoum the following year, was not finally crushed until Kitchener's victory at Omdurman in 1898. After this, while the rest of the Sudan was subject to civil government, the Nubas continued to present a military problem until the end of the First World War.

Percy's involvement, however, ended in 1910, when he became ADC to the Governor-General of Canada, a fellow Northumbrian aristocrat, Earl Grey. This was a much less hazardous role, and his appointment to it may have been related to the death of his elder brother, Henry, as the result of which he became the heir to the dukedom. By all accounts, Percy was a great success in Canada, where his lack of affectation and pretension and his vigorous involvement in outdoor pursuits earned him popularity and approval.

His period as ADC ended two years later in 1912, when he retired from the army. But on the outbreak of the First World War in 1914, he rejoined his regiment and again saw active service, this time in France. His time at the front lasted until 1916, when he was recalled to join the Intelligence Department of the War Office. When, at the end of the First World War, he retired from the army for the second time, he had attained the rank of lieutenant-colonel.

His retirement was not due solely to the war's ending, but also to the fact that earlier in 1918 he had become the eighth Duke of Northumberland upon the death of his father. In this role, he continued his commitment to military life through his presidency of the Northumberland Territorial Force Association and his honorary colonelcy of the Northumberland Fusiliers and the Tyne Electrical Engineers, a unit founded in 1884. In the civil sphere, he was President of the Institute of Naval Architects and, continuing the family tradition, of the Royal Institution. He also assisted the study of Northumberland's history through his chairmanship of the Northumberland County History Committee, formed in the early 1890s to produce a comprehensive history of the county along similar lines to the Victoria County Histories, a project to which all counties save Northumberland were committed. Similarly, he was president of the Newcastle Society of Antiquaries and generously helped to finance their annual publication, *Archaeologia Aeliana*. He was equally concerned to ensure the preservation of the county's physical remains. In 1922, he handed over the ruins of Warkworth Castle to the Ministry of Works (the forerunner of English Heritage), and through his chairmanship of the Roads and Bridges Committee of Northumberland County Council he gave protection to the ancient bridges of the county. He also helped to found the Northumberland and Newcastle Society, which is dedicated to preserving the county's natural and architectural heritage. And in 1929, he succeeded the Earl of Durham as Chancellor of Durham University, which then included the College of Medicine and Armstrong College in Newcastle.

He was also very active in the field of politics, not in seeking office but as a polemicist, a role for which he was greatly suited, since he was both a lucid writer and a fiery and persuasive public speaker. He gained a reputation (which in some quarters amounted to notoriety) for his clear-cut and very definite opinions, which derived from certain basic principles to which he was firmly committed. As a member of the House of Lords, he had a parliamentary platform on which he could expound his views, but he also had ready access to the public via the press as part-owner of a national newspaper, the *Morning Post*, and through his own journal, *The Patriot*. His advocacy of what he believed was always assertive and frequently abrasive; and he was contemptuous of compromise, for he was convinced that he was entirely right and that those who held opposite or different views were totally wrong. Essentially, he was a diehard Tory to whom many contemporary developments and trends were utterly abhorrent. As regards the wider world, he was convinced of British superiority in the matter of government, hence he was strongly opposed to the granting of independence to Ireland (and to any other colony), believing that chaos would ensue, which would require the reintroduction of British rule. This belief also helps to explain his intense dislike of the League of Nations, which he felt was based upon the false premise that war could be avoided. He was entirely clear in his dislike and suspicion of Germany, which he voiced trenchantly both before and after the First World War; and inevitably he was totally opposed to the new USSR, which emerged after the 1917 revolution in Russia, and to Bolshevism, which he saw as a threat to everything he valued.

At home, he was contemptuous of the Liberal Party and its ideals, which he thought had spawned socialism; and he was convinced that the Labour Party, which became a major force in British politics in the 1920s, was a creature of the Soviet government. Of all politicians, he most disliked and despised Lloyd George, not only because he had granted independence to Ireland, but also on account of his cynical practice of raising money for political purposes by the sale of honours. Under the corrupt manipulation of Maundy Gregory, this attained scandalous proportions: the widely recognised prices were £10,000 for a knighthood, £30,000 for a baronetcy and at least £50,000 for a peerage. The extent of this racket and the income it generated can be gauged from the fact that in 1921 and 1922 twenty-six peerages, seventy-four baronetcies and 294 knighthoods were conferred. The duke was one of the most aggressive and tenacious members of the campaign against this practice, which clearly devalued existing titles. In the end, the government capitulated and set up a royal commission, out of which came the Honours (Prevention of Abuses) Act of 1925, which aimed at preventing future abuse of the honours system. At the same time, he was equally forthright in defence of his own interests. He made no apology for the income he derived from coal royalties, arguing that they were the consequence of the entirely legitimate and legal business acumen of his predecessors in buying coal-bearing land, and that in any case most of the money (which amounted to over £82,000 a year) went to the Treasury in the form of taxation. He vigorously defended his role as a coal owner in the meetings of the commission to look into the condition of the coal industry set up in 1919 under the chairmanship of Mr Justice Sankey. His toughness and directness in debate won him a degree of respect from the miners' leaders, who pressed strongly for the nationalisation of the entire industry, a solution which would have meant the expropriation of one of his principal assets.

The duke died suddenly in August 1930. At the time of his death, he was one of the wealthiest men in Britain, and was reckoned to be worth £2.5 million. This was without the estate at Stanwick St John, which he sold in 1921. The sale included the house, Stanwick Park, which had last been occupied by the widow of the fourth duke until her death in 1911.

In doing so, he joined a move by the aristocracy in the immediate post-war years to sell land. It has been argued that this was not due solely or necessarily to the pressure of death duties, although these were raised considerably in 1919. Rather, their aim was to take advantage of the current high price of land and at the same time to reduce their dependence on income from it, which was poor compared with yields from shareholdings and government bonds. Moreover, in most cases what was sold was not core properties, but distant or outlying parts, the effect of which was to produce more compact and logically constructed estates. In this matter, the duke appears to have been at one with many of his fellow aristocrats.

His premature passing meant that he did not live to see the coming to power in Germany of Adolf Hitler and the Nazi Party. It is interesting to speculate how he would have reacted to the events of the 1930s: with his long-standing and forcefully expressed anti-German views he might well have become a serious and significant force in British politics and not merely a polemicist.

The early deaths of Henry and of Alan Percy arguably robbed Britain of two outstanding leaders. Before discussing Alan's successor, mention must be made of his younger brother, Lord Eustace Percy, who also had a distinguished career and in many respects resembled his eldest brother, Henry. Born in 1887, he too had an outstanding career at Oxford, gaining a First in History in 1907, after which he entered the Diplomatic Service. From 1910 until 1914, he was an attaché at the embassy in Washington, but then spent most of the war period in the Foreign Office. Shortly after the end of the war, however, he decided to abandon the civil service for politics. In 1921, he entered the Commons after winning a by-election at Hastings, a seat he retained until 1937. Three years later, his undoubted intellectual ability secured him a seat in the Cabinet in 1924 as President of the Board of Education, a post he held until the fall of Stanley Baldwin's government following the Labour victory in the 1929 election. It is fair to say that he was too concerned with accuracy and truth to be an effective politician, and he never became an impressive or persuasive speaker in Commons debates. These 'defects', which almost inevitably, given his name, led to his being called Lord 'Useless' Percy, together with the fact that he was out of office until 1935, helped to reduce his interest in politics and to lead him to his third career.

In 1933, he was appointed President of Armstrong College in New-castle, which by the Durham University Act of 1935 was joined with the Newcastle College of Medicine to form King's College, the Newcastle Division of Durham University. The new constitution came into opera-tion in 1937, when Percy became Rector of King's College, in effect Vice-Chancellor, on a two-year rotational basis with the Warden of the Durham Colleges, of Durham University. Through his energy, intellec-tual strength and devotion to duty he was the driving force of King's College until his retirement because of ill health in 1952. He guided it through the difficult years of the Second World War and the early phase of the post-war expansion. Although far from being a mere administrator (during the war he had acted as Professor of History), possibly his most important contribution was to secure in 1946 the Compulsory Purchase Order which ensured that King's College (and the much larger university that grew out of it after 1963) had the room to expand on its city-centre site. He was created Baron Percy of Newcastle in 1953, but the title became extinct upon his death in 1958.

In 1911 the eighth duke married Helen Gordon-Lennox, the youngest daughter of the seventh Duke of Richmond and Gordon. In the nineteen years of their marriage, they had six children, the eldest of whom, George, succeeded to the title. The ninth duke was born in July 1912 and was therefore only eighteen years old and still a minor at the time of his accession. As had become normal in the Percy family, he was educated at Eton and Christ Church College, Oxford, after which, as a member of the House of Lords, he embarked upon a political career. In June 1935, he got on to the bottom rung of the promotion ladder when he was appointed Parliamentary Private Secretary to the Lord Privy Seal, the Marquess of Londonderry, but following the election of that year, he was moved to a similar post with the Secretary of State for Air, Viscount Swinton. This must be seen as a promotion, given the rapidly growing importance of that ministry as the likelihood of another war with Germany increased. The duke was only twenty-three years old and the speed with which he had become a member of the government, while doubtless because of his potential, may also have been due to the fact that both ministers whom he served were in the Lords.

The outbreak of the Second World War in September 1939 ended the duke's political career. He became a lieutenant in the 3rd Battalion,

Grenadier Guards, which was part of the 1st Division (commanded by Major-General Harold Alexander, the future Field-Marshal Earl Alexander of Tunis), one of the nine divisions that made up the British Expeditionary Force which crossed to France. In 1940, as a German offensive became imminent, the BEF took up defensive positions between the Belgian Army and the 1st French Army along the west bank of the River Dyle, in the hope of repulsing any German attempt to occupy Belgium. This strategy was totally undermined in mid-May, however, by the surprise advance of the German armoured divisions through the Ardennes and their rapid advance towards the Channel coast. This precipitated a hurried withdrawal from the Dyle, which for the British forces ended in their evacuation, minus most of their equipment, from the beaches of Dunkirk in a nine-day period in late May and early June.

Sadly, the duke was not among those who returned to Britain. By 20th May the British forces had retreated westwards as far as the River Escaut (Scheldt) and the 1st Division was dug in near the village of Pecq. The following morning, under cover of mist, units of the German army crossed the river in an attempt to create a bridgehead. Throughout the morning, several counter-attacks were launched against this bridgehead and it was during one of these that the duke and two of his fellow officers were killed by machine-gun fire. At the end of the day, a Guards patrol discovered that the Germans had abandoned their position and returned to the east bank of the river. This was the result of the single-handed charge of a Lance-Corporal Nichols, who was awarded the VC, thought to be posthumous, until it was discovered that Nichols was recovering from wounds in a German hospital. The duke was one of the first of over twenty peers or the heirs to peerages to be killed in action in the course of the Second World War.

The duke died unmarried at the age of twenty-seven, which meant that the title passed to his younger brother, Hugh, who was two years his junior, having been born in April 1914. He too was educated at Eton and Christ Church, and he also saw service in the Second World War as an officer in the Northumberland Hussars. This severley restricted his scope for exercising his ducal role, but with the coming of peace in 1945 he embarked upon a career lasting over forty years in which he was a model late-twentieth-century aristocrat.

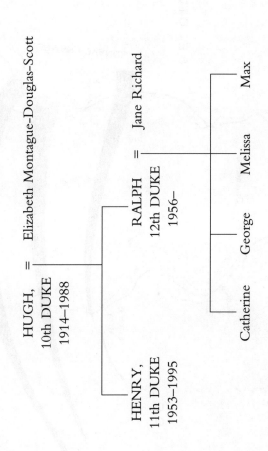

HUGH,
10th DUKE
1914–1988

=

Elizabeth Montague-Douglas-Scott

HENRY,
11th DUKE
1953–1995

RALPH
12th DUKE
1956–

=

Jane Richard

Catherine

George

Melissa

Max

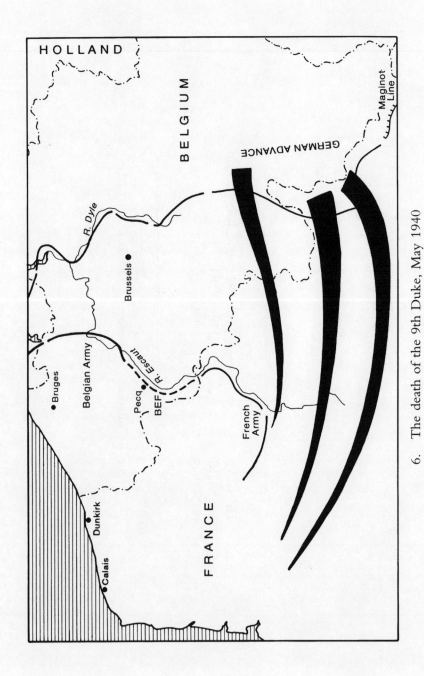

6.   The death of the 9th Duke, May 1940

He was an exemplary landlord, who devoted a great deal of his time to restoring his estates from the neglect of the war years and ensuring that they conformed to the most up-to-date standards of husbandry. The estate in Northumberland, now reduced to around 100,000 acres, was reorganised into a smaller number of larger units, so that the average farm size rose from around 250 to over 400 acres. Mixed woodland was planted at a rate of over 100 acres a year, and large sums were spent on modernising and improving farmsteads and estate houses. His deep interest in and knowledge of farming almost inevitably led to invitations to join national bodies concerned with agriculture. He was Chairman of the Agricultural Research Council (1958–68), then of the Agricultural Economic Development Committee (1971–78); and of the Border Forest Park Committee (1956–68). He also chaired several *ad hoc* committees looking into specific problems, such as that set up in 1968 and 1969 to investigate the problem of foot and mouth disease in cattle. He was also a member of other bodies, notably the National Forestry Committee for England and Wales and the Hill Farming Advisory Committee.

Local and regional matters, both civil and military, also engaged his attention. He served for many years on Northumberland County Council, as a councillor from 1944 until 1955, and then as an alderman until 1967. Like virtually all of his predecessors since the sixteenth century, he was Lord Lieutenant of Northumberland from 1956 until 1984, when he reached the statutory retiring age of seventy. He was Chairman of the Court of Durham University from 1956 until 1964, when he became first Chancellor of the University of Newcastle upon Tyne, created in the previous year by the severance of King's College from the Durham Colleges. On the military side, he remained closely involved with the Territorial Army. As well as being a reserve officer until he was fifty in 1964, he was honorary colonel of the 7th battalion, Royal Northumberland Fusiliers (the Royal was added in 1935), and of the 6th battalion, Royal Regiment of Fusiliers after the amalgamation of regiments in the 1970s. Between 1956 and 1968, he was President of the Northumberland Territorial Army and Auxiliary Forces Association and then, until 1971, of the North of England Territorial Army and Volunteer Reserve Association.

His many other services included the chairmanship of the Medical

Research Council (1969–88), the honorary treasurership of the Royal National Lifeboat Institution, the presidency of the Wildfowl Trust (1968–72) and membership of the Royal Commission on Historic Manuscripts (1973–88), an entirely appropriate role in the light of the hugely important archive at Alnwick. And from 1973 until his death, he was Lord Steward of Her Majesty's Household.

In 1946 the duke married Elizabeth Montague-Douglas-Scott, daughter of the eighth Duke of Buccleuch and Queensberry. They had six children, three boys and three girls. He died in October 1988 and was buried in the family vault in St Nicholas Chapel, Westminster Abbey, the last member of the family to be accorded this privilege. In 1930, after the interment of the eighth duke, it was decided that the vault could accommodate only two further burials. The first of these, in 1965, was that of the dowager duchess, Helen, who was the linchpin of the family in the difficult days following the early death of her husband and that of her son in the Second World War; the other was his own.

The tenth duke was succeeded by his eldest son, Henry, who was born in July 1953 and educated at Eton and Christ Church. In his last year at university he contracted ME (myalgic encephalomyelitis) and thereafter he suffered from poor health until his death in October 1995, at the early age of forty-two. The eleventh duke was an exceedingly shy man who never married. His great interest was films. He built up a collection of 1930s and 1940s films and as duke he formed his own production company, Hotspur Films. In the company's brief career it made three films, one of which, *Lost in Africa*, was shown at the specialist Tyneside Cinema in Newcastle, although it was not generally released. The eleventh duke died of kidney failure in 1995 and was buried in the parish church at Alnwick.

His successor as twelfth duke is his brother, Ralph, who was born in November 1956 and also educated at Eton and Oxford. In 1979, he married Jane Richard of Edinburgh and in doing so continued the well established and, considering the family's long involvement in Border history, happy tradition of finding a Scottish bride. As they have two sons and two daughters, the House of Percy is happily well set to continue.

The duke, who is a qualified Chartered Surveyor, is fully committed to active estate management: in his own words, his aim is to 'protect, preserve and restore'. He is also concerned to ensure that all elements of the Percy inheritance operate efficiently and effectively, especially as the agricultural side is experiencing recession (for the current year the farm tenants have been granted a 15% rent rebate, but the duke does not expect this to result in the erection of another tenantry column at Alnwick!). However, his faith in the long-term future of land is demonstrated by his recent purchase of the Dryburgh Estate in the Scottish Borders. Once again the Percys are established north of the Border, although this time they have come in peace.

Unlike almost all of his predecessors, he is not involved in politics, either locally or nationally, but he does support, as patron, president or chairman, a wide range of charities and institutions, including the Royal Society for the Promotion of Health, the Community Council of Northumberland and the Northumberland Fund of the Tyne and Wear Foundation. He also maintains his family's traditional link with the RNLI and he is a Deputy Lord-Lieutenant of Northumberland and the Hon Colonel of the Northumberland Fusiliers. In all of these activities he has the wholehearted support of the duchess who, in addition to initiating her own ambitious garden project (described in the next section) is supervising a comprehensive programme of restoration of rooms and furniture at Alnwick Castle. Once their northern projects are well under way, the duke and duchess plan to undertake restoration and development schemes at Syon Park.

These last paragraphs show that this book cannot have a conclusion in the normal sense. Perhaps the best note on which to end is to say that, having survived so many misfortunes and played such a notable part in British life for almost all of this present millennium, the Percys may with some confidence face the new millenium which will begin the year after the publication of this book.

Principal Houses and Castles

In the course of its long history, the Percy family has owned a large number of houses and castles: it has been estimated, for example, that in the mid-fifteenth century the total was as high as thirty. Those described below are the ones which were most important in the sense that they were the places most favoured by the heads of the family. For the sake of convenience, they are arranged in three geographical groups: London and the Home Counties; Yorkshire; and Northumberland.

LONDON AND THE HOME COUNTIES

In the south-east of England the Percys have owned five large houses, two of which no longer exist and only one of which is still in their possession. Two, however, are country houses of major importance nationally as regards their contents and gardens, as well as their architecture.

Northumberland House, London

There have been two Northumberland Houses in London. The first was in Aldgate Ward at the corner of Fenchurch Street and an alley (now Northumberland Avenue) that ran through to Crutched Friars. It was built on land acquired in May 1343 by Henry, Lord Percy II. Why he did so is not recorded, but it is reasonably safe to assume that it was connected with his rising importance and the emergence of parliament as a permanent institution of government, which would have combined to make his frequent residence in London a necessity. Virtually nothing is known about it until 1603, when John Stow in his famous book, *A Survey of London,* stated that it had been abandoned by the earls of Northumberland sometime before and, after a period when it was used as a gambling den and a bowling alley, it had been broken up into a large number of small tenements. Sixty-three years later it was destroyed in the Great Fire of 1666.

By that time the earls had acquired another London home, also known as Northumberland House, in the Strand. It had been built on the site of a dissolved medieval hospital by Henry Howard, Earl of Northampton, between 1605 and 1609 and was known as Northampton House. Designed by Bernard Jansen and Gerard Christian, it had three sides, the fourth side remaining open to the river, until an additional wing was built sometime after 1614 by Northampton's successor, Thomas Howard, first Earl of Suffolk. It was then known as Suffolk House until 1642, when it was given by Thomas Howard, second Earl of Suffolk, as part of his daughter's dowry upon her marriage to the tenth Earl of Northumberland. Thereafter, as Northumberland House, it continued to be a Percy property for a further 230 years.

In the 1640s, the tenth earl spent large sums modernising his acquisition, notably reconstructing the south wing facing the river to the designs of Edward Carter, who replaced Inigo Jones as Surveyor of the King's Works. Almost certainly he was encouraged to do so by the ready availability of skilled labour as the result of the departure of the court from Westminster upon the outbreak of war and by his need to spend much time in London on political matters. Later in the seventeenth century, a new west wing was built by the sixth Duke of Somerset. The house achieved its final form in the 1770s, when it was remodelled by Robert Adam for the first Duke and Duchess of Northumberland. It was sold in 1873, with great regret but for £479,000, by the seventh duke to the Metropolitan Board of Works, who demolished it to create the present Northumberland Avenue between the Strand and the Embankment. All was not lost, however, since the panels of Adam's Glass Drawing Room were crated and stored until after the Second World War, when they were sold to an antique dealer, who hired them out as temporary decor for debutante balls. They now have a permanent and more dignified resting place in the Victoria and Albert Museum.

Albury Park, Surrey
Albury is the most recently acquired of the main Percy houses. Its origins are uncertain, but it was a half-timbered Tudor house in the mid-

seventeenth century, when it was rebuilt by the Duke of Norfolk. Among those he employed were John Evelyn and his brother, who created an Italian-style garden, which included an imitation Roman bath in a cavern under the main terrace. This house was burnt down in Queen Anne's reign but was immediately rebuilt by its then owner, the Earl of Aylesford. In the next century and a half, it was remodelled on three further occasions by Sir John Soane, Henry Hakewill and finally by Augustus Welby Pugin, who transformed it both inside and out between 1846 and 1852. The result is a Tudor-style redbrick house with sixty-three chimneys, all of different design. The commissioning owner was Henry Drummond, who bought it in 1819 and made it the centre of an estate he built up in the neighbourhood. Drummond's daughter, Louisa, married the sixth Duke of Northumberland, who inherited the property on his father-in-law's death in 1860. The estate created by Drummond is now controlled by a trust created by the seventh duke in 1918 to provide an income for Earl Percy, the heir to the dukedom, upon reaching the age of twenty-five. The house, however, was sold to the Country Houses Association in 1965 following the death of the Dowager Duchess Helen.

Petworth House, West Sussex

In contrast to Albury Park, Petworth came to the Percys at an early date: it was granted in the middle years of the twelfth century to Agnes de Percy and her husband, Jocelin, Count of Louvain, by his half-sister, Adeliza, the widow of Henry I. It was probably a manor house rather than a castle, since licence to crenellate was not granted until 1309. The chapel is also of this period, suggesting an extensive fourteenth-century recon-struction. But the house is unlikely to have been of major importance to the Percys until the sixteenth century, since their main centres of activity were in the north. Nevertheless, it was not totally neglected: in particular, by purchase and enclosure, the surrounding park was enlarged until by 1621 it covered 400 acres (its present size is 700 acres).

What gave Petworth its importance was the enforced confinement of the eighth and ninth Earls of Northumberland to the south of England. Because of their political untrustworthiness, real or imagined, both Elizabeth I and James I required them to reside at Petworth, well away from their northern power bases and close at hand for instant arrest, if necessary. The consequence was a considerable expenditure on the house

218

and its gardens. The eighth earl is believed to have spent nearly £5,000 on the house and chapel and on constructing a new walled garden. His successor was far more ambitious: while a prisoner in the Tower he had estimates made for a completely new house which would have cost over £25,000 had the project been carried out. The plans were shelved, however, and the earl contented himself with enlarging the existing house and building a magnificent stable block and riding school which, alas, were demolished in the early eighteenth century. The tenth earl, unlike his father and grandfather, was a free agent, but he continued to reside at Petworth out of choice, and it is thanks to his desire to do so that the house has such a notable collection of Van Dyck paintings. There is some indication that in the 1630s he considered reactivating his father's plans for a new house, but then abandoned the idea when he acquired Suffolk House in London. What the eleventh earl would have done cannot be known, since he died only two years after succeeding to his inheritance, but it seems likely that he too would have made Petworth his main residence.

The most extensive Percy developments at Petworth were carried out by the 'Proud Duke', the sixth Duke of Somerset, whose first wife was Elizabeth Percy, the eleventh earl's only surviving child. Between 1688 and 1702, he used his wife's great wealth to rebuild Petworth in the grand manner and in the style popularised by Louis XIV. In part this was the result of his own observations while on the Grand Tour some years earlier; but it is also likely that he was influenced by his stepfather-in-law, Ralf Montague, who had been ambassador to France and whose North-amptonshire house, Boughton, strongly resembles Petworth, and by the French Huguenot architect, Daniel Marot, who had worked for both Montague and William III. The taste and commitment of these men is still magnificently visible in the west front of the house. Internally, he employed a range of craftsmen, including the wood carver, Grinling Gibbons, and his assistant, a local man, John Selden. The result was a seat fit for a man of the duke's high status and self-esteem. But it also needed a grandiose setting, and this too the duke contrived. Again, his huge wealth allowed him to hire the best advice, notably that of the royal gardener, George London. The most impressive outcome was a splendid formal garden at the front of the house. But the duke's interest in gardening went beyond the ostentatious display of wealth, for he had a genuine love of botany and went to great lengths and expense to import exotic species for his gardens and orangery and to ensure that they thrived. The sixth Duke of Somerset may have cut a slightly ridiculous figure in society, but there is no doubt that at Petworth he created one of the most beautiful and impressive houses in Britain.

Percy ownership of Petworth continued for less than fifty years after the completion of the 'Proud Duke's' redevelopments. In 1750, as a result of the settlement created in the previous year, Petworth House, together with the land there and at nearby Sutton and Duncton, passed to Sir Charles Wyndham, who became the second Earl of Egremont. The estate remained in the possession of his descendants until 1947, when the house and the park were made over to the National Trust, although the family continue to live there. In that time there were two major changes. One was the remodelling of the gardens between 1753 and 1765 by Lancelot 'Capability' Brown, which most notably, and perhaps regrettably, involved the destruction of the formal garden at the front of the house and its replacement by a lawn leading to a landscaped park. The other was the extensive alterations, particularly to the south end of the house, carried out by Anthony Salvin in the 1870s.

Syon Park, Middlesex
Syon Park is the only house in the Home Counties still in Percy ownership. Its origins go back to 1415, when Henry V began the task of honouring the promise made by his father to Pope Gregory XII in 1408 to found three monasteries in return for papal forgiveness for the execution of Archbishop Scrope of York. In the event only two were founded, one at Richmond, the other at Twickenham: it was the latter that was the origin of Syon. The monastery belonged to a new order founded in the 1370s at Vadstena by Queen Birgitta (Bridget) of Sweden. Bridgettine houses were 'double' in that, while they were essentially for women and headed by an abbess, they had supporting groups of male priests. The first professions were made in 1420, and by curious coincidence the first Confessor (the title of the leading male member of the community) was a native of Alnwick. However, the original site at Twickenham proved to be too damp and too small and therefore in 1426 the community was given a larger and healthier site at Isleworth, a short distance downriver, to which it moved in 1431 on completion of the buildings.

The most dramatic phase of the monastery's history occurred in the middle decades of the sixteenth century. In the 1530s its abbess, Elizabeth Barton, strongly opposed Henry VIII's divorce from his queen, Catherine of Aragon, and allied herself with Sir Thomas More. As a result, she too was executed in 1535, together with one of the male members of the community, Richard Reynolds, who refused to acknowledge the king as head of the church. Four years later, the house was closed along with all other larger monasteries. But the closure was not final, for in 1557 the catholic queen, Mary I, reassembled the dispersed nuns and reopened the house. The refoundation was short-lived, however, for in the following year Elizabeth I came to the throne and reversed her half-sister's work. Still Syon refused to die: many of the nuns emigrated and in 1594 the house was again refounded, this time in Portugal. There it continued to flourish until 1861, when it returned to Britain and settled at South Brent in Devon. There is a well-known story that, when in Portugal, the second duke visited the monastery where the abbess proudly boasted that she still had the keys to Syon. This thrust was neatly parried by the duke, who replied, 'Indeed madam? But I have altered the locks since then'.

After its closure as a monastery, the buildings at Syon became Crown property and were in occasional use. Queen Catherine Howard was housed there before her execution in 1542, and five years later the body of Henry VIII rested there the night before its interment at Windsor. It was shortly after this that it was converted, as many other monasteries were, into a house by a new owner. This was Edward Seymour, first Duke of Somerset, who with the title of Lord Protector was the ruler of England on behalf of his under-age nephew, Edward VI. Details of the conversion are almost non-existent, but it is almost certain that the shell of the present house is Somerset's work and that it stands on the foundations of the cloister of the former monastery. The new house was the scene of one further important incident before settling down to a half-century of obscurity. In 1553, following the death of Edward VI, an attempt was made by John Dudley, Duke of Northumberland (who had replaced Somerset as Lord Protector), to prevent the accession of Queen Mary, a development which would have ended his political power. It was at Syon that he persuaded Lady Jane Grey, his son's wife, who was the grand-daughter of Henry VIII's sister, Mary, to usurp the throne. The coup failed and both parties died for their attempt to subvert the law of succession.

The Percys obtained Syon in the years between 1597 and 1604. Their interest began in the former year when the ninth earl replaced Robert Knolles as Housekeeper of Syon and Steward of the Manor of Isleworth. Five years later, he was granted a twenty-one-year lease of the properties. Queen Elizabeth's generosity may have been related to the fact that the earl's wife, Dorothy Devereux, had lived at Syon when married to her first husband, Sir Thomas Perrott. But above that was the queen's need to ensure the earl's loyalty in the light of his earlier association with his wife's brother, the rebel Earl of Essex. Two years later in 1604, the lease was replaced by the outright freehold. The grantor was the new monarch, James I, who wished to reward the earl's active help and support during the difficult and dangerous transition period following Elizabeth's death. The earl immediately began to improve his new property, and his effort and commitment were not seriously interrupted by his long incarceration in the Tower following the discovery of the Gunpowder Plot. He was responsible for the corner towers, the battlements, the casements and the leading of the roof. To a very large extent, the external form of the house today is his creation. The earl was equally keen to develop the gardens at Syon, which were already well established before its conversion to a house, so much so that William Turner, a notable botanical author, lived and worked there for twelve years during and after the Duke of Somerset's ownership. Almost immediately, the earl began to create a levelled area for the gardens, which were separated from the water meadows next to the river by a buttress wall. The gardens themselves were surrounded by a fifteen-foot-high wall to provide shelter and warmth. The success of this enterprise can be measured by the fact that grapes were grown as well as native fruits and vegetables.

Syon was much involved in the civil wars of the 1640s. Between 1646 and 1649, it was the home of Charles I's three younger children, when they were committed to the custody of the tenth earl, and consequently it was there that they were visited by their father when he was living at Hampton Court, a short river journey away. The house also suffered damage as the result of its occupation by royalist troops, who are said to have discharged cannons inside the hall. After the end of hostilities the earl had a large and expensive repair bill to meet. The tenth earl also continued to develop the gardens, using the services of a French gardener to create a formal garden, planting a twenty-acre orchard, which included

222

mulberry trees, four of which still survive, and succumbing to the contemporary craze for tulips, on which he spent £21 in obtaining bulbs from Holland.

During the time of the sixth Duke of Somerset and his wife, Elizabeth Percy, Syon played an important but subsidiary role as a residence. But it was the family's main stables and a convenient halfway point between Petworth and Northumberland House in London for personal meetings and for changing horses. The family also used it as a summer alternative to London, which could become very unpleasant and unhealthy in hot weather. With the division of the estate in 1750 and the loss of Petworth, Syon assumed greater importance and therefore it is not surprising to discover that it was under the first Duke and Duchess of Northumberland that it underwent major internal renovation and reconstruction. The architect was Robert Adam, whose plans, drawn up in 1761 and executed by a team of first-rate artists and craftsmen, were to transform the interior of the house. The most outstanding results are perhaps the Great Hall, with its two copies in bronze of ancient Roman statues, the Dying Gaul by Luigi Valadier and Apollo Belvedere by John Cheere, and the Long Gallery (136 feet in length) which Adam designed 'for the amusement and delight of the ladies'. The duke and duchess also transformed the surroundings of the house, notably by employing Lancelot 'Capability' Brown to replace the out-of-date formal gardens by the fashionable 'natural landscape'. They also spent a great deal of money on the gardens, employing between fourteen and sixteen men. One of their head gardeners was William Forsyth, after whom *Forsythia* is named, who later became the royal gardener.

In the nineteenth century, it was probably the third duke who made the greatest impact on Syon. He may not have been a major figure in the public life of his day, but he gave to Syon one of its treasures, the Great Conservatory, which made a major contribution to the nurture of the huge numbers of exotic plants he brought into the country in the middle decades of the century. It was built in the years 1826 and 1827 to the design of Charles Fowler, who was a founder of the Institute of British Architects and the designer of the Covent Garden covered market. Behind this development lay the duke's deep interest in botany, which also extended to generous patronage of leading botanists, including J. C. Loudon. Both the duke and the duchess greatly enjoyed living at Syon

223

and undertook many repairs and renovations. The duke's successor also supported innovative botanical activity at Syon. It was during his time that the giant lily, *Victoria Regia,* was propagated and grown there for display at the Great Exhibition of 1851, after which it was exhibited in various cities around the country

Syon has managed to survive the vicissitudes of the twentieth century. During the First World War, it was used as a military hospital, a use which was the ruination of more than one country house, and during the inter-war years it was threatened with compulsory purchase for the construction of a huge sewage farm. It was restored to its present condition by the tenth duke, who was very fond of it and used it as a summer residence. He regenerated the gardens in conjunction with ICI and restored the metal frame of the Great Conservatory; and in 1968 he opened the first garden centre in Britain and in so doing initiated a major growth sector of the economy. Like so many similar houses, it is now open to the public

YORKSHIRE

As in the south-east, the Percys had five important residences in Yorkshire. Unfortunately, none has survived except as a ruin, and consequently detailed descriptions like those for Petworth and Syon are not possible.

Leconfield Manor, East Riding (East Yorkshire)
Until the Percys were obliged by the Crown to reside at Petworth, Leconfield, located three miles north of Beverley, was, with Wressle, the most favoured residence of the earls of Northumberland. It was essentially a late-medieval manor house, for which licence to crenellate was granted to Henry, Lord Percy I, in 1308. When it was described in 1577, it comprised four ranges, each 324 feet in length, built around a courtyard. The southern range, which was built of brick, contained thirty rooms, including the great hall, the great chamber, parlours and the chapel and was evidently the part occupied by the earl and his family. The other three ranges were timber-framed buildings with brick corner towers and contained offices, lodgings and service areas. Entrance to the courtyard was by a gatehouse of brick in the centre of the north range. The whole

complex was enclosed by a dry moat, which encompassed four acres, and it was set in a park covering 1,420 acres. At the time of this description, it is clear that the house was no longer in serious use and was somewhat dilapidated. It was finally abandoned in the early seventeenth century, when the best fittings were removed and taken to London, presumably to Northumberland House, while the timber framing was sold and other materials were sent to Wressle for use in repairs. There are no vestiges still extant and the site is now occupied by Manor House Farm.

Seamer Manor

Although it appears never to have been the principal residence of the heads of the House of Percy, Seamer Manor deserves to be included since it was a house of some importance until the sixteenth century. Situated four miles south of Scarborough, only one wall remains standing, so until excavations are undertaken, its age and form will remain unclear. It is known to have been in existence in 1304, and subsequent references to it suggest that it was mainly a dower house. In 1555, it was given by Mary I to Sir Henry Gate, and was among the properties the Percys did not regain when Thomas Percy was restored as seventh Earl of Northumberland in 1557.

Stanwick Park, North Riding (North Yorkshire)

Stanwick Park, like Leconfield, has been totally destroyed, although much more recently. It was located at Aldborough St John six miles north of Richmond and a similar distance south-west of Darlington. The earliest known house was built in the seventeenth century, probably in the years immediately after the Restoration, but it was remodelled in the Palladian style in or about 1740. The architect is thought to have been either Lord Burlington or, more likely, his close associate, William Kent. The two dates fit well with the crucial events in the ownership of the property: the acquisition by the first Sir Hugh Smithson following his marriage with the Catterick heiress, and the marriage of the third baronet, the future Duke of Northumberland, and Lady Betty Seymour. The house was of seven bays and had two-and-a-half storeys and was the main country seat of Sir Hugh and Lady Smithson until they acquired Alnwick Castle on becoming Earl and Countess of Northumberland in 1750.

The next period of occupation was in the early nineteenth century, when it was the home of Lord Prudhoe, the second son of the second duke, who succeeded his brother as fourth duke in 1847, and it continued to be the residence in which he and his wife felt most comfortable. The main consequence of this constant use was the addition of a two-storey, three-bay east wing and the restructuring of the stables and servants' quarters to the designs of Decimus Burton. After the fourth duke's death, Stanwick became the dower house for his widow, Duchess Eleanor, who lived there until her death in 1911. Subsequently, it was used only occasionally and in 1921 it was sold when the estate was broken up by the eighth duke. The buyer was a Northallerton man, who sold the fittings and demolished the house.

Spofforth Castle, West Riding (West Yorkshire)

Spofforth, situated four miles south-east of Harrogate, was one of the properties granted by William the Conqueror to William de Percy I, who is known to have built a manor house there. As all trace of this building has disappeared, we have no certain idea of its construction, although it is reasonable to think it was of wood. The earliest fabric still standing is the early thirteenth-century vaulted undercroft, which housed the service departments. Above it are the great hall and solar, which are the outcome of remodelling in the fourteenth and fifteenth centuries. The result is an oblong-shaped building on a north-south alignment measuring 135 feet by 50 feet. The curious feature is the setting of the undercroft against a rock face, so that the upper floor could be entered directly on its east side. Apart from this hall, nothing remains except a few fragments, but these are sufficient to suggest that the hall formed the east side of a quadrangular courtyard.

Licence to crenellate was issued to Henry, Lord Percy I, in 1308, indicating that Spofforth was not a castle but a manor house, which, as the present remains show, it continued to be. As the licence was contemporary with those issued for Leconfield and Petworth, it would seem that Henry, Lord Percy I, was determined to give all his houses greater security. Spofforth decayed as the result of neglect and non-use during the fifteenth and early sixteenth centuries, but it was repaired by the seventh earl in 1559. Its last known period of occupation ended in 1604 and, like so many similar houses, it was reduced to a ruin during the Civil War between 1642 and 1646.

Topcliffe Castle and Cocklodge Manor, North Riding (North Yorkshire)
Very little is known about these buildings, which is regrettable since
Topcliffe was almost certainly the centre of William de Percy I's estate. As
Topcliffe is about nineteen miles north of York and little more than three
miles east of the Great North Road, it was well placed to dominate the
main north-south route along the Vale of York. It is also only about a
mile further in the opposite direction from what is now the A19, the road
from York to the Tees. Clearly, the location was selected for its strategic
importance. The castle was a motte and bailey and was located on a
natural ridge, which was all but surrounded by swampy ground, between
the River Swale and its tributary, the Cod Beck. The height of the motte,
which would have been surmounted by a wooden tower or palisade, was
at least forty-five feet, of which the top ten or twelve feet were artificial.
The bailey enclosed about an acre of land and was formed by the
excavation of a deep, horseshoe-shaped ditch. Many castles of this sort
were later rebuilt in stone, but there is no evidence to suggest that this
happened at Topcliffe. Instead, it was replaced by a manor house known
as Cock Lodge, built on an adjacent site just to the west of the castle.
This house was of considerable size, covering an area 580 by 550 feet.
When it was built is not known, nor is the date of its abandonment,
although this was after the murder of the fourth earl in 1489 and was
probably connected with the sixteenth-century exile of the Percys to
Sussex. Both castle and manor house have disappeared, almost without
trace.

Wressle Castle, East Riding (East Yorkshire)
The remains at Wressle, which are immediately adjacent to the later farm,
are substantial, although, not being in public ownership, they are not
readily accessible. The castle was built on a property that had been in
Percy ownership since at least the early fourteenth century, by Thomas
Percy, the younger brother of the first Earl of Northumberland. He was
made Earl of Worcester in 1397 and was executed in 1403 immediately
after the Battle of Shrewsbury. The castle was in the form of a courtyard
measuring 90 by 85 feet formed by four corner towers linked by curtain
walls and with a gate tower in the centre of the east wall. The site was
further protected by a moat, although whether this was dry or water-
filled is not clear. In size and design, Wressle closely resembles two other

contemporary northern castles, Bolton in Wensleydale and Lumley in County Durham. The strong similarity is no accident: in addition to being built about the same time, it has been pointed out that there were close family ties between Thomas Percy and John Neville, the builder of Lumley, and Richard Scrope, who built Bolton. Wressle was lost as a result of Percy treason in the first decade of the fifteenth century and it became a source of dispute with the Neville family into whose hands it passed in the 1440s. It was, however, recovered by the Percys late in the century following the fall of the Nevilles in the early 1470s. It was not considered to be in good condition when it came into the Crown's hands in 1537 and it must have deteriorated thereafter through neglect and non-use, although, as has been noted, it was repaired in the early seventeenth century with materials brought from Leconfield. This helps to explain why it was still intact in 1650, when, on government orders, it was slighted. By that date, its owner, the tenth earl, who had been a staunch supporter of the parliamentary cause, had withdrawn from political life and no longer had much influence. The south range was left upstanding and was occupied until 1796, when it was destroyed by fire. The remains are in a sorry state and sorely in need of consolidation and excavation, actions which would be expensive but worth the effort.

NORTHUMBERLAND

Although Northumberland is the county with which the Percys are now most closely associated, they had relatively few residences within its bounds, principally because their entry into the county did not occur until the fourteenth century, and even when they became its dominant landowner they tended to prefer living elsewhere.

Alnwick Castle
If the Percy family is associated with any one place, it is with Alnwick. In reality, however, Alnwick came into its possession fairly late and thereafter it was only intermittently the main or preferred place of residence. The first certain owner and lord of Alnwick was Ivo de Vesci, who was granted the barony late in the 1090s or the early years of the twelfth century, and whose descendants held it until very late in the thirteenth

century. It is probable that Ivo built a motte and bailey castle with the motte and its wooden keep situated, as at Windsor, between two baileys. However, it is not until the time of his son-in-law and successor, Eustace Fitz John, who died in 1157, that much is known about it. By that date the original wooden curtain wall had been replaced by one of stone from the line of which there has been virtually no subsequent deviation, although a great deal of repair and reconstruction has taken place. It is possible that by the same date the wooden tower on the motte had also been replaced by a shell keep in stone.

It is unlikely that there were any further substantial changes to the castle during the remainder of the period of de Vesci ownership, which ended with the death of William de Vesci in 1297. Twelve years later the castle, along with the barony, was acquired by Henry, Lord Percy I, from Bishop Antony Bek of Durham. In the course of the next forty years, he and his son and successor, Henry, Lord Percy II, were to effect major developments to the castle, although without fundamentally changing its plan. The defensive capacity of the curtain wall was enhanced by refacing it to increase its thickness and by the addition of nine towers and a number of small turrets known as garrets between them. Similarly, seven towers were added to the shell keep; and a new gatehouse with a barbican was built with a drawbridge over the moat, a portcullis and double doors. By the time the second Lord Percy died in 1352, the castle's outward appearance was very close to what it is today.

The heavy expenditure on these improvements indicates that Alnwick figured prominently in the minds of the first two Lords Percy, although it should be noted that the elder also spent heavily on the defences of Spofforth and Petworth. With the forfeiture of the first earl, the castle probably saw little of the head of the Percy family until the eighteenth century. For many years after 1405 and between 1461 and 1470, 1537 and 1557 and 1569 and 1574, it was in the hands of the Crown as the result of forfeiture. Also, from the late fifteenth century until 1537, the most favoured residences of the earls were Leconfield Manor and Wressle Castle in the far south of Yorkshire, while after 1569 they were required (but later chose) to reside at Petworth. This did not mean that the castle was not in use. Until the end of the Border following the Union of the Crowns in 1603, it continued to be an important fortress under the command of the Warden of the East March, the headquarters of the regional estate administration and from time to time the place where one of the earl's brothers might live.

But, almost inevitably, this varied and intermittent use meant that maintenance was neglected and the fabric became dilapidated. As a result when the first duke and duchess came into ownership in 1750, the castle was in a very poor state of repair. It was they who resolved to restore the castle and to make it their main seat. There were two aspects to their work: the repair of the exterior of the castle, so that its essential medieval form was retained; and the complete recasting of the interior in the fashionable Strawberry Hill Gothick style. The architect principally responsible was, as at Syon, Robert Adam, although James Paine does appear to have been used in the early stages. The result, which was accomplished by the mid-1760s, was a medieval castle the inside of which was a ducal palace furnished to the highest taste and at huge expense. Moreover, the modernised castle was given an appropriate modern setting by the landscape architect, Lancelot 'Capability' Brown, who was commissioned to redesign the park which lay between the castle and the River Aln. Thus, as regards the grounds, the first duke can be seen marching step by step with the second Earl of Egremont, the man with whom he had had to share the great Percy inheritance.

There matters largely rested until the accession of the fourth duke in 1847. By that date, the fanciful style of Adam was out of fashion and the duke undertook the hugely expensive task of remodelling the castle, employing for the purpose one of the most fashionable architects of the day, Anthony Salvin. The work, which began in 1854, but was not quite complete when the duke died in 1865, resulted in a more solidly medieval outside and also a stable court and riding school. Far more radical was the transformation of the interior, where virtually all trace of Adam's work was swept away and replaced by a Renaissance style executed by a number of leading Italian craftsmen and artists, notably Giovanni Montiroli. To a large extent Alnwick today is as the fourth duke planned it, although the seventh duke did add to the medieval authenticity by partially excavating the moat between the gatehouse and the barbican and replacing the paved road across it with a wooden bridge.

The castle has survived the vicissitudes of the twentieth century, in particular the period during and after the Second World War when it was firstly a temporary home for the Newcastle Church High School and then a Teacher Training College for women. Although this use ended in the 1970s, it still accommodates the summer school of St Cloud College, Minnesota, USA.

Throughout the period of the dukes, therefore, the castle has been fully maintained, even though it has not always been their favourite residence. But with the sale of Albury and, as we shall shortly see, Kielder, Percy residence options were much reduced. Happily, the present duke and duchess have made it their home, and at the time of writing the duchess has embarked upon an ambitious and exciting scheme to transform a derelict walled garden at a cost of £15 million. Originally created in 1750, it was redeveloped into an Italianate garden by the third duchess, and it was one of the properties that the fourth duke opened to the townsfolk of Alnwick. Its decline began in the First World War and was completed in the Second World War, when it became a vegetable garden under the 'Dig for Victory' scheme. Plans for the new garden have been prepared by three garden designers, two, Jacques and Peter Wirtz, from Belgium and one, Louis Benech, from France, and a Belgian architect, Paul Robbrecht. If all goes to plan, the garden will open to the public in 2001 and will immediately be seen as one of the world's most exciting gardens. It will also maintain the Percy reputation for innovative interest in, and serious commitment to, horticulture.

Kielder Castle
Kielder is a castle in name only. In reality, it was built as a shooting box by the first duke on the high moorland two miles south of the Border. The architect was a local man, William Newton, and the construction took place between 1771 and 1775. It was most actively used by the fourth duke and duchess, who enjoyed holding small, informal house parties in the peaceful solitude it afforded. An extension was built by the eighth duke in 1926, but four years later the castle and a large tract of land were sold to the Forestry Commission. Now a visitor centre for the Kielder Forest Park, the castle is part of a very different environment from that which existed at the time of its creation in that it is close to a huge reservoir known as Kielder Water and in the middle of an even larger forest covering 148,000 acres, both created since 1930. It is perhaps appropriate that as an artificial castle it now serves two other artificial creations.

231

Prudhoe Castle

In complete contrast, Prudhoe is a genuine castle of great antiquity which, like Alnwick, did not become Percy property until the fourteenth century. It occupies an easily defended site on top of an almost vertical 150-foot spur of land rising from the haughs of the River Tyne. Its position allowed it to dominate the east-west route through the Tyne Gap between Newcastle and Carlisle and it was not far from the north-south Roman road which crossed the Tyne at Corbridge. It is not surprising, therefore, that it was chosen by Robert de Umfraville as the site for the castle he built as the centre of his barony, although the potential was perhaps already indicated by the presence of a building, which may have been the hall of his thanely predecessor, traces of which have been revealed by excavation.

The date of the earliest castle is not certain, but recent research points to the very last years of the eleventh century. Like virtually all castles of this period, it was of wood and comprised an enclosed bailey and a wooden tower on top of a mound, or motte. But rebuilding in stone appears to have begun almost immediately and, as the gatehouse clearly demonstrates, the curtain wall was completed before 1150, although the tower keep was not rebuilt until about 1175. In the following century, as was the case in so many other castles, a barbican was constructed to strengthen the gatehouse, above which a chapel was created.

Prudhoe Castle and its barony came into the hands of the Percys late in the fourteenth century as the result of the marriage in 1381 of the first Earl of Northumberland and Maud, the childless widow of Gilbert de Umfraville, although full ownership did not become effective until her death in 1398. It is clear that the Percys kept the castle in good repair and carried out minor improvements, although as with Alnwick, their presence was occasional following Crown possession as the result of forfeitures and the preference of the earls for their East Riding homes. Consequently, and almost inevitably, the fabric began to decay through neglect from the late sixteenth century. What saved it from complete destruction was its continued use as an administrative centre for the estate and the restoration carried out by the second duke between 1808 and 1817. He repaired the curtain walls and consolidated the tower, and on the foundations of a medieval range he built in the Gothick style what is known as the Manor House, part of which is still in domestic occupation.

Further repairs were carried out in 1912, but in 1966 the castle was placed in the guardianship of what is now English Heritage, although it is still owned by the Percy estate.

Warkworth Castle

Warkworth Castle, like those at Alnwick and Prudhoe, did not come into the hands of the Percys until the fourteenth century and its origins are also obscure. Warkworth was one of the few places in Northumberland that William II and Henry I retained in the hands of the Crown and, as they had castles at Bamburgh and Newcastle, it is far from certain that they developed the defensive capabilities of Warkworth. These may have been created, however, by the earls of Northumbria, either before or after the Norman takeover. Another possibility is that the first castle was the work of Henry, the son of David I of Scotland, who became Earl of Northumberland in 1139 after the county was transferred to his father by the Treaty of Durham. What that treaty did not do was to concede to the Scottish king the castles at Bamburgh and Newcastle. Consequently, Earl Henry had to locate his headquarters elsewhere and Warkworth may have been the place he selected. Even if he was not the founder of the castle, he certainly added to it.

Scottish control of Northumberland lasted until 1157, when the English king Henry II forced his Scottish counterpart, Malcolm IV, to return the county to him. Henry promptly handed over Warkworth with its castle, together with other properties in Northumberland, to Roger fitz Richard. Major improvements to the castle were undertaken by Roger's son, Robert (who succeeded his father in 1177), probably as the result of the weakness revealed during the Scottish invasion of 1173. The castle was again strengthened in the early fourteenth century during the early phases of the Scottish wars, probably by his great-grandson, Robert. Robert died in 1310 and was succeeded by his son, John, who adopted the surname Clavering after the family's property in Essex. John, however, was the last of his line, and upon his death in 1332, Warkworth and the estates attached to it reverted to the Crown, which immediately transferred them to Henry, Lord Percy II, in lieu of the annual fee he was being paid to defend the Border. During the remainder of the fourteenth century, Warkworth appears to have been the favourite residence of the Percys when in Northumberland, and so they did much to improve and modernise it. Although architectural historians are not entirely certain of the details, they believe that it was most probably the first earl who was responsible for its three most notable features. They attribute to him the redesigning and restructuring of the keep, including the addition of polygonal towers to its four sides, and the remodelling of the Great Hall on the western side of the outer bailey. And they also believe that he began to build a church which he intended should house a small college of secular canons. This project was not completed, however, and it is thought that the building may never have risen higher than the present level.

In the course of the fifteenth and sixteenth centuries the Percys lost their estates on several occasions. Nevertheless, when they were in possession and residing in Northumberland, it was at Warkworth that they normally lived. Moreover, when in the sixteenth century they were in disgrace and southerners held the Wardenship of the March, it was at Warkworth that they too resided. Consequently, the castle was maintained in a better state of repair than many similar fortresses. With the end of the Border in 1603 and the ninth earl's incarceration in the Tower and subsequent confinement to Petworth, Warkworth Castle ceased to be of importance to the family or to the Crown and it was allowed to decay through neglect. Its ruin was hastened by the damage done by the parliamentary forces, who occupied it in 1648, and then after the eleventh earl's death in 1670 by the trustees of the estate, who allowed a local man to remove large quantities of materials to build a manor house for himself. In the eighteenth century, the sixth Duke of Somerset considered rebuilding the castle as his northern home, but in the end did not pursue the idea. Nor did the first Duke of Northumberland, who after deliberation decided upon Alnwick as his northern seat. Had he not done so, Warkworth would have been what Alnwick is now. Thereafter, the dukes kept the castle in a reasonable state of repair until 1922, when the eighth duke placed it in the guardianship of the predecessor of English Heritage.

Further Reading

In writing this book, I have consulted all the works listed below. Those marked with an asterisk are wholly or mainly concerned with the Percy family. To highlight individuals may be considered invidious. On the other hand, not to do so would be to fail to give proper recognition to those whose major contributions to our knowledge of the Percys have made this book possible and worthwhile. Those worthy of special note are: G. R. Batho (the career of the ninth earl), J. M. W. Bean (the estates up to the 1537 catastrophe), P. Dalton (the creation of the estate in Yorkshire), M. A. Hicks (the fourth and fifth earls), R. W. Hoyle (the catastrophe of 1537), M. E. James (the fourth, fifth, eighth and ninth earls), D. Spring and F. M. L. Thompson (the estate under the fourth duke), J. A. Tuck (the Percys and Northumberland in the fourteenth century), M. Weiss (the Percys in the fifteenth century).

PRINTED PRIMARY SOURCES

★J. C. Atkinson (ed.), *The Chartulary of Whitby Abbey I,* Surtees Society 69 (1879)

J. Bateson, *The Great Landowners of Great Britain and Ireland,* 4th edition (1883)

★G. R. Batho (ed.), *The Household Papers of Henry Percy, ninth Earl of Northumberland, 1564–1632,* Camden Society, 3rd. series 93 (1962)

J. Caird, *English Agriculture in 1850–51* (1852)

★C. T. Clay (ed.), *Early Yorkshire Charters XI: The Percy Fee* (1963)

G. E. Cockayne, *The Complete Peerage I; revised V. Gibbs (1910), V,* revised H. A. Doubleday, D. Warrand and Lord Howard de Walden (1926), *X,* revised G. H .White (1945), *XII* revised G. H. White (1953)

G. E. Cockayne, *The Complete Baronetage* (1900–1909)

W. Farrer (ed.), *Honours and Knights' Fees III* (1925)

*J. Greig (ed.), *The Diaries of a Duchess* (1926)

*G. B. Harrison (ed.), *Advice to his son by Henry Percy, ninth Earl of Northumberland, 1609* (1936)

*J. C. Hodgson (ed.), *Percy Bailiff Rolls of the Fifteenth Century*, Surtees Society 134 (1921)

*M. E. James (ed.), *The Estate Accounts of the Earls of Northumberland, 1564–1632*, Surtees Society 163 (1958)

*J. McNulty (ed.), *The Chartlulary of the Cistercian Abbey of Sallay in Craven*, Yorkshire Archaeological Record Series 87 (1933)

*M. T. Martin (ed.), *The Percy Cartulary*, Surtees Society 117 (1909)

Victoria County Histories of: *Lincolnshire II*, ed. W Page (1925)

Middlesex III, ed. S Reynolds (1962)

Somerset VI, ed. R W Dunning (1992)

Surrey III, ed. H L Malden (1911)

Sussex IV, ed. L F Salzman (1953)

Yorkshire East Riding IV, ed. K J Allison (1979)

Yorkshire North Riding II, ed. W Page (1925)

Who Was Who 5 volumes 1897–1995

SECONDARY SOURCES

K. R. Andrews, *Ships, Money and Power* (1991)

C. A .J Armstrong,'Politics and the Battle of St. Albans, 1455', *Bulletin of the Institute of Historical Research* 33 (1960)

S. Ayling, *George the Third* (1972)

A. Ayton, *Knights and Warhorses: Military Service and the English Aristocracy under Edward III* (1994)

G. W. S. Barrow, *The Anglo-Norman Era in Scottish History* (1980)

*G. R. Batho, 'Henry, ninth Earl of Northumberland and Syon House, Middlesex 1594–1603)', *Transactions of the Ancient Monuments Society*, new series 4 (1956)

*G. R. Batho, 'The Wizard Earl in the Tower', *History Today* 6 (1956)

*G. R. Batho, 'A Difficult Father-in-Law', *History Today* 6 (1956)

★G. R. Batho, 'Syon House: the first two hundred years', *Transactions of the London and Middlesex Archaeological Society* 19 (1956–58)

★G .R .Batho, 'The Percys and Alnwick Castle' , *Archaeologia Aeliana* 4th ser. 35 (1957)

★G. R. Batho, 'The Percys at Petworth', *Sussex Archaeological Collections* 95 (1957)

★G. R. Batho, 'Notes and Documents on Petworth House, 1574–1632', *Sussex Archaeological Collections* 96 (1958)

★G. R. Batho, 'The Library of the "Wizard Earl": Henry Percy, Ninth Earl of Northumberland, 1564–1632', *The Library 15* (1960)

★G. R. Batho, 'Thomas Harriott and the Northumberland Household', *The Durham Thomas Harriott Seminar* I (1983)

★J. M. W. Bean, *The Estates of the Percy Family, 1416–1537* (1958)

★J. M. W. Bean, 'The Percys' Acquisition of Alnwick', *Archaeologia Aeliana* 4th series 32 (1954)

★J. M. W Bean, 'The Percys and their Estates in Scotland', *Archaeologia Aeliana* 4th series 35 (1957)

M. Beard, *English Landed Society in the Twentieth Century* (1989)

I. F. W. Beckett, *The Amateur Military Tradition, 1558–1945* (1991)

J. V. Beckett, *The Aristocracy in England, 1660–1914)* (1986)

B. W. Beckinsale (ed.), *Elizabeth I* (1963)

B. W. Beckinsale, *Thomas Cromwell: Tudor Minister* (1978)

H. Begbie, *The Windows of Westminster* (1924)

H. Bettenson, *The University of Newcastle upon Tyne, 1834–1971* (1971)

S. Biddle, *Bolingbroke and Harley* (1974)

★J. Bilson, 'Wressle Castle', *Yorkshire Archaeological Journal* 22 (1913)

J. Black, *The War for America* (1991)

W. G. Blaxland, *Destination Dunkirk: the story of Lord Gort's Army, May-June 1940* (1973)

B. Bond, *France and Belgium, 1939–1940* (1975)

★R. C. Bosanquet, 'Memoir of Allan Ian, Eighth Duke of Northumberland KG, President of the Society', *Archaeologia Aeliana* 4th series 8 (1931)

J. Brewer, *Party, Ideology and Popular Politics at the Accession of George III* (1976)

J. Brooke, *King George III* (1972)

M. L. Bush, 'The Problem of the Far North', *Northern History* 6 (1971)

M. L. Bush, *The Pilgrimage of Grace: a study of the rebel armies of October 1536* (1995)

D. Cannadine, *Aspects of Aristocracy: grandeur and decline in modern Britain* (1994)

D. Cannadine, *The Decline and Fall of the British Aristocracy* (1990)

J. Cannon, *Aristocratic Century: the peerage in eighteenth-century England* (1982)

★S. M. Collins, 'The Blue Lion of Percy', *Archaeologia Aeliana* 4th series 24 (1946)

C. Cruikshank, *Henry VIII and the Invasion of France* (1994)

C. Cruikshank, 'Henry VII and Rebellion in North-Eastern England, 1485–1492: Bands of Allegiance and the Establishment of Tudor Authority: *Northern History* 32 (1996)

P. Dalton, *Conquest, Anarchy and Lordship: Yorkshire, 1066–1154* (1994)

P. Dalton, 'The Governmental Integration of the Far North, 1066–1199' in J. C. Appleby and P. Dalton (eds.), *Government, Religion and Society in Northern England, 1000–1700* (1997)

M. W. Daly, *Empire on the Nile: the Anglo-Egyptian Sudan, 1898–1914* (1986)

C. S. L. Davies, 'The Pilgrimage of Grace Reconsidered', *Past and Present* 41 (1968)

N. Denholm-Young, *History and Heraldry* (1965)

Dictionary of National Biography

★M. H. Dodds, 'The Financial Affairs of a Jacobean Gentleman', *Archaeologia Aeliana* 4th series 22 (1944)

D Dunn, 'Margaret of Anjou, Queen Consort of Henry VI: a reassessment of her role, 1445–53', in R. E. Archer (ed.), *Crown, Government and People in the Fifteenth Century* (1995)

★A. E. Ellis, 'Biographical Notes on the Domesday Tenants in Yorkshire', *Yorkshire Archaeological Journal* 4 (1877)

B. English, *The Great Landowners of East Yorkshire, 1530–1910* (1990)

R. Fleming, *Kings and Lords in Conquest England* (1991)

A. J Fletcher, *The Outbreak of the English Civil War* (1981)

A. J Fletcher and D. MacCulloch, *Tudor Rebellions* (1997)

A. Fraser, *King Charles II* (1979)

J. Gillingham, *The Wars of the Roses: peace and conflict in fifteenth-century England* (1981)

★J. P. Gilson, 'St. Julian the Harbinger and the first of the English Percys', *Archaeologia Aeliana* 2nd series (1898)

C. Given-Wilson, *The English Nobility in the Later Middle Ages: the fourteenth-century political community* (1987)

B. Golding, *Gilbert of Sempringham and the Gilbertine Order, 1130–1300* (1995)

A. Goodman, *The Wars of the Roses: military activity and English society, 1452–97* (1981)

H. Gough, *Scotland in 1298* (1888)

J. A. Green, 'Aristocratic Loyalties on the Northern Frontier of England', in D. Williams (ed.), *England in the Twelfth Century* (1990)

S. J. Greenberg, 'Seizing the Fleet in 1642', *Mariners' Mirror* 77 (1991)

E. Gregg, *Queen Anne* (1986)

★R. A. Griffiths, 'Local Rivalries and National Politics: the Percys, the Nevilles and the Duke of Exeter, 1452–53', *Speculum* 43 (1968)

P. J. Gwyn, *The King's Cardinal: the rise and fall of Thomas Wolsey* (1990)

J. Habakkuk, *Marriage, Debt and the Estate System: English Landownership, 1650–1950* (1994)

C. Haigh, *The Reign of Elizabeth I* (1988)

★A. Hamilton Thompson, 'The Monastic Settlement at Hackness', *Yorkshire Archaeological Journal* 27 (1924)

F. Harris, *A Passion for Government: the life of Sarah, Duchess of Marlborough* (1991)

R. Hatton, *George I: Elector and King* (1978)

★L. Hepple, 'Walter le Rey Marchis, a Percy King of Arms and the Falkirk Roll of 1298', *Archaeologia Aeliana* 5th series 24 (1996)

★M. A. Hicks, 'Dynastic Change and Northern Society: the fourth Earl of Northumberland, 1470–1489', *Northern History* 12 (1976)

M. A. Hicks, 'Edward IV and Lancastrian Loyalism', *Northern History* 20 (1984)

★M. A. Hicks, 'The Yorkshire Rebellion of 1489 Reconsidered', *Northern History* 22 (1986)

G. Holmes, *British Politics in the Age of Anne* (1969)

J. C. Holt, *The Northerners: a study in the reign of King John* (1961)

★R. W. Hoyle, 'The Fall of the House of Percy', in G. W. Barnard, (ed.), *The Tudor Nobility* (1992)

★M. W. I'Anson, 'Castles of the North Riding', *Yorkshire Archaeological Journal* 22 (1913)

E. W. Ives, *Anne Boleyn* (1986)

★G. Jackson-Stops, 'Petworth and the Proud Duke', *Country Life* (June 1975)

★M. E. James, 'The Murder at Cocklodge', *Durham University Journal* 57 (1964–5)

★M. E. James, *A Tudor Magnate and the Tudor State: the fifth Earl of Northumberland* (1966)

M. E. James, 'The Concept of Order and the Northern Rising of 1569', *Past and Present* 60 (1973)

G. P. Judd, *Members of Parliament, 1734–1832* (1972)

W. E. Kapelle, *The Norman Conquest of the North: the region and its transformation, 1000–1135* (1979)

L. Keen, 'The Umfravilles, the castle and the barony of Prudhoe', *Anglo-Norman Studies* 5 (1983)

A. D. H. Leadman, 'The Battle of Boroughbridge', *Yorkshire Archaeological Journal* 7 (1882)

Lord Leconfield, *Petworth Manor in the Seventeenth Century* (1954)

Lord Leconfield, *Sutton and Duncton Manors* (1956)

M. Lewis, *A Social History of the Navy, 1793–1815* (1960)

D. Loades, *The Tudor Court* (1992)

J. G. Lockhart and M. Lyttleton, *The Feet of the Young Men* (1928)

R. W. Lockyer, *Buckingham, the life and political career of George Villiers, Duke of Buckingham 1592–1628* (1981)

★W. H. D. Longstaffe, *The Old Heraldry of the Percys* (1860)

M. W. McCahill, *Order and Equipoise: the peerage and the House of Lords, 1783–1806* (1978)

N. D. Mackichan, *The Northumberland Central Railway* (1998)

C. McNamee, *The Wars of the Bruces: England, Scotland and Ireland, 1306–1328* (1997)

★P. McNiven, 'The Scottish Policy of the Percys', *Bulletin of the John Rylands Library* 62 (1980)

K. Mertes, *The English Noble Household, 1250–1600: good governance and politic rule* (1988)

H. Miller, *Henry VIII and the Nobility* (1986)

J. Miller, *Charles II* (1991)

G. E. Mingay (ed.), *The Agrarian History of England and Wales: VI, 1750–1850* (1989)

★T. C. Mitchell, 'Maiden's Bower near Topcliffe', *Yorkshire Archaeological Journal* (1886)

D. Nichol, *Thurstan, Archbishop of York, 1114–1140* (1964)

M. Nichols, *Investigating the Gunpowder Plot* (1991)

★M. Nichols, 'As Happy a Fortune as I Desire', *Historical Research* 65 (1992)

M. W. Ormrod, *The Reign of Edward III: the crown and political society in England, 1327–1377* (1990)

N. Pevsner, *The Buildings of England: Middlesex* (1951), *Northumberland*, revised edition (1992), *Surrey* (1971), *Sussex* (1965), *Yorkshire, East Riding* (1972), *Yorkshire, North Riding* (1966), *Yorkshire, West Riding* (1967)

J. H. Philbin, *Parliamentary Representation 1832, England and Wales* (1972)

A. J. Pollard, *North-Eastern England during the Wars of the Roses* (1990)

A. J. Pollard, 'St Cuthbert and the Hog', in R. A. Griffiths and J Sherborne (eds.), *Kings and Nobles in the Later Middle Ages* (1996)

A. J. Pollard, 'The Crown and the County Palatine of Durham 1437–94', in A. J. Pollard (ed.), *The North of England in the Reign of Richard III* (1996)

★R. Pollitt, 'The Defeat of the Northern Rebellion and the Shaping of Anglo-Scottish Relations', *Scottish Historical Review* 64 (1985)

M. C. Prestwich, *War, Politics and Finance under Edward I* (1972)

M. C. Prestwich, *The Three Edwards: War and State in England, 1272–1377* (1980)

D. B. Quinn and A. D. Ryan, *England's Sea Empire, 1550–1642* (1993)

R. R. Reid, 'The Rebellion of the Northern Earls, 1569', *Transactions of the Royal Historical Society* 20 (1906)

C. Richmond, 'The Nobility and the Wars of the Roses', *Nottingham Medieval Studies* 21 (1977)

R. Rinehart, *Lord President Sussex and the Rising of the Northern Earls 1569 - 70* (1975)

K. Robbins, *Sir Edward Grey* (1971)

H. C. B. Rogers, *The British Army of the Eighteenth Century* (1977)

W. D. Rubinstein, 'British Millionaires, 1809–1949' *Bulletin of the Institute of Historical Research* 47 (1974)

C. Russell, *The Fall of the British Monarchies* (1991)

G. W. M. Sewell, *The North British Railway in Northumberland* (1991)

K. Sharpe, *The Personal Rule of Charles I* (1992)

★J. Sherborne, 'Perjury and the Lancastrian Revolution of 1399', in J. Sherborne (ed.), *War, Culture and Politics in the Fourteenth Century* (1994)

J. W. Shirley, *Thomas Harriott: A Biography* (1983)

E. A. Smith, *The House of Lords in British Politics and Society, 1815–1911* (1992)

D. Spring, *The English Landed Estate in the Nineteenth Century* (1963)

★S. P. H. Statham, 'The Parentage of William de Percy', *Yorkshire Archaeological Journal* 28 (1926)

★G. Tate, *History of Alnwick,* 2 vols. (1868)

F. M. L. Thompson, *English Landed Society in the Nineteenth Century* (1965)

R. F. Treharne, *The Baronial Plan of Reform, 1258–1263* (1932)

R. F. Treharne and I. J. Sanders, *Documents of the Baronial Movement of Reform and Rebellion* (1973)

J. A. Tuck, *Richard II and the English Nobility* (1973)

★J. A. Tuck, 'Richard II and the Border Magnates', *Northern History* 6 (1968)

J. A. Tuck, 'Northumbrian Society in the Fourteenth Century', *Northern History* 6 (1971)

J. A. Tuck, 'War and Society in the Medieval North', *Northern History* 21 (1985)

★J. A. Tuck, 'The Emergence of a Northern Nobility', *Northern History* 22 (1986)

R. V. Turner, 'The Exercise of the King's Will in the Inheritance of Baronies: King John and William Briwerre', *Albion* 22 (1990)

★M. J. Vine, 'Two Yorkshire Rebels: Peter de Brus and Richard de Percy', *Yorkshire Archaeological Society* 47 (1975)

R. Walcott Jnr., *English Politics in the Early Eighteenth Century* (1956)

C. R. Warn, *Main Line Railways of Northumberland* (1976)

C. R. Warn, *Rural Branch Lines of Northumberland* (1975)

E. Waterson and P. Meadows, *Lost Houses of York and the North Riding* (1990)

★M. Weiss, 'A Power in the North: the Percys in the Fifteenth Century', *Historical Journal* 19 (1975)

J. Wood, 'The Architectural Patronage of Algernon Percy, 10th Earl of Northumberland', in E. Bold and E. Chaney (eds.), *English Architecture: Public and Private* (1993)

C. Woodam-Smith, *Queen Victoria: her life and times I 1819–1861* (1972)

Index

243

Index

Index

Index